NON
OBVIOUS

D0068621

ALSO BY THE AUTHOR:

Personality Not Included: Why Companies Lose Their
Authenticity -- And How Great Brands Get It Back

Likeonomics: The Unexpected Truth Behind Earning Trust,
Influencing Behavior, and Inspiring Action

ePatient: 15 Surprising Trends Changing Healthcare
(with co-author Fard Johnmar)

Always Eat Left Handed: 15 Surprising Secrets
For Killing It At Work And In Real Life

ABOUT THE NON-OBVIOUS TREND SERIES

—

Wall Street Journal Best Seller

Winner of the Axiom Business Book Award
In Business Theory (Silver Medal)

Shared By Over 1 Million Readers Online

#1 Amazon Business Book (All Categories)

For the past eight years, the Non-Obvious Trend Series has been one of the most widely read curated annual predictions about business and marketing trends in the world with over 100 trends predicted since 2011.

This is the ALL NEW 2018 Edition of the Wall Street Journal Best Seller and features 15 new trends as well as updated analysis on over 100 previously predicted trends.

PRAISE FOR NON-OBVIOUS

"

"Non-Obvious is a sharp, articulate, and immediately useful book about one of my favorite topics: the future. Filled with actionable advice and entertaining stories, Rohit offers an essential guidebook to using the power of curation to understand and prepare for the future of business."

—DANIEL H. PINK, Author of *To Sell Is Human* and *Drive*

There are very few books that I read hoping that no one else around me will. They're the books that are so insightful, so thought provoking and so illuminating that they provide powerful competitive advantage. Non-Obvious is one of those. Pass on it at your own peril.

—SHIV SINGH, SVP Global Head of Digital & Marketing Transformation at VISA and author of *Social Media Marketing For Dummies*

This is one of those rare books that delivers insights that are both useful and help illuminate where business is going. It's a great read.

—CHARLES DUHIGG, Author of the bestseller *The Power Of Habit*

The insights in Rohit's Non-Obvious Trends are an invaluable guide to understanding our customer's customer. His predictions are useful and highly anticipated within our group across the globe every year. As a B2B marketer and leader, this is one of my rare must-read recommendations for my entire team.

—NAVEEN RAJDEV, *Chief Marketing Officer, Wipro*

It doesn't take a crystal ball to predict that digital is the future. Rather than tell you what you already know, Rohit sets his sights on something much more important: helping you adopt a more curious and observant mindset to understand the world around you. If you believe in a lifetime of learning, read this book!

—JONATHAN BECHER, *Chief Marketing Officer, SAP*

A lot of books promise to help you see things differently but Rohit's book actually delivers. His insightful blend of visual thinking and business strategy shows you how to find meaningful patterns that others miss. A real mind-opener.

—SUNNI BROWN, Author, Gamestorming and *The Doodle Revolution*

❝

Shatter your magic crystal ball, and toss out the tea leaves. In this book, Rohit shows us how and where to find the future trends that will shape your business, your brand, and even your own decision-making.

—SALLY HOGSHEAD
NY Times bestselling author of *How The World Sees You*

Lots of books tell you to "think different" but Non-Obvious is one of the few books that actually teaches you how to do it. Whether you are trying to persuade clients, motivate a team, or just impress a demanding boss —Non-Obvious can help you succeed. I've already purchased copies for my entire team.

—JOHN GERZEMA
New York Times best-selling author and social strategist

The best books approach their topic with a spirit of generosity. Rohit's new book offers insight into the business and cultural trends that matter. And why they do. And what actions they might inspire. But more than that, it also generously teaches you how to develop your own process, for evaluating the trends that matter and those that don't. Also, it's well-written. Which makes it a joy (and not a chore!) to read!

—ANN HANDLEY
Chief Content Officer, MarketingProfs

Non-Obvious is simple, elegant and powerful - one of those intensely engaging books that I couldn't put down. Every year I use the ideas in this book to help my team see new opportunities and out think our competition.

—HOPE FRANK
Chief Marketing and Digital Officer + Futurist

Rohit Bhargava's *"Likeonomics"* is the gold standard on understanding the social economy. His new book had me at "predict the future" but there's much more than that in here. It's about seeing the world in a new way —plus a powerful argument for how curation can change your organization.

—SREE SREENIVASAN
Former Chief Digital Officer, The Metropolitan Museum of Art

"

Rohit provides a goldmine of ideas and trends that will shape the future of marketing and product development. Read this book to get in front of the herd.

—GUY KAWASAKI
Chief Evangelist of Canva. , Author of *The Art of the Start, 2.0*

Our industry is all about the future – the future of kids, the future of schools, the future of education. In the admissions office, the ability to recognize and leverage that future is an indispensable skill. In Non-Obvious, Rohit provides us the tools we require to perform those functions with precision and get better at predicting what will be important tomorrow based on improving your observations of today.

—HEATHER HOERLE
Executive Director, The Enrollment Management Association

Seeing things that others don't is perhaps the highest form of creativity that exists. Unlock the Non-Obvious approach and you can write your ticket to success in any field.

—JOHN JANTSCH
Author of *Duct Tape Marketing* and *Duct Tape Selling*

In Non-Obvious Rohit shares valuable tips, tricks, methodologies and insightful curated trends to help readers navigate the future. Recommended!

—ROSS DAWSON
Chairman, Future Exploration Network

Very few people understand the world of digital business better than Rohit and I have introduced my clients to his ideas for years. His new book is a must-read resource for learning to see patterns, anticipate global trends, and think like a futurist every day!

—GERD LEONHARD
Author and Keynote Speaker Basel / Switzerland

Non-Obvious should be called oblivious since that's how you'll be if this book isn't on your shelf. I actually wish some of Rohit's predictions won't come true ('Selfie Confidence'!? Nooo!) ... but usually they do. He's the best at this, and this book shows you why.

—SCOTT STRATTEN
Four time Best-Selling Author, including 2014 Sales Book of the Year: *UnSelling*

"

Artfully lacing stories together to pull out simple, yet powerful trends, Rohit offers a blueprint for making trend identification a key component of your business strategy. The format of his book makes it easy for the novice to adopt these principles, and for the expert to glean pearls of wisdom. While the title is Non Obvious, your next step should be obvious —read this book today!

—JOEY COLEMAN
Chief Experience Composer at Design Symphony

Non-Obvious is a powerhouse 'must read' for corporate executives, marketeers and product and service developers. Rohit Bhargava provides valuable, entertaining and easily understood sideways insights into critical trends shaping the near future. He lifts the lid on the myths surrounding the dark arts of trend prediction and offers very practical guidance on how to spot, curate and capitalize on Non Obvious trends.

—ROHIT TALWAR
Global Futurist and CEO Fast Future Research

NON OBVIOUS

IDEAPRESS
PUBLISHING

ROHIT BHARGAVA

IDEAPRESS
PUBLISHING

COPYRIGHT © 2018 BY ROHIT BHARGAVA

All rights reserved.

Published in the United States by Ideapress Publishing.

IDEAPRESS PUBLISHING | WWW.IDEAPRESSPUBLISHING.COM

All trademarks are the property of their respective companies.

Cover Design by Jeff Miller/Faceout Studios

Cover Photo by Javier Pérez

Cataloging-in-Publication Data is on file with the Library of Congress.

ISBN: 978-1-940858-42-5   ISBN: 978-1-940858-52-4 (e-book)

PROUDLY PRINTED IN THE UNITED STATES OF AMERICA

BY SELBY MARKETING ASSOCIATES

SPECIAL SALES

Ideapress Books are available at a special discount for bulk purchases for sales promotions and premiums, or for use in corporate training programs. Special editions, including personalized covers, custom forewords, corporate imprints and bonus content are also available. For more details, email info@ideapresspublishing.com.

To my parents – for always giving me
a chance to see the world in my own way...
even if it wasn't always non-obvious.

CONTENTS

—

Part I

THE ART OF CURATING TRENDS

Part II

THE 2017 NON-OBVIOUS TREND REPORT

CULTURE & CONSUMER BEHAVIOR TRENDS

MARKETING & SOCIAL MEDIA TRENDS

MEDIA & EDUCATION TRENDS

Part III

THE TREND ACTION GUIDE

Part IV

PREVIOUS TREND REPORT SUMMARIES
(2011-2017)

AUTHOR'S NOTE:
The 2018 Edition – What's New and Non-Obvious?

—

This is a book about learning to predict the future.

It is also printed with a date on its cover, reflecting the fact that every year I rewrite and replace about 40% of this book with all new content.

The simple belief of this book is that the secret to predicting the future is to get better at understanding the present. The only difficulty is, the present is always evolving.

Throughout the year my team and I spend more than a thousand hours scanning tens of thousands of stories, conducting dozens of interviews, attending and speaking at over 50 events, reading or reviewing more than 100 new books and then combining all that research to identify 15 trends that will change the world in the coming year.

Whether you have read a previous edition of this book or not, a lot has changed in this year's edition. Here's a quick summary:

✓ All new interior design featuring easier to read charts and layout
✓ Updated Appendix featuring ratings of over 100 past trends
✓ Completely updated and rewritten Parts I and III
✓ And of course, 15 more trends for 2018 featured in Part II

While it will be tempting to focus only on the new, I highly encourage you to check out the past and previously predicted trends as well. You will find the answer there to the one question everyone asks: did your predictions come true? The other thing you will discover is that new trends don't make old trends irrelevant.

Rather, trends are meant to describe an accelerating idea and if those past predictions were actually "non-obvious" when predicted, then they may become more obvious over time–but still ring true.

Whether you actively seek to understand the future or find yourself curious about the past, this book can help. The most important thing I hope you will take away is the belief that there is real value in seeing the world in a more "non-obvious" way and curating ideas and trends for themselves. The world needs your innovation and ideas. I can't wait to see what you come up with.

Rohit Bhargava
Washington DC
December 2017

PART I

THE ART
OF TREND
CURATION

INTRODUCTION

—

"I am not a speed reader, I am a speed understander."

ISAAC ASIMOV, Author, Historian and Biochemist

—

Nearly 150 years ago the Dewey Decimal Classification System ambitiously introduced a method to break down the published volumes of the world into ten main categories. Isaac Asimov has written at least one book in nine of them.

In his prolific lifetime, he wrote nearly five hundred books on topics ranging from his beloved science fiction series to a two-volume work explaining the collected literature of William Shakespeare. He even wrote a reader's guidebook to the Bible.

Though he was celebrated for his science fiction, Asimov never defined his work using a single category. When asked to name his favorite book, he often joked, "the last one I've written." He cannot be described only as a scientist or a theologian or a literary critic.

He was, without question, a writer and thinker with an incredible curiosity for ideas. In fact, he used this curiosity to maintain his grueling schedule of publishing, which at its peak resulted in about fifteen books per year. His secret, if there was just one, seemed to be in his ability to juggle multiple projects at once.

When he became stuck during writing (which indeed happened to him just as it does to any writer), Asimov would simply move on to one of his other in-progress projects. He never stared at a blank sheet of paper.

He credited his ability to focus on so many areas at once to his voracious appetite for reading and his capacity for being a "speed understander." What if you could become a speed understander like Asimov?

I believe we all can.

The simple aim of this book is to teach you how to notice the things that others miss. I call this "non-obvious" thinking and learning to do it for yourself can change your business and your career.

The context within which I'll talk about this type of thinking is business trends. For better or worse, most of us are fascinated by trends and those who predict them. We anticipate these predictions as a glimpse into the future and they capture our imagination.

There's only one problem—too many trends are based on guesswork or lazy thinking. In other words, they are obvious instead of non-obvious.

This book was inspired by the landslide of obvious ideas we are surrounded with and our desire to do something better with them.

In a world where everyone is one click away from being a self-declared expert, learning to think differently is more important than ever. Observing and curating ideas can lead to a unique understanding of why people choose to buy, sell, or believe anything.

—

A non-obvious trend is a unique curated observation about the accelerating present.

—

Unlike many other far-future predictions, the trends and methods in this book are designed to help you right now. There are plenty of people who can tell you what the world might be like twenty years from now. Sadly, many of those are guesses or wishful thinking. How many trend forecasters do you think predicted the rise of something like Twitter back in 1996? Exactly Zero.

Yet this doesn't mean curating trends (or honing your ability to predict them) is useless. The most powerful trends can offer predictions for the short-term future based on observing the present. The truth is, knowing the short-term future is more valuable than you may think.

Why Does Trend Curation Matter?

Most of our life decisions happen in the short-term, though we may describe them differently. You choose to start a business in the short-term. You choose who to marry in the short-term. You change careers from one role to the next, all in the short-term.

Long-term decisions start in the short-term, so understanding how the world is changing in real time is far more valuable in your day-to-day career and life than trying to guess what will happen in the world twenty years from now.

When I speak at industry events, I often describe myself first as a "trend curator." The reason I use that term is because it describes my passion for collecting ideas and taking the time to see the patterns in them to describe the world in new and interesting ways. In this book, you will learn the exact step-by-step method I use and how to become a trend curator yourself.

The result of all of my idea collection is that for the past eight years I have published an annual list of fifteen trends that will shape the business world in the year to come. Across that time, I have advised some of the largest brands in the world on business strategy, taught several courses at Georgetown University, and been invited to speak at events in thirty-two countries around the world.

All of this gives me the valuable chance to gain firsthand insight into dozens of different industries and to study media, culture, marketing, technology, design, and economics with an unfiltered eye. Adding to these real-life interactions, I also read or review dozens of books and buy magazines on everything from cloud computing to Amish farming methods.

My philosophy is to collect ideas the way frequent fliers collect miles—as momentary rewards to use for later redemption.

Why I Wrote Non-Obvious

When I first started writing an annual list of predictions in 2011, my intent was to share trends as ideas that didn't have a home with any project I was working on at the time in my role at a large marketing agency. In 2015 the first edition of this book expanded beyond the trends themselves to feature an inside look at my process for curating trends and detailed instructions for how you can learn to curate your own ideas.

The book is divided into four parts.

Part I is dedicated to sharing my methods of trend curation, which I have usually only taught in depth through private workshops or with my students in class. You will learn the greatest myths of trend prediction, five essential habits of trend curators, and my own step-by-step approach to curating trends, which I call the Haystack Method.

Part II is the 2018 edition of the Non-Obvious Trend Report, featuring fifteen new ideas that will shape business in the year to come. Each trend features supporting stories and research, as well as an outline for why that trend matters and concrete ideas for how to apply the trend to your own business or career.

Part III is filled with tips on making trends actionable, including a short description of workshops you can host yourself to bring these trends to life in your organization. In this section, I also discuss the importance of anti-trends and how to use "intersection thinking" to see the patterns between industries and stories.

Finally, Part IV is a candid review of 105 previously predicted trends from the past seven years along with an honest assessment and rating for how each one performed over time, all sourced from a combination of conversations with industry insiders and a review panel of trusted colleagues.

You can choose to read this book in the order that it's presented or you can skip back and forth between trends and techniques. Whether you choose to focus on my predictions for 2018 or jump to the last part to see how previously trends rated, this book can be read in short bursts or all at once.

Either way, like Asimov, you don't need to be a speed reader.

Being a speed *understander*, however, is a worthy aspiration. It's my hope that this book will help you get there.

1

≋

THE NORWEGIAN BILLIONAIRE:
Why Most Trend Predictions
Are Spectacularly Useless

—

In 1996 Christian Ringnes was a billionaire with a first-world problem—he was running out of space for his favorite collection.

As one of the richest men in Norway, Ringnes is well known as a flamboyant businessman and art collector whose family started the country's largest brewery more than a hundred years ago. In his hometown of Oslo, Ringnes owns several restaurants and museums and has donated more than $70 million for the creation of a large sculpture and cultural park, which opened in 2013.

In his heart, Ringnes is a collector. Over decades he has built one of the largest private collections of art in the world. Yet his real legacy may come from something far more unique: his lifelong obsession with collecting mini liquor bottles.

This fixation began for Ringnes at the age of seven when he received an unusual present from his father: a half-empty mini liquor bottle. It was this afterthought of a gift that led him on a path toward amassing what is recognized today as the largest independent mini-bottle collection in the world, with more than 52,000 miniature liquor bottles.

Unfortunately, his decades-long obsession eventually ran into an insurmountable opponent—his late wife, Denise.

As the now legendary story goes, Denise wasn't too pleased with the disorganization of having all these bottles around the house. After years of frustration, she offered him an ultimatum: either find something to do with all those bottles or start selling them.

Like any avid collector, Ringnes couldn't bear the thought of selling them, so he created a solution based on his wealth and personality.

He commissioned a museum.[1]

"To Collect Is Human"

Today his Mini Bottle Gallery, located in downtown Oslo, is one of the world's top unique museum destinations, routinely featured in irreverent travel guides and global lists of must-see Scandinavian tourist attractions. Beyond providing a place for Ringnes to store his collection, the gallery, which has a restaurant, is also a popular venue for private events.

It was here, while in Oslo for a conference dinner that included a tour of the Mini Bottle Gallery, that I got my first personal introduction to Ringnes and his story.

—

I have 52,500 different miniature bottles in a museum in Oslo. They're completely useless. But men, we like collecting. We like having things. That's human. Once you get fascinated by something, you want it and then you start collecting.

CHRISTIAN RINGNES, Founder, The Mini Bottle Gallery

—

The museum lived up to its quirky reputation.

The entrance is a bottle-shaped hallway leading into an open lobby with a champagne waterfall. As you move through over 50 unique installations spanning three floors, each features its own composed soundtrack, customized lighting, and even some unique smells. Like all great museum experiences, the rooms of the Mini Bottle Gallery are carefully curated.

The mini bottles are grouped into themes ranging from a brothel-inspired Room of Sin with mini bottles from De Wallen (Amsterdam's red-light district), to a Horror Room featuring liquor bottles with trapped objects such as mice and worms floating inside.

There's a Jungle Room, a Room of Famous Persons, and rooms themed around sports, fruits, birds, circus performers, and the occult. There's even a room featuring the iconic porcelain series of the Delft Blue KLM houses, a series of tiny Dutch rowhouse-shaped liquor bottles given away to passengers by KLM Airlines for more than five decades.

Across all these rooms, the tour mentions that the gallery typically has more than 12,000 bottles on display. Apart from the scope of the themed rooms, one of the most interesting elements of this story is what the gallery does with the bottles that aren't on display.

An Accidental Trend Curator

Like any other museum, the Mini Bottle Gallery never uses its entire collection. Instead, they only display about 20% of Ringnes's full collection at any time, and carefully keep the rest in storage. This thoughtful curation adds value to the experience of seeing them.

Curation is the ultimate method of transforming noise into meaning.

If you consider the amount of media any of us is exposed to on an average day, the quest to find meaning among the noise is a challenge we all know personally. Navigating information overload requires the same discipline as deciding what bottles to put on display so those that visitors see can tell a better story.

Without curation, themes would be indecipherable and the experience would be overwhelming, downright noisy.

It was only on my flight home from Oslo after that event that I realized how important curation had become for my own work.

Just a few months earlier I'd published the first edition of my Non-Obvious Trend Report, inspired by an idea to publish an article from the many ideas I'd collected over the past year but had never written about. What I was already doing without realizing it was collecting intriguing ideas and saving them in perhaps the most disorganized way possible—by writing them down randomly, printing them or ripping them out of magazines, and then stashing everything in a well-worn folder on my desk.

In producing that first report, my ambition had been to describe patterns in the stories I had collected that went beyond the typical obvious observations I was always reading online. My goal was to find and develop insights that others either hadn't yet noticed and that were not getting the attention they warranted.

To get a different output, sometimes you need a different input.

On that flight home from Norway, I realized that my accidental method for getting different input—collecting ideas for a year and waiting months before analyzing them—could be the very thing that would set my insights apart and make them truly non-obvious.

The Non-Obvious Trend Report (my annual list of fifteen trends) was born from this desire to collect underappreciated ideas and connect them into predictions about the future.

The Underappreciated Side of Data

Now, if you happen to be an analytical person, this process will hardly seem rigorous enough to be believable. How can collecting ideas and waiting possibly be a recipe for developing genuine insights? What about first-hand research, surveys, and focus groups? What about trend panels and using a global army of trend spotters? What about the *data*?

While it's easy to assume that data means putting numbers into a spreadsheet or referencing some piece of analytics published in a journal—the truth is that data has a forgotten side that has little to do with devising experiments and far more to do with training your powers of observation.

When you think about the discipline that goes into scientific research to produce raw data, research can seem like a task only performed by robot-like perfectionists. The truth of scientific research, just like the truth behind many equally complex areas of study, is that experiments aren't the only way to gather data—nor might they even be the most accurate.

Trends, like science, aren't always perfectly measured phenomena that fit neatly into a spreadsheet without bias. Discovering trends takes a willingness to combine curiosity with observation and add insight to create valuable ideas that you can then test to ensure they are valid.

The one thing that I don't believe describes this method is, ironically, the one term that comes to many people's minds as soon as the art of predicting the future is mentioned: "trend spotting." The term itself is a symbol of the biggest myths we tend to believe about those who predict or describe the future.

Let's explore these myths and the reasons behind their popularity.

The 5 Myths of Trend Spotting

Trend spotting is not the key to predicting the future.

Unfortunately, the bias toward trend-spotting has created an unreasonable portrait of the type of person who can put the pieces together and anticipate the future. Consider this infuriatingly common definition for what it takes to become a so-called trend spotter:

—

To become a trend spotter, someone usually receives extensive education and training in the industry he or she is interested in working for. After receiving a thorough grounding...the trend spotter could start working in company departments which predict trends.[2]

—

The assumption that you need to be working in "company departments which predict trends" is just plain idiotic—and wrong.

I believe anyone can learn the right habits to become better at curating trends and predicting the future for themselves. You just need to develop the right habits and mindset.

Before we start learning those habits, however, it's important to tackle the biggest myths surrounding trends and explain why they miss the mark so badly.

MYTH #1 - TRENDS ARE SPOTTED

The concept of trend spotting suggests that there are trends simply sitting out there in plain sight ready to be observed and cataloged like avian species for birdwatchers. The reality of trends is far different. Trend spotters typically find individual examples or stories. Calling the multitude of things they spot the same thing as trends is like calling ingredients such as eggs, flour, and sugar the same thing as a cake. You can "spot" ingredients, but trends must be curated from these ingredients to have meaning.

MYTH #2 - TRENDS ARE PREDICTED BY INDUSTRY EXPERTS

It's tempting to see industry expertise as a prerequisite to being good at curating trends, but there's also a predictable drawback: blind spots. The more you know about a topic, the more difficult it becomes to think outside your expertise and broaden your view. There's no single expertise required to curate trends, but psychologists and business authors have long pointed to this "curse of knowledge" as a common challenge for anyone who builds any type of expertise.[3] To escape it, you need to learn to engage your greater curiosity about the world beyond what you know and learn to better empathize with those who don't share your same depth of knowledge.

MYTH #3 - TRENDS ARE BASED ON "HARD" DATA

When it comes to research, some people rely only on numbers inserted into a spreadsheet as proof and they conveniently forget that there are two methods to conducting research: the quantitative method and the qualitative method. Qualitative research involves using observation and experience to gather mainly verbal data instead of results from experiments. If you are uncovering the perfect pH balance for shampoo, you certainly will want to use quantitative research. For curating trends, you need a mixture of both, as well as the ability to remember that research data can often be less valuable than excellent observation.

MYTH #4 - TRENDS ONLY LAST FOR A SHORT TIME

The line between trends and fads can be tricky. Although some trends seem to spotlight a currently popular story, good ones need to describe something that happens over a span of time. Fads, in comparison, describe an idea that's popular in the short term but doesn't last. Great trends do reflect a moment in time, but they also describe more than a fleeting moment.

MYTH #5 - TRENDS ARE HOPELESSLY BROAD PREDICTIONS

Perhaps no other myth about trends is as fueled by reality as this one. The fact is, we encounter hopelessly broad trend predictions in the media all the time. Therefore, the problem comes in concluding that trends should be broad and all encompassing. Good trends tend to be more of the opposite: They define something that's concrete and distinct, without being limiting.

For example, someone once asked me after an event if I had considered the rise of 3D printing as a trend. I replied that I had not, but the "Makers Movement"—which was a well described trend that focused on the human desire to be a creator and make something (which 3D printing certainly enabled)—was a worthwhile trend. The point was, a trend is never a description of something that just exists—like 3D printing.

Instead, a trend must describe what people do or believe as a result. Once you know that the "Makers Movement" describes the human desire to make something, for example, you can think about how to offer that type of fulfillment to your customers in how they interact with you. IKEA has benefitted from this trend for years—because people often feel a disproportionate emotional connection to furniture they had to work to assemble themselves. Psychologist have dubbed this the "IKEA effect."

Now that I've shared the most common myths about trend predictions, let's consider why so many trend predictions involve self-indulgent guesswork or lazy thinking. What exactly makes them so useless?

To answer this question, let me tell you a little story.

Why Most Trend Predictions Are Useless

A few years ago, I picked up the year-end edition of *Entrepreneur* magazine, which promised to illuminate trends to watch in the coming year. Earlier that same week, a special double issue of *BusinessWeek* magazine had arrived in the mail making a similar promise.

It was the end of the year and the trend season was in full swing.

Just like New Year's resolutions to lose weight, trend forecasting is popular in December (one of the reasons why each annual edition of Non-Obvious is usually published in December as well). Unfortunately, the side effect of this annual media ritual is an abundance of lazy predictions and vague declarations.

For entertainment, I collect these year-end trend forecasts and keep them as standing memorials to the volume of pitiful predictions that bombard us as we look to the year ahead.

Here are a few of the worst-offending, most obvious "trends" I've seen. For the sake of kindness, I haven't tagged them with their sources or authors:

- "It's all about the visuals."
- "Streaming video content."
- "The Year of Drones has arrived. Really."
- "Content Marketing will continue to be the place to be."
- "Fantasy Sports"
- "Virtual Reality"
- "Change will be led by smart home technology."

Virtual Reality? Really?

Not to ruin the suspense, but I don't believe any of these should be described as trends. Some are just random buzzwords or the names of platforms. Others are hopelessly broad, useless, and, yes, obvious.

None of them fit my trend definition of a unique idea describing the accelerating present.

Meanwhile, all of us as media consumers read these predictions with varying levels of skepticism. To better understand why, let's review the four main reasons why most trend predictions fail the believability test.

REASON #1 - NO OBJECTIVITY

If you sell drones for racing, declaring 2018 the "Year of Racing Drones" is clearly self-serving. Of course, most bias isn't this easy to spot and objectivity is notoriously difficult for any of us. Our biases are based on our expertise and the world we know. This is particularly true in business, where we sometimes need to believe in an industry or brand in order to succeed. The problem is that losing objectivity usually leads to wishful thinking. Just because we want something to be a trend doesn't make it one.

REASON #2 - NO INSIGHT

Trends need to do more than repeat common knowledge. For example, saying that "more people will buy upgraded smartphones this year" is obvious—and useless, because it lacks insight. The biggest reason that most trend predictions share these types of obvious ideas is because it's easier to do so. Lazy thinking is always easier than offering an informed and insightful point of view.

—

*Great trends are never obvious declarations
of fact that most people already know.*

—

Instead, they share new ideas in insightful ways while also describing the accelerating present.

REASON #3 - NO PROOF

Sharing a trend without specific examples is like declaring yourself a musician by simply buying a guitar. Unfortunately, many trend predictions similarly coast on the power of a single story or example. Exceptional examples and stories are powerful parts of illustrating why a trend matters. They are necessary elements of proving a trend. Only finding one example and declaring something a trend without more evidence is usually a sign that a so-called trend is based on little more than guesswork.

RREASON #4 - NO APPLICATION

Perhaps the most common place where many trend predictions fall short is in the discussion of how to apply them. It's not enough to think about trends in the context of describing them. The best trend forecasts go further than just describing something that's happening. They also share insights on what it means and what you can or should do differently as a result of the trend. In other words, trends should be actionable.

How to Think Different About Trends

Now that we have examined the many myths and reasons for failure, let's focus on what makes a non-obvious trend:

—

A Non-Obvious Trend is a curated observation that describes the accelerating present in a new, unique way—usually by looking at the intersection of multiple industries, behaviors, and beliefs.

—

Over the next two chapters, you'll learn the step-by-step technique that can help you think differently about trends and escape the trap of lazy thinking that leads to obvious ideas. In doing that, you'll immediately find yourself having more insights than your peers around you and seeing the connections between industries and stories in a way that most people don't.

The key to the method you're about to learn is a willingness to go outside your usual sources of information and open your mind to unconventional ways of thinking and brainstorming. As a result, you'll become better at spotting the connections between the things you read, what you see, and the conversations you have.

There's magic to be found in thinking like a trend curator. Let's talk about how to find it.

2

≋

THE CURATOR'S MINDSET:
Learning the 5 Essential Habits
of Trend Curators

—

"You never learn anything by listening to yourself speak."

SIR RICHARD BRANSON, Entrepreneur and Founder of the Virgin Group

Across decades of research with grade school students, interviewing professional athletes and studying business leaders, renowned Stanford psychology
professor Carol Dweck has developed an elegant way to describe why some
people manage to exceed their potential while others peak early or never
achieve that same success.[1]

According to Dweck, it all depends on your mindset.

People with *fixed mindsets* believe that their skills and abilities are set.
They see themselves as either being good at something or not good at something, and therefore tend to focus their efforts on tasks and in careers where
they feel they have a natural ability.

People with *growth mindsets* believe that success and achievement are the
result of hard work and determination. They see their own (and others') true
potential as something to be defined through effort. As a result, they thrive
on challenges and often have a passion for learning.

When it came to setbacks, people with a growth mindset are more likely to treat failure "like a parking ticket instead of a car wreck."[2] They're more resilient, have more self-confidence, are less focused on getting revenge for any perceived wrong, and tend to be happier.

Despite the many benefits of adopting a growth mindset, the sad reality is that as soon as children become able to evaluate themselves, some of them become afraid of challenges and failure. They become afraid of not being smart. This is a tragedy, because it's a limitation that they will continue to impose upon themselves into adulthood, sometimes without realizing it.

—

I have studied thousands of people . . . and it's
breathtaking how many reject an opportunity to learn.
– CAROL DWECK (from *Mindset*)

—

The first and most important key to becoming a better collector of ideas and thinking more innovatively is the deceptively simple decision not to limit yourself.

What if you were capable of more than just that narrowly defined list of things you believe you are naturally good at? Learning to curate ideas into trends, like playing an instrument or being more observant, is a skill that's within your grasp to learn and practice—but only if you venture outside of your mental comfort zone and adopt a growth mindset.

Does this mean anyone can transform themselves into a professional flamenco guitarist or a full-time trend forecaster with enough practice? Not necessarily. Aptitude and natural talent still play an important part in succeeding at anything on a professional level.

Yet the past decade of my work with thousands of executives and students at all levels of their careers has proved to me that the skills required for trend curation can be learned and practiced, just as the growth mindset can be taught and embraced. When you learn these skills and combine them with the right mindset, they can inform your own view of the world and power your own future success.

After understanding your mindset, the next step on your path to predicting the future is learning five core habits. To start learning them, let me share a story of the most famous art collector most people had never heard of—until he passed away a few years ago.

The World's Most Unknown Art Collector

By the time eighty-nine-year-old Herbert Vogel passed away in 2012, the retired New York City postal worker had quietly amassed one of the greatest collections of modern art in the world.

Vogel and his wife, Dorothy, were already local legends in the world of art when Herbert passed away. News stories soon after his death told the story of five large moving vans showing up at the Vogel's rent-controlled, one-bedroom Manhattan apartment to pick up more than five thousand pieces of art. The Vogel Collection, built over decades, was offered a permanent home as part of the archives and collection at the National Gallery of Art in Washington, DC.

The Vogels had always said the only thing they did was buy and collect art they loved.[3]

This passion often led them to find new young artists to support before the rest of the world discovered them. The Vogels ultimately became more than collectors. They were tastemakers, and their fabled collection featuring art from hundreds of artists, including pop artist Roy Lichtenstein and post-minimalist Richard Tuttle, was the envy of museums and other private collectors around the world.

The same qualities that drive art patrons like the Vogels to follow their instincts and collect beautiful things are the ones that make great curators of any kind. Museums and the art world are a fitting place to start when learning how to be a curator.

The Rise of "Curationism"

Museum curators organize collections into themes that tell stories. Whether they're quirky like those told in the Mini Bottle Gallery, or an expansive exhibit covering eighteenth-century pastel portraits at the Metropolitan

Museum of Art, the goal of curation is always to take individual items and examples and weave them together into a narrative.

Curators add meaning to isolated beautiful things.

I'm inspired by curators—and I'm clearly not alone. The business world has turned toward the longtime practice of curation with such growing frequency that even artists and art critics have noticed.

In 2014, art critic and writer David Balzer published a book with the brilliant title *Curationism* (a play on "creationism") to examine how "curating took over the art world and everything else." His book explores the evolution of the curator as the imparter of value and what the future of curation looks like in a world where so many from outside the art world or without the usual training start to use the principles of the field for their own purposes.

Though the book is an academic read intended mainly for the curatorial circles within which he works, he shares the valuable caution that this rise in curationism can sometimes inspire a "constant cycle of grasping and display," where we never take the time to understand what the individual pieces mean.

In other words, curation is only valuable if you follow the act of collecting with enough moments of quiet contemplation to truly understand what all of it means.

This combination of collection and contemplation is central to being able to effectively curate ideas and learn to predict the future.

The 5 Habits of Trend Curators

I realize that calling yourself a "curator" of anything can seem like a stretch.

Curator is often a job title applied to someone who has years of expertise in historical studies or the evolution of an industry, but curators today can come from all different types of backgrounds.

Some focus on art and design while others may look at history or anthropology. Some have professional training and degrees while others are driven by passion alone, like Herbert and Dorothy Vogel. No matter their background, every one of them exhibits the same types of habits that help them to become masters at adding meaning to collected items.

Curation doesn't require you to be an expert or a researcher or an academic. Learning these five habits will help you put the power of curation to work to help you discover better ideas and use them to develop your own observations about the rapidly accelerating present.

THE 5 HABITS OF TREND CURATORS

BE CURIOUS – always asking why, investing in learning, and improving your knowledge by investigating and asking questions.

BE OBSERVANT – learning to notice the small details in stories and life that others may ignore or fail to recognize as significant.

BE FICKLE – moving from one idea to the next without becoming fixated or overanalyzing each idea in the moment.

BE THOUGHTFUL – taking time to develop a meaningful point of view and considering alternative viewpoints without bias.

BE ELEGANT – seeking beautiful ways to describe ideas that bring together disparate concepts in a simple and understandable way.

How to Be Curious

—

Being more curious means asking questions about why things work the way they do and embracing unfamiliar situations or topics with a sense of wonder.

—

Bjarni Herjulfsson could have been one of the most famous explorers in the history of the world.

Instead, his life has become a cautionary tale about the historic consequences of lacking curiosity. In the year AD 986, he set off on a voyage from Norway with a crew to find Greenland. Blown off course by a storm, his ship became the first European vessel in recorded history to see North America.

Despite his crew pleading to stop and explore, Herjulfsson refused and guided his ship back on course to eventually find Greenland. Years later, he told this tale to a friend named Leif Erikson, who became inspired, purchased Herjulfsson's ship, and took the journey for himself. Erikson is now widely remembered as the first European to land in North America—nearly five hundred years before Christopher Columbus landed in the Bahamas and "discovered" America.[4]

Herjulfsson, on the other hand, has been mostly forgotten and his story illustrates exactly why curiosity matters: it's a prerequisite to discovery. Humans are naturally curious. The challenge is to continually find ways to allow yourself to explore your curiosity without it becoming an ongoing distraction.

When noted chef and food pioneer Ferran Adrià was once asked what he likes to have for breakfast, his reply was simple: "I like to eat a different fruit every day of the month." Imagine if you could do that with ideas. Part of being curious is wanting to consume stories, ideas, and experiences to earn greater knowledge of the world, even if that knowledge doesn't seem immediately useful.

3 WAYS TO BE MORE CURIOUS TODAY

✓ **Consume "Brainful Media."** Sadly, we are surrounded with "brainless media," including reality shows featuring unlikeable people doing unlikeable things (sometimes on islands, sometimes in our backyards). While they can be addictively entertaining, brainless media encourages vegetation instead of curiosity. Curiosity is fueled by consuming media that makes you think, such as a short documentary film or an inspirational seventeen-minute talk from TED.com

✓ **Empathize with Magazines.** One of my favorite ways to see the world through someone else's eyes is buying niche magazines to learn about unfamiliar topics. Simply walking into the magazine section of a bookstore offers plenty of options. For example, Modern Farmer, Model Railroader, and House Beautiful are three vastly different magazines. Flipping through the stories, advertisements, and imagery in each will do more to take you outside of your own world than almost any other quick-and-easy ten-minute activity.

✓ **Ask Bigger Questions.** A few years ago, I was invited to deliver a talk at an event for the home interior paint industry. It's an industry I know very little about and so it was tempting to show up, deliver my keynote, and then leave. Instead, I stayed and walked around the exhibit hall asking questions. In less than thirty minutes I learned about how paint is mixed and what additives are typically used. I heard about the industry debate between all-plastic cans versus steel and the rise of computerized color-matching systems. Thanks to that small investment of time on my part, the talk I gave was far more relevant.

BE CURIOUS: WHAT TO READ

✓ **Historical Fiction.** Every great piece of historical fiction was inspired by a writer who found a story from the past that was worth sharing with the world. By reading books such as Erik Larson's *The Devil in the White City* (about murder at the 1893 Chicago World's Fair) or Simon Winchester's *The Professor and the Madman* (about the creation of the Oxford English Dictionary), you can give yourself a wonderful gateway to start thinking about the world in unexpected ways.

✓ **Curated Compilations.** There are many books that bring together real-life stories or essays to help you think about new and interesting topics. A collection of shorter topics and stories is sometimes far easier to use for engaging your curiosity than a longer book. For example, the *This Will Make You Smarter* series edited by John Brockman or any book by *You Are Not So Smart* podcast host and psychology buff David McRaney are perfect, bite-sized ways to inspire your curiosity without requiring a huge time investment.

How to Be Observant

—

*Being more observant means training yourself to
notice the details that most others often miss.*

—

I was invited not long ago to a formal dinner connected to an event in
New York. The venue was a beautiful restaurant, and after our meal the waiter
came around to take our dessert orders from one of two set menu options.
Less than ten minutes later, a team of six people, not including our waiter,
came and delivered all the desserts to our large table of thirty people, getting
each order perfectly right without saying a word to anyone.

As they delivered the desserts, I started to wonder how that one waiter
who took our orders had managed to relay all those choices perfectly to a team
of six in such a short time.

By observing the wait staff for a moment, I quickly figured out the simple
trick our head waiter had used. If you had picked dessert option one, he had
placed a dessert spoon on the table above your plate. If you picked option two,
he placed the spoon to the right of your plate.

When the team of food runners came to the table, all they needed was the
"code" to decipher the spoon positioning and they could deliver the desserts
to the right people with ease and accuracy.

Perhaps you already knew that spoon trick, but imagine if you didn't. Simply observing it gives you a glimpse into the little processes that we rarely pay
attention to that keep the world moving along. Now, you might be thinking,
Who cares how waiters deliver dessert?

Of course, understanding how dessert is delivered will hardly change your
life, but imagine that moment multiplied out to a thousand different situations. Observing details can lead to understanding something insignificant,
but it can also lead to your next big business idea.

Learning to be more observant isn't just about seeing the big things.
Instead, it's about training yourself to pay more attention to the little things.

What can you see about a situation that other people miss? What can the details you're noticing teach you about people, processes, and companies that you didn't know before?

This is the power of making observation a habit.

3 WAYS TO BE MORE OBSERVANT

✓ **Explain the World to Children.** If you're fortunate to have children in your life, one of the best ways to hone your skills of observation is to explain the world around you to them. For example, when one of my kids asked me recently why construction vehicles and traffic signs are orange but cars that most people drive aren't, it forced me to think about something I would otherwise have easily ignored, even if I didn't have the perfect answer to the question.[5]

✓ **Watch Processes in Action.** Many interactions in life, from how the coffee shop makes your latte to who gets an upgrade on a flight are controlled by a scripted process. Next time you engage with one of these processes, pay attention to the details. What does a typical interaction look like? How does it differ from person to person? Learning not to ignore these common processes in everyday life is great training for being more observational in situations where it really matters.

✓ **Don't Be Observationally Lazy.** Aside from being really good at capturing our attention, our devices can keep us from seeing the world around us. Rather than switching to autopilot to navigate daily tasks like walking down the street or buying groceries while trying to avoid any or all eye contact, train yourself to put your phone down, see the world, and maybe even have a conversation.

BE OBSERVANT: WHAT TO READ

✓ *What Every Body Is Saying,* **by Joe Navarro.** If you need to learn the art of interpreting body language or detecting lies, a former FBI agent like Joe Navarro is probably the ideal teacher. In this bestselling book from 2008, Navarro shares some of his best lessons on how to spot "tells" in body language and use them to interpret human behavior. His work on situational awareness and teaching people how to be more observant to assess people and situations for danger and comfort is a book that should be on your reading list no matter what you do. It also happens to be a perfect supporting book to teach you how to be more observant.

How to Be Fickle

—

Being fickle means capturing ideas without needing to fully understand or analyze them in that same moment.

—

People often cast the idea of being fickle as a bad thing. When we hear the word, we tend to think of all the negative situations where we abandon people or ideas too quickly, but there is an upside to learning how to be purposefully fickle.

On the surface, this may seem counterintuitive. After all, why wouldn't you take the time to analyze a great idea and develop a point of view? There are certainly many situations when you do this already.

But you probably never do the opposite. A key element of becoming an idea curator is saving ideas for later digestion. As you will see in Chapter 3, where I share my specific methods for curating trends, this idea of saving an idea so I can return to it later when it may have more value is a very fundamental part of the method I use for trend curation.

Often the connection between ideas will only come from the discipline of setting them aside and choosing to analyze them later, when you have more stories and added perspective to see the connections. Being fickle isn't about avoiding thought—it's about freeing yourself from the pressure to recognize connections immediately and making it easier to come back to an idea later for analysis.

3 WAYS TO BE MORE FICKLE

✓ **Save Ideas Offline.** There are countless digital productivity tools, such as Evernote, but they can be hard to manage and navigate when you need them. Instead, I routinely print articles, rip stories out of magazines, and put them all into a single trend folder that sits on my desk. Saving ideas offline allows me to physically spread them out later to analyze more easily.

✓ **Use a Timer.** To avoid the temptation to overanalyze an idea in the moment, set a timer as a reminder to go back. It will help you to clear your mind in the interim. The other benefit of using a timer is that it can force you to evaluate things more quickly and just focus on the big picture.

✓ **Take Notes with a Sharpie.** I mark the many articles and stories I find throughout the year with a few words to remind me of the theme of the article and story. I use a Sharpie marker because the thicker lettering stands out and encourages me subtly to write less. This same trick can help you to make only the most useful observations in the moment and save any others for later.

BE FICKLE: WHAT TO READ

✓ *The Laws of Simplicity,* **by John Maeda.** Maeda is a master of design and technology, and his advice has guided many companies and entrepreneurs toward building more amazing products. In this short book, he shares some essential advice for learning to see the world like a designer and how to reduce the noise in order to see and think more clearly.

✓ *How to Make Sense of Any Mess,* **by Abby Covert.** I have read many books on the art of organizing information, but this one, with its smart reasoning and simplified approach, is one of my favorites. The author is an Information Architect who goes by the pseudonym "Abby the IA" and shares methods based on more than ten years of teaching experience that are worth adopting and sharing with your entire team.

How to Be Thoughtful

—

Being thoughtful means taking the time to reflect on a point of view and share it in a considered way.

—

In 2014, after ten years of writing my business and marketing blog, I decided to stop allowing comments. For some readers, this seemed counter to one of the fundamental principles of blogging, which is to create a dialogue.

The reason I stopped was simple. I had noticed a steady decline in the quality of comments. What was once a robust discussion involving thoughtfully worded responses had devolved into a combination of thumbs-up–style comments and spam.

Thanks to anonymous commenting and the ease of sharing knee-jerk responses, comments had lost their thoughtfulness—and people were starting to notice. Thus, I turned off the comments.

The web is filled with this type of "conversation." Angry, biased, half-thought-out responses to articles, people, or media. Being thoughtful is harder to do when the priority is to share a response in real time. Yet the people who are routinely thoughtful are the ones who gain and keep respect. They add value instead of noise... and you can be one of them.

3 WAYS TO BE MORE THOUGHTFUL

✓ **Wait a Moment.** The beauty and challenge of the Internet is that it occurs in real time. It's easy to think that if you can't be the first person to comment on something, your thoughts are too late. That's rarely true. "Real time" shouldn't mean sharing a comment from the top of your head within seconds. Take your time before writing a comment or sharing a link and consider what you're about to say—and whether you'd still be proud to say it twenty-four hours from now.

✓ **Write and then Rewrite.** When it comes to being thoughtful with writing, all of the most talented writers take time to rewrite their thinking instead of sharing the first thing that they write down. The process of rewriting can seem like a big-time commitment, but the fastest form of writing is dialogue—so when in doubt, write it like you would say it.

✓ **Embrace the Pauses.** As a speaker, becoming comfortable with silence took me years to master. It's not an easy thing to do. Yet when you can use pauses effectively, you can emphasize the things you really want people to hear and give yourself time to craft the perfect thing to say.

BE THOUGHTFUL: WHAT TO READ

✓ *Brain Pickings,* **by Maria Popova.** Popova describes herself as an "interestingness hunter-gatherer," and she has one of the most popular independently run blogs in the world. Every week she publishes articles combining lessons from literature, art, and history on wide-ranging topics like creative leadership and the gift of friendship. The way she presents her thoughts is a perfect aspirational example of how to publish something thoughtful week after week.

How to Be Elegant

—

Being elegant means developing your ability to describe a concept in a beautiful and simple way for easy understanding.

—

Jeff Karp is a scientist inspired by elegance . . . and jellyfish.

As an associate professor at Harvard Medical School, Karp's research focuses on using bio-inspiration—inspiration from nature—to develop new solutions for all types of medical challenges. His self-named Karp Lab has developed innovations such as a device inspired by jellyfish tentacles to capture circulating tumor cells in cancer patients and better surgical staples inspired by porcupine quills.

Nature is filled with elegant solutions, from the way that forest fires spread the seeds of certain plants to the way termites build porous structures with built-in heating and cooling.

I believe it's this idea of simplicity that's fundamental to developing elegant ideas. As Albert Einstein famously said, "make things as simple as possible, but not simpler."

A good example of things described beautifully is in what talented poets do. Great poetry has simplicity, emotion, and beauty because superfluous words are edited out of the verse. Poets are masters of elegance; they obsess over language and understand that less can mean more.

You don't need to become a poet overnight, but some of these principles can help you get better at creating more elegant descriptions of your own ideas. To illustrate how, here's the process I used to name my trends in previous reports.

3 WAYS TO THINK MORE ELEGANTLY

✓ **Start with the Obvious.** One of the most popular trends from my 2015 Non-Obvious Trend Report was something I called "Selfie Confidence." The name was a play on "self-confidence" and was written to force people to see something they were already familiar with in a new way. Selfies are often criticized as demonstrations of narcissism, but the trend also suggested the idea that selfies might contribute to helping people to grow their self-esteem.

✓ **Keep It Short.** One thing you'll notice if you look back on any of the previous years' trends (including this year) is that the title for most trends are no longer than two words. Elegance often goes hand in hand with simplicity, and this usually means using as few words as possible.

✓ **Use Poetic Principles.** Poets use metaphors and imagery instead of obvious language. In Chapter 3 you'll get an inside look at how I use techniques borrowed from poetry as part of the naming process I use every year for trends. A quick scan of past trends will also illustrate how I've used these principles to describe trends like "Preserved Past" or "Lovable Unperfection."

BE ELEGANT: WHAT TO READ

✓ *Einstein's Dreams,* **by Alan Lightman.** This book, written by an MIT physicist and one of my favorites, creatively imagines what Einstein's dreams must have been like and explores them in a beautiful way through short chapters with interesting assumptions about time and space. This is not a book of poetry, but it'll introduce you to the power of poetic writing while also offering the most elegant description of the nature of time that you'll ever read.

✓ **Any Book by Dr. Seuss.** This may seem like an odd suggestion, but Dr. Seuss had a great talent for sharing big ideas with simplicity and elegance. You probably already know some of his brilliance: "Today you are you, that is truer than true. There is no one alive who is youer than you." Reading his work, though, will remind you of the power of finding just the right words while inspiring you to do more with less.

Why These 5 Habits?

Do these five habits for helping you to learn the art of curating ideas seem a bit surprising? The fact is, the process of how I came to these five involved an exercise of curation in itself.

Over the past several years, I read interviews with professional art curators and how they learned their craft. I bought more than a dozen books written by trend forecasters, futurists, and innovators. I interviewed dozens of top business leaders and authors. I carefully studied my own behavior. I tested the effectiveness and resonance of these habits by teaching them to my students at Georgetown University and professionals in private workshops.

Ultimately, I selected the five habits presented here because they were the most helpful, descriptive, easy to learn, and effective once you learn to put them into action.

As a recap before we get started with a step-by-step approach to curating trends, let's do a review:

5 HABITS OF TREND CURATORS

BE OBSERVANT
See What
Others Miss

BE CURIOUS
Always Ask
Why

BE FICKLE
Learn to
Move On

BE THOUGHTFUL
Take Time
to Think

BE ELEGANT
Craft Beautiful
Ideas

3

≡

THE HAYSTACK METHOD:
How to Curate Trends for Fun and Profit

—

"The most reliable way to anticipate the future is to understand the present."

JOHN NAISBITT, Futurist and Author of *Megatrends*

—

In 1982, a book called *Megatrends* changed the way governments, businesses, and people thought about the future.

Author John Naisbitt was one of the first to predict our evolution from an industrial society to an information society, and he did so more than a decade before the advent of the Internet. He also predicted the shift from hierarchies to networks and the rise of the global economy.

Despite the book's unapologetic American-style optimism, most of the ten major shifts described in *Megatrends* were so far ahead of their time that when it was first released one reviewer glowingly described it as "the next best thing to a crystal ball." With more than 14 million copies sold worldwide, it's still the single bestselling book about the future published in the last forty years.

For his part, Naisbitt believed deeply in the power

of observation to understand the present before trying to predict the future (as the opening quote to this chapter illustrates). In interviews, friends and family often described Naisbitt as having a "boundless curiosity about people, cultures and organizations," even noting that he had a habit of scanning "hundreds of newspapers and magazines, from *Scientific American* to *Tricycle*, a Buddhism magazine" in search of new ideas.[1]

John Naisbitt was and still is (at a spry eighty-eight!) a collector of ideas. For years, his ideology has inspired me to think about the world with a similarly broad lens and has helped me to develop the process I use for my own trend work, which I call the Haystack Method.

Inside the Haystack Method

It's tempting to describe the art of finding trends with the cliché of finding a "needle in a haystack." This common visual reference brings to mind the myth of trend spotting that I discounted in Chapter 1. Uncovering trends hardly ever involves them sitting in plain sight waiting for us to spot them.

—

The Haystack Method describes a process where you first focus on gathering stories and ideas (the hay) and then use them to define a trend (the needle), which gives meaning to them all collectively.

—

In this method, the work comes from assembling the information and curating it into groupings that make sense. The needle is the insight you apply to this collection of information to describe what it means—and to curate information and stories into a definable trend.

While that describes the method with metaphors, to learn how to do it for yourself we need to go deeper. Starting with the story of why I created the Haystack Method in the first place.

Why I Started Curating Ideas

The Haystick Method was born out of frustration.

In 2004, I was part of a team that was starting one of the first social media–focused practices within a large marketing agency. The idea was that we would help big companies figure out how to use this new platform as a part of their marketing efforts.

The aim of our team was to help brands work with influential bloggers, because in 2004 (prior to Facebook and Twitter) "social media" mainly referred to blogging. There was only one problem with this well-intentioned plan—none of us knew very much about blogging.

So we did the only thing that seemed logical to do: each of us started blogging.

In June of that year I started my "Influential Marketing Blog" with an aim to write about marketing, public relations, and advertising strategy. My first post was on the dull topic of optimal screen size for web designers. Within a few days I ran into my first challenge: I had no plan for what to write about next.

How was I going to keep this hastily created blog current with new ideas and stories when I already had a full-time day job that wasn't meant to involve spending time writing a blog? I realized I had to become more disciplined about how I collected ideas.

At first I focused on finding ideas for blog posts, usually collected by scribbling them into a notebook or emailing them to myself. Then I decided to include ideas from the daily brainstorming meetings I attended. Pretty soon I expanded to saving quotes from books and ripping pages out of magazines.

Those first four years of blogging helped me land my first book deal with McGraw-Hill. Several years later, in 2011, the desire to write a blog post about trends based on ideas I had collected across the year led me to publish the first edition of my Non-Obvious Trend Report.[2]

My point in sharing this story is to illustrate how the pressure to find enough ideas worth writing about consistently on my blog helped me to get better at saving and sharing ideas that people cared about. Blogging helped me become a collector of ideas, which is the perfect introduction to the first step in the Haystack Method.

THE HAYSTACK METHOD

1

GATHERING

Save
Interesting
Ideas

2

AGGREGATING

Curate
into
Clusters

3

ELEVATING

Identify
Broader
Themes

4

NAMING

Create
Elegant
Descriptions

5

PROVING

Validate
without
Bias

Step 1—Gathering

—

*Gathering is the disciplined act of collecting stories
and ideas from reading, listening and speaking to different sources.*

—

Photo: Sources used for gathering information.

Do you read the same sources of media religiously every day? Or do you skim social media occasionally and sometimes click on the links your connections share to continue reading? Regardless of your media diet, chances are you encounter plenty of interesting stories or ideas. The real question is: Do you have a useful method for saving them? The key to gathering ideas is making a habit of saving interesting things in a way that allows you to find and explore them later.

My method involves always carrying a small passport-sized notebook in my pocket and keeping a folder on my desk to save media clippings and printouts. By the time you read these words, that folder on my desk has changed color and probably already says "2019 Trends" on the outside of it. In my process, I start the clock every January and complete it each December for my annual Non-Obvious Trend Report (see Part II of this book). Thanks to this deliverable, I have a clear starting and ending point for each new round of ideas that I collect.

You don't need to follow as rigid a calendar timetable as I do, but it is valuable to set a specific time for yourself to review and reflect on what you have gathered in order to uncover the bigger insights (a point we will explore in subsequent steps).

IDEA SOURCES: WHERE TO GATHER IDEAS

1. Personal conversations at events or meetings
2. Listening to live speakers or TED Talks
3. Entertainment
4. Books
5. Museums
6. Magazines and newspapers
7. Travel!

This list of sources might seem, well, obvious. It's rarely the sources of information themselves that will lead you toward a perfectly packaged idea or trend. Rather, mastering the art of gathering valuable ideas means training yourself to uncover interesting ideas across multiple sources and become diligent about collecting them.

Tips & Tricks: How to Gather Ideas

✓ **Start a Folder.** A folder on my desk stores handwritten ideas I find interesting, articles ripped out of magazines and newspapers, printouts of articles from the Internet, brochures from conferences, and the occasional odd object (like a giveaway from a conference or a brochure received in the mail). This folder lets me store things in a central and highly visible way. You might choose to create this folder digitally or with paper. Either way, the important thing is to have a centralized place where you can save ideas for later digestion.

✓ **Always Summarize.** When you're collecting ideas on a longer time scale (i.e., across an entire year), it's easy to forget why a story seemed significant in the first place. To help yourself remember, get into the habit of highlighting a few sentences or writing down a few notes about your thoughts on the idea (usually using a Sharpie pen - which is also suggested in Chapter 2). Later, when you're going through your gathered ideas, these notes will be useful in recalling what originally sparked your interest.

✓ **Seek Concepts, Not Conclusions.** As we learned in Chapter 2, a key habit of good curating is the ability to be fickle. In practice, this means not getting too hung up on the need to quantify or understand every idea you save in the moment. Many times, the best thing you can do is to gather something, save it, and then move on to your next task. Perspective comes from taking time and having patience.

Step 2—Aggregating

—

Aggregating involves taking individual ideas and disconnected thoughts and grouping them together to try and uncover bigger themes.

—

Photo: Example of aggregating possible trend topics.

After gathering ideas, the next step is to combine the early results of your observation and curiosity with some insights about how ideas might fit together. Using a series of questions can help you do that. Here are a few of my favorites.

AGGREGATING QUESTIONS: HOW TO GROUP IDEAS

1. What broad group or demographic does this story describe?
2. What is the underlying human need or behavior?
3. What makes this story interesting as an example?
4. How is this same phenomenon affecting multiple industries?
5. What qualities or elements make me interested in this story?

At this stage a common trap is to start grouping all the stories from one industry together. Resist the temptation to do that and try aggregating based on insights and human motivations instead.

In this second step, it's not important to come up with a fancy name for your ideas or even to do extensive research around any one them. Instead, the aim is to start building small clusters of ideas that bring together stories into meaningful clusters.

Tips & Tricks: How to Aggregate Ideas

✓ **Focus on Human Needs.** Sometimes focusing on a bigger underlying human emotion can help you see the basis of the idea and why it matters. For example, the basic human need for belonging fuels many of the activities people engage in online, from posting social comments to joining online communities. The key is to connect the ideas you have gathered with the basic human needs behind them.

✓ **Recognize the Obvious.** Along the path to uncovering "non-obvious" insights, there's some value in recognizing and even embracing the obvious. In a grouping exercise, for example, you can often use the obvious ideas (like multiple stories about new wearable technology products) as a way of bringing things together and later you can work on discovering the non-obvious insights between them.

✓ **Follow Your Intuition.** When you train yourself to be more observant, you might also find that you start to develop a feeling for stories that are interesting or somehow feel significant—even though you may not be able to describe why. Embrace that intuition and save the story. In later phases of the Haystack Method, you can try to connect this story to a broader idea.

Step 3—Elevating

—

Elevating involves finding the underlying themes that connect groups of ideas to describe a single, bigger concept.

—

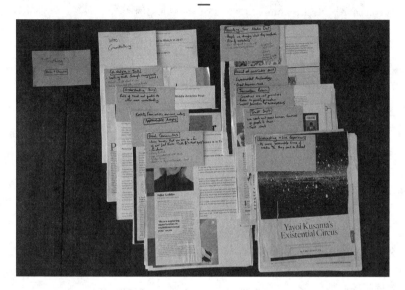

Photo: Examples of groups of stories elevated together for a trend.

If you've gone through gathering and aggregating ideas—this is the point where you'll probably confront the same problem I do every year: there are too many possibilities!

When I go through my annual exercise of curating trends, the first time I aggregate my ideas into clusters it usually yields between seventy and a hundred possible trend topics. That's far too many, and a clear sign that there's more work to be done.

How do you know what to focus on in order to build out into a trend? The goal in this third step is to try and take a bigger view and connect your smaller clusters of ideas together into larger ones that describe even bigger and potentially more powerful ideas. More than any other step, this is where the breakthroughs and inspiration usually come.

ELEVATING QUESTIONS:
HOW TO THINK BIGGER ABOUT IDEAS

1. What interests me most about these ideas?
2. What elements could I have missed earlier?
3. What is the broader theme?
4. How can I link multiple industries?
5. Where is the connection between ideas?

This third step can be the most challenging phase of the Haystack Method, because the process of combining ideas can also lead you to unintentionally make them too broad (and by definition, obvious). Your aim in this step, therefore, should be to elevate an idea to make it bigger and more encompassing of multiple stories without losing its uniqueness.

For example, when I was producing my 2014 Non-Obvious Trend Report I came across an interesting healthcare startup called GoodRx, which had a tool to help people find the best price for medications. It was simple, useful, and the perfect example of an evolving shift toward empowering patients in healthcare, which I wrote about in my earlier book *ePatient 2015*.

At the same time, I was seeing retail stores, such as Macy's, investing heavily in creating apps to improve their in-store shopping experience and a number of new fashion services, like Rent the Runway, designed to help people save time and money while shopping.

On the surface, a tool to save on prescriptions, an app for a department store, and an optimized tool for renting dresses don't seem to have much in common. I had therefore initially grouped them separately. While elevating trends, though, I realized that they all had the underlying intent of helping to optimize a shopping experience in some way.

I grouped them together as examples of a shared trend which I called *Shoptimization*. The trend described how technology was helping consumers optimize the process of buying everything from home goods and fashion to medical prescriptions.

In the next step, I'll discuss techniques for naming trends (including how I named *Shoptimization*), but for now my point in sharing that example is to illustrate how elevation can help you make the connections across industries and ideas that may have initially seemed disconnected and meant to fall into different groups.

The difference between aggregating ideas and elevating them may seem very slight, but there are times when I manage to do both at the same time, since the act of aggregating stories can help to broaden your conclusions about them.

In the Haystack Method, I choose to present these steps separately because most of the time they do end up as distinct efforts. With practice though, you may get better at condensing these two steps together.

Tips & Tricks: How to Elevate Your Ideas

✓ **Use Words to Elevate.** When you have groups of ideas, sometimes boiling them down to a couple of words to describe them can help you to see the common themes between them. When I was collecting ideas related to entrepreneurship, for example, a word that kept emerging to describe the growing ecosystem of on-demand services for entrepreneurs was "fast." It was the theme of speed that helped me to bring the pieces together to eventually call that trend "Instant Entrepreneurship."

✓ **Combine Industry Verticals.** Despite my own cautions against aggregating ideas by industry sector, sometimes a trend ends up heavily focused in just one sector. When I see one of these clusters of ideas predominantly focused in one industry, I always try to find another batch of ideas I can combine it with. This often leads to bigger thinking and helps to remove any unintentional industry bias I may have had earlier in the process.

✓ **Follow the Money.** With business trends, sometimes the underlying driver of a trend is who will make money from it. Following this trail can sometimes lead you to make connections you might not have considered before. This was exactly how studying a new all- you-can-read ebook subscription service and the growth of cloud-based software led me to write about the trend of "Subscription Commerce" several years ago.

Step 4—Naming

—

Naming is the creative art of finding the right words to describe an elevated idea as a trend in an easily understandable and memorably branded way.

—

Photo: Sources used for names and word lists.

Naming a trend is a little bit like naming a child—you think of every way that the name might unintentionally be dooming your idea to a life of ridicule and then you try to balance that with a name that feels right.

Naming a trend also involves the choice of sharing a specific point of view in a way that names for kids generally don't. Great trend names convey meaning with simplicity—and they're memorable.

For that reason, this is often my favorite part of the Haystack Method, but also the most creatively challenging. It's focused on that critical moment when you brand an idea that will either stick in people's minds as something new and important, or will be immediately forgotten.

The title for my second book, *Likeonomics,* came from one of these trend-naming sessions. The concept took off immediately because people understood the idea and the name was just quirky enough to inspire a second look. Finding the right name for an idea can do that.

An effective title can inspire people. It can help a good idea capture the right peoples' imaginations and urge them to own and describe it for themselves. Of course, that doesn't make naming any easier to do.

In fact, naming a trend can take just as long as any other aspect of defining or researching a trend. In my method, I try many possibilities. I jot down potential names on Post-it notes and compare them side by side. I test them with early readers and clients. Only after doing all of that do I finalize the names for the trends in each of my reports.

NAMING QUESTIONS: HOW TO ENSURE YOU HAVE AN EFFECTIVE TREND NAME

1. Is the name not widely used or already well understood?
2. Is it relatively simple to say out loud in conversation?
3. Does it make sense without too much additional explanation?
4. Could you imagine it as the title of a book?
5. Are you using words that are unique and not cliché?
6. Does it build upon a topic in an unexpected way?

So how did 2018's trend names turn out? The full list is outlined in Part II and the backlist of trend names is included in the Appendix, but here are a few of my favorite trend names from previous reports along with a little of the backstory behind the development and selection of each one:

✓ **Virtual Empathy (2016 + 2018).** During a time when virtual reality was a hot topic, the underlying theme behind VR was how it managed to amplify a sense of empathy in anyone who used it. As a result, I paired the term "virtual" with "empathy" instead to create a new way of thinking about the powerful effects of Virtual Reality. In this year's report (Chapter 12), the *Virtual Empathy* trend is revisited within a new, broader context, but the name still works.

✓ **Experimedia (2015).** The name for this trend came together quite quickly after finding several articles all talking about how social experiments were creating a new category of media stories. Putting "experiment" together with "media" works because the prefix of "experiment" remains unchanged, and a new ending creates a word that engages people's curiosity while still being clear enough that you could guess the meaning.

✓ **Obsessive Productivity (2014).** As the life-hacking movement generated more and more stories of how to make every moment more productive, I started to feel that these tools and advice about helping each of us optimize every moment were bordering on an obsession. The naming of this trend was easy, but to me it worked because it combined a word most people associate as negative ("obsessive") with one that is usually discussed as a positive ("productivity"). I used the same principle to name "Fierce Femininity" in 2017.

While there are many ways inspiration can strike as you name your own ideas, the following tips and tricks share a few of the techniques that I tend to use most often in naming and branding the trends in my reports.

Tips & Tricks: How to Name Your Ideas Powerfully

✓ **Mashup.** Mashups take two different words or concepts and put them together in a meaningful way. *Likeonomics* is a mashup between likeability and economics. *Shoptimization* is a mashup between shopping and optimization. Using this technique can make an idea immediately memorable and ownable, but can also feel forced and artificial if not done artfully. There is a reason I didn't call my book

Trustonomics. The best mashups are easy to pronounce and are as close to sounding like the original words as possible.

✓ **Alliteration.** When naming a brand, this technique is commonly used and the virtues are obvious: think Coca-Cola and Krispy Kreme. The idea of using two words beginning with the same consonant is one I have used for trends such as "Reverse Retail" and "Disruptive Distribution." Like mashups, it can feel forced if you put two words together that don't belong, but the technique can lead you toward a great trend name.

✓ **Twist.** The technique involves taking a common idea or obvious phrase and inserting a small change to make it different. The name should employ a term that's already commonly used and then twisted a bit to help it stand out. One of my favorite examples was a trend from 2015 called "Small Data" to counter all the discussion about Big Data. The "Unperfection" trend, which was first published in 2015, used a similar method—just enough of a twist on the actual word "imperfection" to feel new and different.

Step 5—Proving

—

Proving is the final step where you evaluate your ideas, seek out more research where needed and make a case for why an idea describes the accelerating present.

—

Photo Credit: Tech.co (Tech Cocktail Sessions DC)

Though my Haystack Method relies heavily on analyzing stories and ideas that have been published, there is also a consistent thread of conversations, speeches, and interviews that inform the trend spotting process. I'm lucky to be able to speak at fifty or so events every year, and my team and I routinely deliver dozens of workshops at companies in almost every industry.

The result of these interactions is a consistent stream of ideas as well as the opportunity to interview the visionary keynote speakers I'm sharing the stage with, which allows me to test new trend ideas and approaches with some of these groups before publishing the new trends..

I believe that trends are curated based on observing behavior, identifying patterns, and assembling the pieces of a puzzle. You can't make a puzzle by showing someone a piece and surveying them about what they think the rest of the puzzle might be.

I don't mean to discount the value of focus groups or surveys as input. The truth is, the more analytical or scientific your stakeholders and audience, the more likely it is you'll need some of this type of data to support your curated trends. But I'm neither a behavioral psychologist nor a market researcher. There are people who are excellent at this, and I would much rather read that research and have a conversation with them—and then use those insights to inform my curation of trends and help to prove them in this final phase of the Haystack Method.

The framework my team and I use, and teach our clients to use, to prove ideas is based on a formula of looking at three critical elements: idea, impact, and acceleration.

3 ELEMENTS OF TRENDS

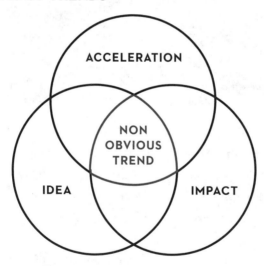

1. **Idea.** Great trend ideas are unique descriptions of a shift in culture, business, or behavior in a concise enough way to be meaningful without being oversimplified.
2. **Impact.** Impact comes when people start changing behavior or companies start to adapt what they are selling or how they are selling it.
3. **Acceleration.** The last critical element is how quickly a trend is affecting business and consumer behavior and whether that's likely to grow.

Since we started publishing our trend research, this is the central filter my team and I have used to measure trend concepts and whether they are provable. To do this, one technique we use is to consistently ask five questions as we finalize our trend list.

PROVING QUESTIONS: HOW TO QUANTIFY A TREND

1. Is the trend idea unique enough to stand out?
2. Has anyone published research related to this trend idea?
3. Is the media starting to uncover examples or focus on it?
4. Are there enough examples across industries?
5. Is the trend likely to continue into the foreseeable future?

In your own efforts to curate trends, when you go through this list of questions—it's possible you'll find that some of the trend ideas that you've curated, analyzed, elevated, and even created names for may not satisfy all these criteria.

Unfortunately, you have now reached the toughest step in the Haystack Method: leaving behind trends that you cannot prove. Abandoning ideas is brutal—especially after you have become attached to them. It probably won't help that in this chapter I've already advised you to name them before you prove them—which seems logically wrong. You never name something you're going to leave behind, right?

Well, as true as that may be, the problem is that you *need* to name the trends before you can assess its importance. The process of naming helps you understand what a trend is and how you might prove it, but it doesn't mean you're finished.

This is the phase of the process where I find discipline. It forces me to go back and either do more research and sometimes even change the original concept of the trend to be broader or narrower.

Grading all the past identified trends (see Appendix) was eye opening when my team and I first decided to add it in the 2016 edition of the book. It was clear that the trends where we had more discipline in the proving phase were the ones that fared better over time. Those were the best ideas, and the ones that you can and should aspire to have, too.

Tips & Tricks: How to Prove Your Trend Ideas

- ✓ **Focus on Diversity.** One of the biggest mistakes people make in trend curation is only seeking out examples in a single industry, category, or situation. If a trend is going to have a large impact on how business is done or how consumers behave, it should be supported by examples or cases in other industries.

- ✓ **Watch Your Biases.** Nothing will cloud your judgment more quickly than finding a trend that somehow helps your own industry, product, or career. This is a tricky subject because part of the intention of curating your own trends may specifically be to support a product or belief. Yet it's also where many of the trends that are oversimplified or just plain wrong come from. Non-obvious trends don't have apparent industry biases and are not gratuitously self-serving.

- ✓ **Use Authoritative Sources.** When it comes to the examples and research that you find to support a trend, the more authoritative sources you can find, the better. What this means in practice is using examples that people may recognize or finding research from reputable organizations or academic institutions. These sources can make the difference between selling your vision or having your audience question your conclusions because they don't believe your sources.

Let's bring the five elements of the Haystack Method to life through a step-by-step analysis of how the process helped define a trend from one of the past reports.

The following description takes you through all five steps of the Haystack Method to gather, aggregate, elevate, name, and prove a single trend from the 2015 Non-Obvious Trend Report: "Engineered Addiction."

Case Study: How to Curate a Non-Obvious Trend
Engineered Addiction

STEP 1—Gathering

One of the earliest stories I saved, more than a year before this trend was published, was about Dong Nguyen, the creator of mobile game Flappy Bird, which became one of the most downloaded apps of the year in 2013. After millions of downloads, Nguyen suddenly removed the game from the iTunes and Android stores. In the interview I had saved, he shared how his unusual move had fueled a consuming worry that the game was negatively affecting people's lives because it had become "addictive."

His unexpected choice seemed significant—though I wasn't yet sure exactly why—so I saved it. Months later, I read a book called *Hooked,* by Nir Eyal, which explored how Silicon Valley product designers were increasingly building "habit-forming products" that seemed to describe perfectly what Nguyen had unintentionally done (and felt so guilty about). I saved that idea, too.

STEP 2—Aggregating

At the end of that year, I began the process of aggregating ideas to start to identify trends. This was the moment where I started seeing a pattern in examples that seemed to focus on some type of addictive behavior. The Flappy Bird story was about game design that seemed to lead to addiction. The book *Hooked* was about product design and using it to create addictive habits in people. As I grouped these ideas together, I focused on the role that interface design seemed to be playing in creating all these addictive experiences. I stapled these stories together and put an index card on top, where I wrote the words "Addictive Design" with a black Sharpie. It was a guess about what I thought the trend could be.

STEP 3—Elevating

When I stepped back to look through my initial list of possible trend ideas (which usually numbers about seventy-five once I make it through the first two phases of the Haystack Method), there were several other trend concepts that seemed to possibly be related to this idea of Addictive Design.

One of them was a grouping of stories that were all about the use of gamification techniques to help people of all ages learn new skills. For that group, I had an index card on top that said "Gamified Learning," and inside were stories about the Khan Academy using badges to inspire learning and a startup called Curious that was making learning addictive by creating bite-sized pieces of learning on interesting topics.

Another group of ideas was inspired by a book I had read earlier that year called *Salt Sugar Fat* by Michael Moss, which had focused on the idea of addiction related to food. The book exposed how snack foods, such as Oreos and Cheetos, had been created to offer a "bliss point" that mimicked the sensations of addiction in most people.[3] Along with the book, I also had several other articles with similar themes that were grouped together and stapled with an index card that said "Irresistible Food."

In this third phase of elevation, I realized that what seemed like three unique ideas (Gamified Learning, Addictive Design, and Irresistible Food), might actually be elements of a single trend. This broader idea seemed to describe a growing instance where experiences and products of multiple types were increasingly being created to be intentionally addictive.

I put all the stories for each of these three aggregated concepts together and called the elevated grouping "Ubiquitous Addiction."

STEP 4—Naming

Now that I had examples as disparate as food manufacturing and online learning, it was time to pick a name that would effectively describe this trend. I had already come up with several to consider. As I reviewed, I dismissed "Addictive Design," because it was too small and didn't describe the food related examples. "Gamified Learning" was also tossed aside as too obvious and niche. The elevated name I had later defined of "Ubiquitous Addiction," also didn't exactly roll off the tongue and seemed to imply that more people are getting addicted to things than in the past, which I didn't believe properly described the trend.

None of the earlier names worked and I knew I needed something better.

The final clue as to what the name of the trend could be came from another interview article I read featuring Nir Eyal. In the article, he described himself as a "behavioral engineer." This idea of "engineering" instead of just design immediately seemed far better suited to describing what I felt the trend was.

After testing a few versions of using the word "engineering" in the title of the trend, I settled on "Engineered Addiction" as the most descriptive and memorable way to describe this trend and all of its components.

STEP 5—Proving

Once the name was in place, I had a way to talk about and share the trend to test it further. I already knew that I had stories across multiple industries and the trend had several dimensions. To get even more proof, I sought out more examples and research focused on intentionally addictive products and experiences that had been "engineered."

My research led me to a recently published Harvard study showing why social media had become so addictive for so many, and then later to a body of research from a noted MIT anthropologist Natasha Dow Schüll, who spent more than fifteen years doing field research on slot machine design in Las Vegas.[4]

Her book, *Addiction by Design,* exposed the many ways that casinos use the experience and design of slot machines to encourage addictive behavior. Together, these were the final elements of proof that would help me tell this story completely.

Engineered Addiction made my 2015 Non-Obvious Trend Report, and, ultimately, it became one of the most talked about trends that year.

Avoiding Future Babble

Now that we have gone through the process for curating trends, I want to share a final caution: the dangerous potential for much of trend forecasting to sink into nonsense.

Despite my love of trends and belief that any of us can learn to curate them, the fact remains that we live in a world frustrated with predictions, and for good reason.

Economists fail to predict activities that lead to global recessions. Television meteorologists predict rain that never comes. And business trend forecasters are perhaps the worst offenders, sharing glassy-eyed predictions that seem either glaringly obvious or naively impossible.

In 2011 journalist Dan Gardner wrote about this mistake-ridden obsession with the future in his insightful book *Future Babble*. Gardner illuminated the many ways that so-called experts and pundits have led us down mistaken paths and caused more harm than good.

He builds his argument based on the widely known but rarely heeded research of psychologist Philip Tetlock, who spent more than twenty years interviewing all types of experts and collected of their 27,450 predictions and ideas about the future. Tetlock then analyzed these predictions against verifiable data and found that the experts' predictions were no more accurate than random guesses.[5]

When Tetlock confronted some of these experts on how flawed their predictions had been, he found that the experts who had fared worst were the ones who struggled with uncertainty. These "hedgehogs," as Tetlock describes them, were overconfident, described their mistaken predictions often as being "almost right," and generally had an unchanging worldview.

—

"At least 50% of pundits seem wrong all the time.
It's just hard to tell which 50%."

DAN GARDNER (FROM *FUTURE BABBLE*)

—

On the other side were experts who didn't follow a set path. They were comfortable with being uncertain and accepted that some of their predictions could be wrong. These experts are "foxes" and their defining characteristics included modesty about their ability to predict the future and a willingness to express doubt about their predictions.

How can you tell which predictions to trust and which to discount? And how can you improve the accuracy of your own predictions?

The Art of Getting Trends Right (and Wrong)

I shared Dan Gardner's caution about the dangers of false certainty and skepticism about future predictions for a reason. If you are going to build your ability to curate trends, you must also embrace the idea that sometimes you will be wrong.

In Part IV, you will see a summary of previous trends along with a corresponding letter grade and a retrospective analysis of its longevity.

Some of them are embarrassingly off the mark.

The reason I share them candidly anyway is partly to illustrate Gardner's point. I want to be as honest with you as I try to be with myself and my team after each year's report. Foxes, after all, are comfortable with uncertainty and know they may sometimes be wrong. I know I'm sometimes wrong, and I guarantee that you will be, too.

Why write a book about predicting the trends and describe the entire process if we both might be wrong at the end of it? A fear of failure should not hold you back from applying your best thinking and exploring big ideas. More important, the Haystack Method may be a way to curate trends, but it's also a way to think about the world that involves finding more intersections and avoiding narrow-minded thinking.

Learning to predict the future, in other words, has a valuable side effect: it can make you more curious, observant, and understanding of the world around you. It's this mental shift that may ultimately be the greatest benefit of learning to see and curate trends.

Oscar Wilde wrote that "to expect the unexpected shows a thoroughly modern intellect."[6] *Non-Obvious* is about helping you to build this type of modern intellect through noticing the things that others miss, thinking differently, and curating ideas to describe the accelerating present in new and unique ways.

Now that we've achieved that, let's turn our attention to the trends for this year.

PART II

THE 2018
NON-OBVIOUS
TREND REPORT

What is a trend? *A trend is a unique curated observation about the accelerating present.*

Culture & Consumer Behavior: Trends in how we see ourselves and patterns in popular culture

TRUTHING

ENLIGHTENED CONSUMPTION

UNGENDERED

Marketing & Social Media: Trends in how brands are trying to influence and engage consumers.

BRAND STAND

BACKSTORYTELLING

OVERTARGETING

Media & Education: Trends in information impacting how we learn, think or are entertained.

MANIPULATED OUTRAGE

LIGHT-SPEED LEARNING

VIRTUAL EMPATHY

Technology & Design: Trends in innovation, technology and product design impacting our behavior.

PREDICTIVE PROTECTION

HUMAN MODE

DATA POLLUTION

Economics & Entrepreneurship: Trends in business models, industry or the future of work or money.

APPROACHABLE LUXURY

DISRUPTIVE DISTRIBUTION

TOUCHWORTHY

4

TRUTHING

What's the Trend?

—

As a consequence of eroding trust in media and institutions,
people are engaging in a personal quest for the truth based on
direct observation and face-to-face interaction.

—

I remember once browsing the Internet I encountered a headline that seemed too ridiculous to be true: "Harry Potter Books Spark Rise In Satanism Among Children." Indeed it turned out to be a joke – and it was one of the first times that I read *The Onion*, a comedy news site that takes modern stories and creates intentionally hilarious twists on them designed to entertain. At the time that story was quickly uncovered to be a work of satire. Today the line between truth, lies, satire and fiction has become much harder to distinguish.

The truth has a media problem.

The term *fake news*, which had no meaning two years ago, has become one of the most popular accusations traded back and forth between politicians and media personalities alike. We are surrounded by routine sensationalism peddled by 24-hour news channels desperate to invent a perpetual stream of "breaking news." Lost in the midst of all this televised finger wagging is a shared sense of reality. Thankfully, that hasn't stopped one underappreciated group of truth seekers.

On July 5, 2017, a dedicated group of 190 top fact-checkers from 54 countries attended the Poynter Institute's fourth annual Global Fact-Checking Summit (Global Fact). Their mission never felt more urgent. In the time since they had last met, Donald Trump had taken office, fake news had become an everyday term, and casual indifference toward the truth seemed to be growing.

Only a month earlier, a widely shared study found that around 59 percent of links shared on social media had never been clicked, including links that went viral and were shared thousands of times.[1] The conclusion: People were actively sharing stories based on headlines alone, without reading the article. But even a headline can mislead a large group of people, sparking a growing need for objective ways to confirm the accuracy of the news we read.

—

"*Forget clickbait. We're living in the age of sharebait now.*"
CAITLIN DEWEY, *Washington Post*

—

At Global Fact, participants celebrated the international growth of fact-checking as a discipline. The participating organizations were impressive and spanned the globe. Faktisk, for example, is an independent group founded by journalists from four competing Norwegian media organizations. La Silla Vacía is a Colombian news site that uses the messaging app WhatsApp to distribute fact-checked media and track false content or stories. Julien Pain, the editor-in-chief of France 24's program *Observateurs*, started an online live streaming program called *Instant Détox* to talk to people about media, misinformation, and rumors on the street. The goal is to debunk them in real time and to provide unbiased, transparent corrections.

This global quest for truth through fact-checking and on-demand transparency is also attracting some wealthy sponsors. Philanthropic investment firm the Omidyar Network announced that it would donate $100 million to support investigative journalism, fight misinformation, and take on hate speech. In one of his first projects since leaving Microsoft, former CEO Steve Ballmer led the creation of USAFacts.org, a comprehensive database of facts that is designed to offer more transparency regarding how the US government spends its money.

All of these organizations are responding, in various ways, to the reality of a world in which people are forced to doubt everything they see on social and mainstream media, hear from companies, politicians, and are told by their own social connections. The defining question of media today has become who can you believe?

Considering this context, the average person looks around and decides that the only trustworthy person is themself. This makes things even worse. As more of us look inward for our own definitions of the truth, the result is a trend we call *Truthing*, when the personal quest for facts leads each of us (for better *and* worse) to rely on direct observation, personal experience, face-to-face-interactions, and the opinions of those who look, talk, and think like we do.

Reengineered Media Diets and the Rise of Curators

Some of these seemingly trustworthy opinions come from intellectually superior cable news hosts who specialize in delivering a steady stream of sound bites taken severed from their context, and outrage-inducing monologues (see Chapter 10 on *Manipulated Outrage*). In response, people are turning to more approachable curators of news to help explain the world in a more human voice—like a slightly opinionated but non-judgmental big sibling who is always in-the-know.

The continued popularity of curated daily email newsletter theSkimm is a perfect example of this. theSkimm essentially offers "all the news you need to start your day," and founders, former TV news producers Danielle Weisberg and Carly Zakin, strike a conversational tone that invites trust from their readers, many of whom are female Millennials as well. This large audience feels comfortable relying on them for their news, and in a little over five years, their newsletter has attracted more than 5 million subscribers.

Other email newsletters like Brain Pickings, which is published every Sunday by writer Maria Popova, the daily *NextDraft,* which is published by writer Dave Pell, are also examples of people's growing reliance on trusted curators to help them make sense of the news. The Coral Project is an open-source organization created to help journalists get closer to the communities they serve by offering tools for better interaction (including curating more valuable stories).[2] These efforts even inspired me to write a curated newsletter, where I share non-obvious ideas and underappreciated innovation, marketing, and business stories every week. Each week I try to offer a fresh take on the stories of the week along with a quick insight about why it matters for my readers.

What these personal news sources aim to do is help each of us to reshape our media diets from something sensationalist to something more relatable. It is an example of *Truthing* because people are seeking out new sources of information to inform their perception of the world instead of ceding control of their news flow to the mainstream media.

Activism 2.0: User-Generated Truth (UGT)

For years people have talked about the power of user-generated content (UGC) as a way for real voices to break through the clutter of media. The exaggerated potential for UGC was even predicted by some to lead to a demise of advertising agencies, an idea that was bolstered as more brands featured user-created content in Super Bowl ads.

Today, UGC is being augmented by something my team and I have started describing as user-generated truth (UGT), a phenomenon where content is shared from some of the most underrepresented parts of the world to tell the story of what those places are really like. One recent example of UGT and its potential to empower people to search for the truth is the United Nations' "Not a Target" campaign. In it, the UN leveraged Facebook's newest live streaming technology to let citizens and humanitarian workers in conflict zones tell their stories directly to an online audience. The videos they shared through live streaming were haunting and eye-opening. Civilians in Syria reclaimed the stories being told about their homelands and declared themselves "Not A Target" through sharing personal, unfiltered stories.

The result of widespread access to this type of technology increases awareness of issues that don't make the front page, which, in turn, shows people that if they want the truth, they will have to go beyond mainstream media.

As Witness (witness.org) program manager Jackie Zammuto explains: "More and more people, not just in the US, are using video to document police violence, especially in places like Brazil, Mexico and all across Latin America. Of the refugees that are coming through Europe, a lot more people are taking to social media and live video to document their voyage."

This documenting of human suffering is more difficult to ignore, shaping people's understanding of the truth about the world around them and prompting them to ask more questions. (This point is also further explored in Chapter 12 on *Virtual Empathy*).

—

"This is happening. You cannot deny that this is happening because it's happening live in front of your face."
JACKIE ZAMMUTO, Witness.org Program Manager[3]

—

Live streaming technology is also changing news media coverage. *The Guardian* newspaper in the UK launched a 360-degree virtual film called "Limbo" to take users inside the process that asylum seekers go through while waiting for a decision about whether they can stay in the UK.

Free video on-demand news channel Euronews expanded its climate reporting with a 360-degree video view of several of Europe's climate change hot spots to provide real-time access to a visual representation of the effects of global warming. In the coming years, virtual tools like this will continue to bring the actions of people, corporations, governments to our computer or mobile screens in more visceral, real and unfiltered ways, which in turn feeds both our need and ability to seek out the truth for ourselves.

Tech-Enabled Truth Warriors

At the core of the rise in this UGT are improvements in the tools that are now available to tell our stories to the world. As part of its annual coverage of "10 Breakthrough Technologies," the MIT *Technology Review* routinely covers topics like the future of gene therapy and cyberwar. Last year, the review featured something that seemed a bit out of place alongside deeply scientific topics: 360-degree cameras.

Thanks to technology, 360-degree cameras are increasingly available to a public eager to share stories in a new way. The *Technology Review* cited examples as varied as videos that share a virtual forest experience and a livestream of a medical procedure used to create an interactive learning experience for surgical residents.[4] Each of these take us a little further toward the truth by presenting the world as unfiltered as it can possibly be... with nothing but a live stream from a camera trained upon it.

Photo: Samsung Gear 360 Spherical Camera

Live streaming is another new form of storytelling emerging through the same trend; YouTube and Facebook are in a race to add more live streaming features to their platforms. According to one analyst, the market for video streaming could top $70 billion by 2021 (more than double its current size).[5]

For at least half a decade the business world has been talking about the potential of UGC. The term typically describes the growing ranks of amateur content creators who make everything from Super Bowl ad competition submissions to online makeup tutorials. With 360-degree video and live streaming technology, these creators are increasingly moving from sharing entertainment to recording the truth.

Why We Trust Older Products

In our personal quests for the truth, nostalgia is a powerful force. Historian Gary Cross explores this idea in his book *Consumed Nostalgia,* in which he looks at the intersection of what we buy and the sense of nostalgia and returning to our past that those products offer. Cross writes that this nostalgia allows us to "recall a 'naïve' simpler time when there were fewer goods that lasted longer and still played an important part in family life."[6]

Why is nostalgia such a meaningful method for us to seek out the truth today? As psychologist and nostalgia expert Constantine Sedikides says, "in difficult situations it appears that nostalgia grounds you. It gives you a base on which to evaluate the present."[7]

Anytime truth feels out of reach, people tend to look into the past to products and services that were more trustworthy. In 2016 we first wrote about a trend we called *Strategic Downgrading* to describe how people sometimes opt for the older and less digital versions of products because they prefer the experience. Nostalgia in this sense, offers a powerful emotional metric for whether a product or experience is "telling the truth." Evoking this sense of nostalgia, when done right, can help consumers decide what to trust or believe.

Truth Seeking Through Nostalgia

This year Kodak announced that it would bring back its iconic Ektachrome film, and excited photographers went wild with speculation. Given the popularity of Kodak's rereleased Super 8 video camera the year before, a return to Ektachrome seemed like the natural next step. Capitalizing on the resurgent popularity of the analog camera, Kodak even published a new magazine called *Kodachrome*, which focuses quarterly on the rise of analog culture.

When Nintendo launched its throwback Nintendo Classic gaming system last year, it was in such demand that some consumers took to Ebay with an intent to sell it for 10 times the original retail price.

Sales of vinyl records over the past year hit a 25-year high, fueled by a return to tangible music and the recent death of several music legends, including David Bowie and Prince.[8]

Nokia even relaunched its iconic 3310 phone in 2017 as the ultimate backup phone, with a battery life that lasts for days and features that allow you to complete only the most necessary of mobile phone activities: calling and texting.

All of these nostalgic products are popular in part because they remind people of a simpler time when the world seemed more trustworthy, choices seemed fewer, and everything was simpler. This may or may not be true—but it certainly feels true for most people, and ultimately that is what *Truthing*

Photo: Nokia 3310 (new edition)

drives each of us to seek: not a perfect truth, but rather one that we find more palatable and believable, and that fits our own view of the world, even if that view might be different than the person right next door.

Why It Matters

The truth has perhaps never been so openly debated as it is today. To navigate this, people are exercising a behavior we call *Truthing,* and this has serious consequences for anyone who must earn the trust of audiences or consumers. Retailers must acknowledge people's skepticism and allow consumers to uncover your brands trustworthiness on their own. This creates a need for far deeper transparency about sourcing, manufacturing and environmental records—even in some cases offering direct connections with the real people making those products.

Organizations of all kinds must be prepared for these more informed customers. Health-care providers must cater to the empowered patient. Media companies must take on the challenge of regaining the public's trust. The ultimate result of *Truthing* means that the new metric for engagement is no longer determined by providing the best information or selling the best solution. Instead, companies and organizations of all kinds will need to focus on *proving* the truth of their claims with an audience that is increasingly training itself in how to spot dishonesty.

How to Use This Trend

✓ **Curate a media diet.** Just as you would never have the same food at every meal, your media diet needs to have enough variety. The problem is, people often fall back into the same sources of media—or tend to respect the same forms of media as organizations—when it comes to developing media outreach programs or advertising plans. Finding the right range in a media diet is something that organizations and people alike can do, but it requires you to start with the decision to do it.

✓ **Make it easy for customers to find truth.** Every organization needs to find new ways to win over a skeptical audience. When it comes to *Truthing*, this means finding the information sources people are most likely to trust and connecting with them. This could mean seeking out peer-to-peer validation or sharing testimonials, or finding the right influencers (or more niche *microinfluencers*) who believe in your business and are willing to speak out on your behalf.

5

UNGENDERED

What's the Trend?

—

Shifting definitions of traditional gender roles are leading some to reject the notion of gender completely, while others aim to mask gender from products, experiences, and even their own identities.

—

Ten years ago I embarked on a mission to bring attention to the 40 stories of successful and pioneering women. It was called *The Personality Project* and it started my decade long fascination with studying the steady cultural shifts of gender.

In 2013, our Trend Report first introduced *Powered by Women* as a trend to describe the significance of this shift. A year later, we proposed *Anti-stereotyping* in response to the growing examples of how traditional gender roles in everything from parenting to corporate culture were evolving. In 2017 one of our most popular trends was *Fierce Femininity* – a term inspired by many examples of women taking back their voices and speaking up.

Together, this work illustrates a track record for defining trends that are changing one of the most fundamental elements of our culture – how we see and understand gender. This year our research has led us to the growing truth that gender itself is becoming a dated idea. To see how, a good place to start is with the research of one of the foremost thinkers on the topic of gender.

Why Testosterone is Overrated

A psychologist and professor at the University of Melbourne, Cordelia Fine first shook the world in 2010 when her second book *Delusions of Gender* challenged the assumption that men's and women's brains were inherently different.

The common theory that the brain is hardwired at birth with traits exclusive to one gender or another is usually explained by the effect of testosterone on the human brain. The assumption is that this hormone makes men better suited for some tasks and women better suited to others. Disputing that theory, Fine and many other prominent feminist researchers have branded this an unacceptable form of *neurosexism*.[1]

In her new book, *Testosterone Rex: Myths of Sex, Science, and Society*, Fine breaks down common gender-based assumptions.[2]

Her ideas are so unconventional, there are some who read them as a personal attack on gender. Just six months after her book was first published, 47% of all the reviews on Amazon gave it just one star—an unusually high number that most likely reflects the polarized political response to her research rather than its inherent value.

Though the topic clearly makes many people uncomfortable and even angry, it is a symbol of the transformation occurring in how we understand, relate to, and discuss gender issues.

Gender Optional

In February 2017, around the same time that Fine was taking on her critics writing op-eds and doing interviews to promote *Testosterone Rex*, *National*

Geographic magazine devoted an entire issue to "the gender revolution." The series of articles was turned into a documentary film about gender identity, produced and narrated by Katie Couric.

As Couric traveled the US to talk with scientists, psychologists, activists, authors, and families about gender, the series asked all kinds of questions that would have been unimaginable just a few decades ago: What is gender? What is intersex? How many gender classifications do we need?

None of those questions have a definitive answer. Even the words we can use to describe gender today are expanding: non-binary, genderless, nonconforming, gender fluid, trans, asexual, and polygender, to name a few.

Four years ago Facebook changed their gender dropdown option housed in each profile to allow for more than 50 gender identities. Just a few months later, the company expanded the list to 71 options. Less than a year after the original announcement, they decided to replace the options with an empty, fill-in-the-blank box to allow each user to define himself or herself as they please.

Photo: Gender options on Facebook.

Gender, at least on Facebook, has become as non-binary as you can imagine.

———

"I think we're seeing a new gender revolution.
It's erased boxes and created gender infinity instead."
DIANE EHRENSAFT, Clinical Psychologist[3]

———

As a result, we are seeing a shift toward a safer, more inclusive and *Ungendered* way of thinking that is affecting everything from entertainment and products to marketing, recruiting and workplace practices.

The Third Gender ... and More!

When Asia Kate Dillon was cast as Taylor Mason on the Showtime original series *Billions*, one of the earliest scenes in the show was particularly true to life. In the scene, Dillon—a self-identified non-binary actor—walks into the office of hedgefund manager Bobby Axelrod and says to him, "These are my pronouns." Those pronouns —*them* and *they*—describe how Taylor (and Dillon in real life) prefer to be called, instead of the traditional, gendered pronouns *he* and *she*.

The scene introduced the concept of non-binary gender to a mainstream audience, and has been so successful that it brought along with it an unexpected problem for Dillon: how to submit a nomination for the gender-based Emmy awards for their performance. Ultimately, they chose Best Actor because it felt less gendered.

Seeing characters like this on television matters because it humanizes the *Ungendered*.

While this might still seem like a fringe idea, there are signs that a more mainstream acceptance for this often-misunderstood group is growing across the world. For example, several US states, including California, New York, and Oregon have passed legislation allowing individuals to select a gender-neutral choice of X (this is actually the letter used instead of M or F) on their driver's licenses and ID cards.

Internationally, Australia is generally credited as the first country to allow a gender-neutral option to be selected on national passports or ID cards and has since been joined by a growing list of just under 10 countries (so far), including Germany, Canada, and India, that also allow for a third gender option.[4]

For the digital world, there is even an ungendered emoji option. Created by Google employee and designer Paul Hunt, who is gay, a series of genderless emojis were approved by the Unicode Consortium (the little-known nonprofit based in Silicon Valley that is responsible for standardizing emojis worldwide).

Photo: Ungendered emoji

For many years gender was the ultimate binary choice, with a few exceptions. It was a statement to be made about yourself and a fundamental element of your identity, no matter how you chose to describe it. Today, gender has become a question to be explored.

Pink Legos and Genderfluid Fashion

The role of gender shaping our children has become a widely debated topic among those who make products for kids. Many have created more gender-neutral packaging. Retail stores have stopped using separate "boy" and "girl" aisles for toys in stores.[5]

And then there is the unique case of Lego. The Lego Friends line was originally designed primarily for girls after years of research on the different ways that girls and boys play. Despite their research-driven approach, the 2012 product launch was met with near universal criticism; one writer even describing the line as having "a color palette so sugary you can almost feel it rotting your teeth."[6] The problem was not Lego's research or even the popular Lego Friends product line, but rather that the brand seemed to fall into the same trap as many manufacturers of clothing or toys did: they made a pink product and tried to sell it to girls.

Photo: Lego Friends Packaging

The fashion industry has perhaps pushed this trend the furthest. Earlier this year, UK retailer John Lewis announced that it would be removing gender-specific labels from clothing. Target had already removed gender-based signage from its stores, and in anticipation of the back-to-school season in the fall of 2017, the retailer partnered with global kids brand Toca Boca to launch a gender-neutral kids' clothing collection.

In fashion, one of the first brands to test the *Ungendered* idea was Zara, which created a line of unisex clothing (which happened to be called

Ungendered) in March 2016. Unfortunately, the line was a flop mostly because it consisted of plain-looking sweatpants and t-shirts: two clothing options that seemed fairly gender neutral anyway.

In the year since, Ungendered fashion has far surpassed lazily rebranded sweatpants. *T Magazine,* the New York Times' style publication, featured a cover story with women wearing suits and traditionally male clothing in August 2017. Calvin Klein's Raf Simons has been credited with breaking convention by putting men and women in the same runway show and promoting an idea of gender fluidity.

Nasty Boys In Nigeria

When speaking about gender, it can be easy to focus on issues like gender equality, which tend to center on discussions about how to improve salaries, representation, agency, or opportunities for women. The flip side of the *Ungendered* trend is the corresponding shift in how we are starting to view masculinity.

Nigerian-born Richard Akuson, former fashion editor of *Cosmopolitan Nigeria,* is one voice leading this charge. In Africa's most populous country and in its largest economy, every detail of his newest publication seems designed to make some people uncomfortable … starting with its name: *A Nasty Boy.*

In a recent interview, Akuson shared:

The stories and visuals we create and share are laced with the quiet voices of the world we imagine where people do not have to feel different because of how they dress or who they are attracted to. Being a man is a diverse thing. Masculinity can and should be inclusive. I want the world to recognize that holding our boys and men to a singular definition is not fair. It alienates those who don't fit the definition, and that is incredibly emotionally damaging.[7]

Early on, *A Nasty Boy* has provided a platform for designers who have an uneasy role in a country like Nigeria, where homosexuality has been criminalized. Its goal, though, is not to enact political or policy change, necessarily, but rather to change the way their readers see the world by breaking down stereotypes about gender.

One of the most popular trends from our annual trend report last year was *Fierce Femininity*—a term created to describe the growing fierceness of how women were being depicted in everything from Hollywood films to household products. The wildly popular *Wonder Woman* film starring fierce actress Gal Gadot (who also spent two years in the Israeli Defense Forces) is one example. Brawny paper towels symbolically replacing their rugged, flannel-wearing lumberjack icon "Brawny Man" with a similarly dressed and equally tough "Brawny Woman" is another.

Photo: Brawny packaging for #Strengthhasnogender campaign.

Over the past year, men have also experienced an evolution when it comes to their expected roles in society, particularly regarding what it means to be a nurturing father. According to the "Making Dads Present" study recently released by Saatchi & Saatchi advertising agency, three in four millennial dads are resentful that advertisers and marketers are out of touch with them and their contributions to family life.

While traditional representations of stay-at-work dads portray them as out of touch or domestic screw-ups, a new generation of dads has become much more engaged and capable when it comes to domestic matters. The Saatchi & Saatchi report goes on to share that most dads (84%) say they are confident with their parenting abilities, and the majority (85%) believe they know more than people give them credit for.[8]

Advertisers are starting to take notice. Barbie dolls are increasingly marketed to dads along with kids. The UK-based Advertising Standards Authority (ASA) has not only banned ads that portray women as expert domestic cleaners, but also ads that reinforce stereotypes, such as men who are incapable of washing the dishes.

Rise of Anonymity

In addition to the challenging of gender stereotypes is the rise of anonymity as a way to mask gender in situations where revealing it may encourage unfair treatment, prejudice, or judgment in the workplace.

Over the past year, our team has been tracking a dramatic growth in technology platforms and solutions aimed at solving the problem of gender bias at work. Platforms like Blendoor, Nottx, and GapJumpers all offer some type of blind hiring technology to allow recruiters to protect themselves from unintentional gender bias when screening applicants for jobs.

In 2016, the Canadian government made a commitment to testing a name-blind hiring policy. In Argentina, the Buenos Aires–based team at Wunderman advertising agency built a browser plugin called "No Gender Profiles" to allow HR and hiring professionals to mask people's names and genders when visiting their LinkedIn profile pages.

One of the most advanced platforms in this space is Interviewing.io, which offers a suite of tools that add more anonymity and equity to the hiring process. The site also offers practice interview tools for applicants and real-time voice-masking technology to use *during* interviews.

Why It Matters

Perhaps no other trend in this book confronts something that feels so fundamental to our culture as gender. Remembering to refer to people with a third pronoun is difficult, as is reimagining the role of gender in one's own identity. It is also tempting to dismiss this trend as only important for those who work with young people. *Ungendered is not a trend about youth.*

Ungendered matters because it challenges us to rethink long-held assumptions and see the world with more empathetic and understanding eyes. In addition, it is causing companies to reevaluate how they talk and market to consumers, design products, and sell them. We are finding a growing number of our clients are focusing their attention in hiring for more diversity, encouraging more inclusivity in their workplace cultures, and contending with the difficulty of doing this in a multi-generational workforce where there are traditions, mindsets and people who are resistant to change.

In the future, we believe the most successful companies will find new ways to create inclusive training, transformational experiences to drive more workplace empathy, and stop needlessly gendering items or using stereotypical messaging. Instead, they will treat people simply as people, and attract new audiences (and employees) in the process that were previously hard to spot when limited by a more gendered point of view.

How to Use This Trend

✓ **Conduct an Ungendered audit.** The first step in putting this trend into action within any organization is an honest assessment of current materials and policies to see where an *Ungendered* approach could help expand or contract your market, or better engage your employees. The best audits will review a variety of variables, including color choice, language and context, channel bias, and implied assumptions and gender-bias in product purchase or use.

✓ **Experiment for gender sensitivity.** Different industries and audiences will have different levels of care required when considering how gender biases apply to customers and employees. The right balance for a fashion brand may be different than what's required for an automobile manufacturer, but every industry will need to find their ideal calibration. Using gender-view task teams, asking for feedback more proactively and conducting test marketing or PR campaigns are just a few of the methods which can help to understand how to put the *Ungendered* trend into action.

6

ENLIGHTENED CONSUMPTION

What's the Trend?

—

Empowered with more information about products and services,
people are choosing to make a statement about their values and the
world today through what they buy, where they work, and how they invest.

—

In the late 18th century, many Europeans were afraid to eat tomatoes.

The fruit was known morbidly as a "poison apple" and was believed to cause illness and even death among the aristocrats who ate it.[1] What no one thought to check was the plates they had been using. It turned out the acidity in tomatoes was reacting with the pewter plates in use at the time, and that the cause of death was actually lead poisoning.

These days, it is easy to assume that confusion of this sort would be unlikely. Our science is far too advanced for us to make this type of mistake again, right? Perhaps not.

Less than 50 years ago, complaints from people who were suffering from symptoms like "numbness and a general feeling of weakness" prompted the *New England Journal of Medicine* to issue a warning for what they called "Chinese Restaurant Syndrome." This dangerous-sounding epidemic was blamed for the presence of large quantities of monosodium glutamate (MSG) in Chinese food. For decades, MSG was so vilified that food packaging frequently included the words *MSG-free,* and even Chinese restaurants began declaring that they prepared food without the chemical. After decades and hundreds more studies, the link between MSG and this so-called "Chinese Restaurant Syndrome" was never found. In fact, it turned out that high levels of MSG are found in many foods that we love, including parmesan cheese or an aged steak. [2]

Science on food and nutrition in particular seems filled with this type of contradictory advice, and has been for hundreds of years. What is different today is that the pace at which these sorts of revelations are coming out seems to be accelerating, thanks to the vast amount of knowledge we have accumulated about the food we eat.

Every week there is a new miracle food and so we engage in a desperate and futile quest to find a way to integrate it into our diets. If only there were a perfect recipe to combine quinoa, acai, coconut water, kimchi, and cricket flour.

Yet with this abundance of "knowledge" often comes confusion. Coffee is unhealthy, and then it isn't. You should avoid alcohol but also drink a glass of red wine a day. Chocolate is good for you, but only if its *dark* chocolate. Fats can make you fat. Or maybe it's carbohydrates. Or perhaps it's sugar.

A recent revelation about sugar recently made big headlines, as a *Journal of the American Medical Association Internal Medicine* paper reported that the sugar industry had paid for scientists to produce research that would downplay the link between sugar and heart disease in the 1960s. [3]

When it comes to food, the science seems to change so frequently that it is hard to know if anything is good for you anymore. Added to that is the challenge of knowing whether any study is truly unbiased or whether it may have been funded by industry players with ulterior motives. Yet there is more transparency today than there ever was, mainly because consumers are demanding it. Releasing a single manipulated study published by scientists on the payroll is no longer enough. As access to information grows, consumers expectations for knowing how the products and services they buy were produced have increased.

We call this trend *Enlightened Consumption:* Consumers and workers are demanding to know exactly how the products and services in every category that they consume will affect their own happiness, health, the environment, and society.

—

"What you wear, eat, and consume says more about who you
are than about where you come from."
GILLES LIPOVETSKY, Philosopher, Professor, and Writer

—

Tools For "Applightenment"

Technology is a constant enabler of our newfound ability to experience products and services from a position of enlightenment, where we know more about how they were created.

Thanks to technology, today one can find information about how products are sourced, produced, shipped, distributed, and packaged in real time, even as one is making a decision about a purchase.

Now consumer-friendly apps like Barcoo (Germany), Good On You (Australia), the Good Shopping Guide (UK), and dozens of others are meeting consumers' high demand for information about the products they are considering. These apps offer information on all kinds of issues, including treatment of animals, carbon footprints, ethnical labor practices, diversity of hiring, and political affiliations.

People often use their mobile phones in stores to research products immediately before purchasing.[4] These apps make it easier to get an instant scorecard on the product you are thinking about buying so that you can decide for yourself if it aligns with your ethics. On the business side, a lack of transparency and ethical lapses have led to millions of dollars of lost revenue and market share for brands that have not been able to grasp the power of today's enlightened consumers.

After allegations of sexual harassment, stealing trade secrets, and profiteering, Uber has gone from claiming 91% of the ride-sharing market in the US to just 74% in two years.[5] In late 2017, the company lost its license to operate in London because of "a lack of corporate responsibility in relation to a number of issues which have potential public safety and security implications," according to a statement from London transport authority Transport for London (TfL).[6]

Other major cities are considering taking similar moves to ban the service. While they may manage to turn the situation around by making concessions for drivers or implementing other changes, Uber has become a go-to case study on the dangers of ignoring how much customers care about how the businesses they support are run.

B2B Sustainability

Aside from empowering customers to vote with their wallets, *Enlightened Consumption* is also changing the way that companies buy goods and services. More B2B suppliers are finding ways to do business ethically, diversify their management teams, focus on sustainability, and boost other positive elements of their operations. In conversations with our clients working in diversity and procurement, a similar theme runs through their efforts to try and ensure they are buying ethically, focusing specifically on finding partners who have diverse female or minority owners.

Enabling this drive to do business in a more enlightened way, companies like Netherlands-based ChainPoint and Germany-based Thinkstep have built software solutions to help companies add more transparency to their supply chains, so they can share information about their operations with procurement managers who are increasingly demanding this type of transparency from the vendors they buy from.

A good example is Stony Creek Colors, which offers a new environmentally friendly way to manufacture colored dye. Rather than using toxic chemicals, Stony Creek's blue dye is produced using indigo plants grown by farmers. These farmers once grew tobacco, but now they have replaced it with Indigo. It is a perfect example of non-obvious thinking: simultaneously Stony Creek can meet buyer needs and help struggling farmers to support their families, create sustainable jobs and renew their sense of purpose. The dye has become so popular that the company is now scaling efforts and using a combination of plant breeding and chemical engineering to change the way dye is made and purchased.

Another example is the efforts of fashion industry titan François-Henri Pinault, the CEO of Kering (parent company for 16 fashion brands including Gucci, Boucheron, and Yves Saint Laurent).[7] After acquiring Puma, Pinault was inspired by the brand's idealistic CEO Jochen Zeitz to create a new way to measure the impact of sustainability. His EP&L (environment profit and loss) metric is now helping Kering's house of brands rethink the way they produce around the world.

Transformative Travel & The World's Quietest Place

Gordon Hempton has spent decades seeking the one sound that has become increasingly hard to find on Earth: silence.

Hempton, also known as The Sound Tracker® (his trademarked name), practices "acoustic ecology" and describes silence as an endangered species. He has traveled the world in pursuit of Earth's rarest sounds and recently started working with a Seattle based tour provider on an experience that promises to take travelers into a place he calls "One Square Inch – a sanctuary of silence."

—

"I think we're realizing quiet is important, and we need silence; that silence is not a luxury, but it's essential. It's essential to our quality of life and being able just to think straight. When we become better listeners to nature, we also become better listeners to each other"

Gordon Hempton, Sound Tracker®

—

The curated quest for deep silence is a perfect example of what many industry insiders believe to be the future of travel: an experience that is not only unique and interesting, but also promises some sort of transformative experience.

This desire for "transformative travel" gained so much attention over the past year that *Vogue* magazine declared it "the travel trend of 2017." The term was described as travel motivated and defined by "a shift in perspective, self-reflection, and development, and a deeper communion with nature and culture."

Catering to this desire for transformation, travel tour operator Thread Caravan offers hands-on experiences like farm-stays in Peru where you can learn to sheer llamas, spin wool and weave it into textiles.

The successful multi-year Incredible India tourism campaign actively promotes the country's longstanding reputation as a destination that offers spiritual enlightenment.

Photo: Incredible India tourism campaign.

Ugly Fruits and Selling Your Leftovers

Turning back to the food industry, growing concern over the amount of food thrown away every year has led to a staggering amount of innovation in food recycling and upcycling in order to reduce waste in a world that is currently throwing away 30 to 40 percent of the food we grow or produce.[8]

In Italy, renowned chef Massimo Bottura founded a restaurant to serve meals to the poor and homeless using surplus and donated food. It is called Food for Soul and it exists in an abandoned Milanese theater donated by a Catholic Church.

Tech-savvy entrepreneurs in Finland have created apps like Neighborfood (which allows anyone to sell their leftover food locally) and ResQ (a tool through which restaurants can sell surplus food at a discount). The FoodforAll app offers the same service for restaurants in the United States.

Quirky Portland-based ice-cream maker Salt & Straw is putting a spotlight on food waste by featuring flavors like Curds & Whey or Spent Grains & Bacon S'mores, which use non-obvious thinking to incorporate by-products from local farms and offer a highly visible example of how we can reuse products that might otherwise be wasted.

Grocery stores are also targeting the enlightened customer in novel ways. Intermarché in France and Walmart in the United States (along with many smaller grocery stores) have committed to selling ugly fruits and vegetables, misshapen, bruised, or lumpy produce that is still fresh and tasty, despite its appearance.

Photo: "Inglorious Fruits and Vegetables" campaign

A German supermarket named The Good Food in Cologne sells only salvaged food that would have otherwise been wasted. To help put all this ugly salvaged food to use, celebrity chef Mario Batali even published *Ugly Food,* a free cookbook in celebration of Earth Day this past year.

Just outside of New York in the Bronx, fruit and vegetable processor Baldor has built a 172,000 square-foot facility where they not only wash, chop, and package fruit and produce for grocery stores and restaurants, but also bag vegetable scraps to sell to juicers and chefs. The company has even begun blending scraps into new products such as a mix of 20 dehydrated vegetables that can easily be added to certain recipes.

This groundswell of retailers, chefs, and restaurants believe that doing good and helping the environment is important, and, as we help our clients understand, doing good does not need to constrain your business but can catalyze non-obvious thinking and innovation. Companies like these and others understand that connecting with enlightened consumers through a shared sense of responsibility inspires belief, fosters innovation and drives purchases.

Enlightened Investing

There is no doubt that people are giving more thought to where they put their money. Sustainable investing is now a $9 trillion market[9] with dedicated attention from major players in the finance industry like Morgan Stanley's Institute for Sustainable Investing.[10]

Some of these groups are creating new models for how investments can and should be tracked based on more than just the simplistic method of performance of the share price. Ethical financial firm Aspiration, for example, built a proprietary Aspiration Impact Measurement (AIM) program which analyzes thousands of data points to generate two scores for corporations: one for their treatment of people and another for their sustainability practices. These "People" and "Planet" numbers are integrated into purchase behavior so their customers can measure in real time the ultimate impact of their purchase, as well as their investments.

Despite what most people assume, sustainability investing is not only for high-net-worth individuals either. An investing app called Swell offers anyone the chance to invest in one of six socially responsible investment portfolios with a minimum investment of just $500. Portfolio categories include renewable energy, clean water, disease-eradication, healthy living, green tech, and zero waste.

Stash is another startup tool that democratizes sustainable investing even further, with a minimum investment of just $5. To entice millennials who are probably investing for the first time, the team behind the app keeps the initial investment minimum low and arranges investments in relatable, consumer-friendly categories such as the Global Citizen fund (including companies from around the world) or Clean & Green (for companies that produce solar, wind, or other forms of renewable energy).

As more people aspire to be more intentional with what they consume, this is also affecting the way they invest and the portfolio of companies they choose to support and believe will grow in the future.

Enlightened Employment

In 2015, one of the most powerful predictions in our Non-Obvious Trend Report was *Mainstream Mindfulness*, a trend we used to describe a growing shift among companies to mindful management and leadership practices in the workplace. Since that time, the trend has grown dramatically.

One of the strongest voices heralding the connection between mindfulness and *Enlightened Consumption* is Paresh Shah, a Harvard MBA turned Yogi. Paresh is a respected strategy and leadership consultant who, after intensive studies in mindfulness, became a wisdom and yoga instructor. Based on his research and corporate work, Shah describes the mindsets and skills of an essential group of workers he calls "Lifters."[11]

Shah defines this growing group in this way:

"Lifters are everyday ordinary workers who know how to elevate their companies, coworkers, customers and community all at once. As employees,

they know that everything and everyone is connected, and that purpose, positivity and social responsibility can lead to 10 X performance."

Unlike demographics that thinly slice people into segments (often based on their year of birth such as Millennials), Shah's research shows Lifters span all ages or race boundaries and he presents the persuasive case that we are seeing a major shift in how people and corporations are starting to think:

"This shift is bigger than the Internet Revolution – we have entered a new era defined by Connectedness, Compassion, Creativity and Consciousness. Just as the nerds and geeks were indispensable heroes of the Information Age, disrupting industry after industry, Lifters are the emerging motive force within organizations (and quite a few of them are nerds and geeks too!)."

Shah's research indicates that organizations that embrace and cultivate Lifter Leadership™ mindsets and skills will have higher performance and be best equipped to solve the biggest problems companies face, including worker motivation, innovation, customer engagement and social responsibility.

What It Means

There was a time when questionable product sourcing or unethical labor practices were once more easily ignored or handled with a well-crafted press release and charitable donation. Today unethical choices are more easily exposed, sometimes by those who see this as their own personal moral crusade (read more on this in Chapter 10 on *Manipulated Outrage*).

There is a race happening now among companies to try and find the right ways to tell their stories of doing business and helping the world without resorting to unbelievable claims of "greenwashing." This is not just a marketing challenge but also affects the board room where pioneering leaders are forced to explain their decisions to often skeptical stakeholders and investors.

The good news is, we are seeing more and more research proving that doing business in more ethical, conscious and "enlightened" ways can lead to higher return on investment, greater innovations and greater worker and customer engagement. Over the coming year, thanks to this growing movement, we will see more organizations invest deeply in mindfulness, purpose, sustainability, diversity and inclusiveness, and community social responsibility.

How to Use This Trend

✓ **Hire and cultivate enlightened workers.** Hire people within your organization (Lifters, as Mr. Shah calls them) that represent the enlightened mindset to help you understand how the enlightened consumer thinks and to drive conscious, mindful practices across your business. Conduct systematic assessments of each product and service to identify areas that require "upgrades" to serve enlightened consumers (materials, labor, environment, use of diversity, etc.).

✓ **Develop and track softer metrics.** Just as Kering developed its EP&L in order to track its own performance, develop a visible score¬card to track real progress in key dimensions and share and engage employees on how to continuously make improvements.

✓ **Find unexpected ways to give back.** Do you have materials or supplies in your business that could be reused or repurposed into new products? One of the ways to give back could be by getting more inventive about how to reduce waste and operate with more sustainability programs both in-house and with external partners.

7

OVERTARGETING

What's the Trend?

—

*Lured by the promise of big data, organizations segment
audiences too narrowly and unintentionally end up abandoning
large groups of potentially lucrative customers.*

—

Last year, I made the mistake of purchasing a bow tie. To be more specific, I made the mistake of *searching* for a bow tie online. It wasn't really the bow tie that caused the problem. It was the ads. For weeks after I had conducted that online search, everywhere I looked online, ads for bow ties seemed to be following me around like banner equivalents of the paparazzi, and it was just as annoying.[1]

The ads went through a predictable script outlining incentives to complete that purchase. Would I like to receive 20% off? What about free shipping? Did I know they had a two-for-one special sale coming up?

The automated ad sequence was working so hard to convert me into a buyer, I even coined a term to describe the situation, joking in a blog post that I was being *adverstalked*.

The reason the script had targeted me in the first place was no surprise. I visited one fashion e-retailer's website and spent about 20 minutes browsing their collection. I had even added multiple products to my shopping cart before eventually abandoning that cart. According to any metric, I should have been an easy customer to convert.

The information they did not have was that I had never worn a bow tie in my life, and that I only needed one because I had a formal event coming up in two days. When I had trouble finding one that could be shipped fast enough to arrive in time for my event, I abandoned my online search and drove myself to a local store and bought a bow tie in person instead. At that point, I was no longer a bow tie customer.

Of course, there was no way for the algorithm to know that in real life, I had gone from an interested shopper to an unlikely one within the span of a few hours. The algorithm had no way of knowing how rarely I even think of wearing bow ties, and that this first bow tie would probably also be my last.

All the data tagged me as a prospective customer who just needed the right offer to convert. And all the marketing dollars spent to reach me were wasted. This is *Overtargeting* and the sad truth of online marketing today is that this is surprisingly common—and it is not accidental. There are plenty of unscrupulous people and companies who are profiting from this arrangement.

The New Snake Oil Salesman

In his book, *Clicksand*, author Bill Troy writes about the biggest problem with many online marketing consultants today. Like modern day snake oil salesmen, they promise the world and deliver hardly any results. Most of them promote the practice of remarketing to hyper-targeted customers and describe it as the *most* efficient type of online advertising money can buy.[2]

Along with a widespread belief in the power of remarketing among online marketers, there has been an explosion of so-called "martech" (marketing technology) companies ready to help companies put their big data to work through supposedly better segmenting and perfectly automated sequences of glorified spam masquerading as personalized marketing.[3]

The prevalence of these tools is a plague that is destroying the credibility of online marketing and it is a devolution that I have witnessed firsthand. As a senior leader in a digital focused group for nearly ten years at one of the biggest agencies in the world, we would routinely see clients burned by the illusion of ROI these companies would present.

In 2016, journalist Dan Lyons published a book titled *Disrupted,* about his time as a content creator inside the offices of Hubspot, one of the leaders in martech automation. He writes, "online marketers have invented euphemisms to make the work they do sound less awful. For example, we're told that our email campaigns do not involve badgering people, or pestering them—rather, we're 'nurturing' them ... if someone doesn't open our first email, we'll keep on nurturing them."[4]

He exposed many flaws in the system, but perhaps the most dangerous was this idea that if you can just create more targeting and more segmentation, then you can fully automate every interaction. The truth is, just because something *can* be automated doesn't mean that it *should*. For instance, what if the key to effective marketing had less to do with how narrowly you could define your audience and more to do with how compelling you could make your story?

B2Beyond Marketing

In our report from two years ago, I wrote about a trend called *B2Beyond Marketing* where a growing number of B2B companies were starting to realize the benefits of not over segmenting their audiences and instead creating content and marketing with a more widespread appeal.

Illustrating this trend in action, I wrote about examples like Volvo creating a Super Bowl ad featuring actor Jean-Claude Van Damme to promote its automatic steering feature used on trucks, and construction vehicle manufacturer Caterpillar creating a viral video showing their products deftly moving heavy wooden blocks in an epic game of Jenga.[5]

Photo: Caterpillar #Builtforit campaign

The examples illustrated a truth about B2B marketing that seemed to fly in the face of what most people assumed at that time: smaller professional audiences were not always better, because reaching a broader audience could build more buzz even it you ended up reaching people who were not part of the target audience.

This is the big idea that has also helped an eight-year-old marketing book from Australia become one of the most popular ideas among senior marketing leaders over the past year.

The Myth of Modern Marketing

In 2010 an Australian professor named Byron Sharp wrote a book titled *How Brands Grow* which challenged the popular belief that 20% of customers drive 80% of revenue.

Instead of trying to sell more or increase brand loyalty from that small group of people who are already buying from you, Sharp suggested that marketing dollars and resources might be far better spent on efforts that generate *broader* reach and influence the other 80%. The key to growth in his model is to generate *more* sales from these light or non-buyers. This is exactly the opposite of what they teach in most graduate-level marketing programs. And it is changing how some of the world's largest marketers already think.

To prove his theory, Sharp uses data to examine everything from why price promotions don't usually work (they usually only reward customers who have purchased your discounted product in the past) to how true loyalty among consumers doesn't really exist (which explains why you probably have more than one brand of shampoo in your shower).

—

"If you get too targeted, you reinforce people who love your brands to use more. There are only so many cups of tea you can drink in a day."

KEITH WEED, Unilever

—

It took several years of slow, word of mouth sharing of Sharp's research before it finally got the attention of a small, well-connected group of early disruptors. Among them was Unilever chief marketing officer Keith Weed, an influencer who controls about $8 billion of marketing budget across all of Unilever's brands worldwide.[6]

Weed and other marketers introduced the book to *their* teams of brand directors, agencies, and others who worked with them. The growing influence of Sharp's work year after year generated a buzz that eventually exploded this past year, igniting a new discussion within the marketing industry.

And then the industry saw $140 million disappear overnight.

How the Marketing Industry Lost $140 Million

If anyone deserves the credit for jumpstarting an industry-wide urgency to improve marketing efficiency and get smarter about *Overtargeting*, it is Procter & Gamble's chief brand officer Marc Pritchard.

Also a fan of Sharp's book, Pritchard cited his deep dissatisfaction with how digital advertising was becoming far too focused on niche targeting when he announced that P&G would be slashing $140 million in digital advertising spending. The move was a response to a growing concern about bot traffic causing empty impressions (which advertisers still were paying for) and the potential risk that ads would appear next to objectionable content.

It was also a wakeup call for the industry to refocus on quality. For years lazy media buyers had simply followed the biggest numbers plugged into a spreadsheet to buy the largest pool of impressions available. Now one of the world's biggest advertisers was exposing the charade and demanding more accountability.

A few months after the announcement, P&G released the even more concerning conclusion that cutting over $100 million from its digital media spending had *no appreciable effect* on its business or sales figures.[7]

After the announcement, media measurement company comScore released a report suggesting that marketers need to take a more disciplined approach to online advertising campaigns and that "marketers, once enamored with reaching highly targeted audiences at bargain-basement rates, are encountering unanticipated problems. In some cases, they are overtargeting consumers at the expense of the broader reach needed to grow their brands."[8]

Don't Kill Demographics, Understand Them

Some brands are looking to blame demographics and plenty of marketing experts have called for an end to using demographics for targeting because they are so notoriously flawed. Demographics rarely reflect differences in customer needs; instead they use the easiest possible data points to segment a particular group (e.g., single versus married, age, geographic location). In this model, demographics are an easy scapegoat and I admit that I have probably expressed disdain for their use in the past. The real problem with demographics is not that they exist, but that we tend to rely on them in incorrect ways.

Demographics were created to help people other than marketers to understand the composition of populations of people. By looking at demographic factors like gender, age, income, births, deaths, or incidence of disease, city planners could build models to understand where different types of people live, what areas require more infrastructure and how that population might then interact with the environment around them.

A major problem today is that while demographics were never intended to describe how people *think*, marketers mistakenly make use of demographics to attempt to do so. When you target the "18-to-34-year-old" demographic, you make an assumption about how everyone in that group thinks and behaves based solely on that person's age. As most of us know, people's behavior and motivations don't fit neatly into those well-defined boxes.

When tech entrepreneur Gina Pell wrote about this problem, she suggested an end to the days of targeting people by their age or generational descriptors like Boomer, Millennial, or Gen Z.

—

"Perennials get involved, stay curious, mentor others, are passionate, compassionate, creative, confident, collaborative, global-minded, risk takers who continue to push up against our growing edge and know how to hustle. We comprise an inclusive, enduring mindset, not a divisive demographic. Perennials are also vectors who have a wide appeal and spread ideas and commerce faster than any single generation."[9]

GINA PELL, Entrepreneur and Writer

—

Pointing to how Amazon and Netflix tailor recommendations to us based on what we watch (and not by how old we happen to be), Pell suggests that the first step to treating people as individuals with varying preferences and desires is to do away with using these generational terms altogether.

When brands do manage to avoid the temptation of segmenting their audience too narrowly and avoid *Overtargeting*, they often will find success by embracing unexpected groups of customers. Let's consider a few examples of this.

Green Grandmas and Girls Riding Harleys

When Maura McCarthy, the co-founder of eco-friendly home builder Blu Homes, first discussed marketing strategy with her team, it all started with an assumption that they knew who their ideal customer was. Given that their product was modern, custom-built homes, it seemed obvious that the target should be hip 30-somethings looking to settle down and buy their first home.

That is, until a group McCarthy would later describe as the *green grandmas* came along.[10]

These financially secure, affluent customers in their 60s were a much better target customer for Blu Homes in every way. They knew what they wanted and were decisive. They were more financially stable. The streamlined building approach created by Blu to deliver a home faster appealed to them. And the stress-free fixed pricing model helped to build trust and close the deal.

As McCarthy learned from interactions with customers who began to walk through her doors, she could pivot her strategy to focus on these forward-thinking grandmas along with those 30-somethings.

Harley-Davidson is another brand that has managed to make a major pivot in their business in order to embrace an entirely new audience. After years of mainly targeting middle-aged white men, the brand worked hard to appeal to women and younger customers. Despite sluggish motorcycle sales overall, there are signs that these efforts are paying off.[11]

Photo: Harley Davidson Advertising - Old vs. New

Unfortunately, too many companies fail to do what Blu Homes and Harley-Davidson have done. Like the clueless online bow-tie retailer, they blindly rely on what their data is showing them and spend too much time, too much money, and too many resources *Overtargeting* their customers.

Why It Matters

The death of mass marketing has been declared numerous times over the past 20 years, but companies on a quest for that shrinking audience of perfect customers are slowly starting to realize that much of this promised automation is an illusion. Instead, companies need to stop thinking about audiences as one narrowly defined segment with a short, predictable list of priorities and motivations, and see them more as people whose behavior and choices change frequently depending on context and circumstances.

Rather than blindly following bad data, the smartest companies are starting to question these numbers, dig further, and sometimes even counterintuitively opt for targeting *broader* audiences when it makes sense. The truth is, this can be done without diluting the message. It is not about being everything for everyone. Being what you are to more people, though, is strategy worth considering.

How to Use This Trend

✓ **Demand transparency from partners.** Just as P&G has demanded more accountability from their vendors (and pulled budget to make the point), you have the ability to do the same. This doesn't require having a big budget, but rather changing the way that you hire and evaluate the companies you work with. Ask questions about their compensation models. Ensure they are not getting paid by vendors and are looking after your best interests. Bring an unbiased expert to evaluate how they operate. These are just a few of the ways you can make sure that you are getting the most from your partners.

✓ **Remap your customer segments.** Once many companies decide who their customers are, this assumption can become sacred and feel impossible to question. Avoid falling into this trap and conduct a new customer-mapping exercise. Speak to your surprising customers. Take the time to understand not only who is buying from you now, but who could be if you only started speaking to them as well.

8

BRAND STAND

What's the Trend?

—

Reacting to a polarized media atmosphere, more brands feel compelled to take a stand and highlight their core values rather than try to be all things to all people.

—

Hamdi Ulukaya was once an anticapitalist shepherd in a cheese-making family in Turkey. Today, he is the founder and driving force behind the Chobani yogurt brand, which, has led a renaissance for Greek yogurt over the past decade and dominates the $3.6 billion yogurt industry.[1]

His rise has all the signature elements of a Hollywood rags-to-riches tale. There are competitors with deep pockets, bouts with bankruptcy, finger-wagging naysayers, and a bold risk to start it all by borrowing more than half a million dollars in 2005 to buy an abandoned yogurt factory no one wanted. Yet for all the drama of his backstory, Ulukaya received the most attention for a choice that would propel him into the center of political controversy and make him an unlikely hero for a group of people who needed the most help.

In 2010, while struggling to manage Chobani's explosive growth, Ulukaya turned to a well-known social services organization called the Mohawk Valley Resource Center for Refugees (MVRCR) located in Utica, New York. He needed workers—and fast. The MVRCR helped place a small group of refugees at Chobani's nearby South Edmeston plant. Over time, they added dozens more, and when Chobani opened a plant in Twin Falls, Idaho, the collaboration continued.

Today, about 30% of the company's workforce are immigrants and about 400 are refugees. Beyond providing jobs, Ulukaya has taken several other market-defying steps to treat his employees as if they were part of his family. In addition to unusually high salaries and six weeks of paid parental leave (rare for the food service industry), Ulukaya even set up a program to give up to 10% of the company's equity to employees.

His generosity has also extended outside America through a $5 million training initiative to support up-and-coming Turkish entrepreneurs and a collaboration with a local grant incubator program for food startups in Australia. Together, his efforts earned him a spot on *Time*'s "100 Most Influential People" list and he was recently invited to speak at the World Economic Forum in Davos, Switzerland. At that annual gathering of policy makers, thinkers, and academics, Ulukaya stood out. As one event attendee later recalled, "[Ulukaya] was quite a sensation there. Here was someone who went beyond the well-meaning chatter of Davos and was walking the walk."[2]

Unfortunately, not everyone was lining up to congratulate him. During the 2016 US election, his efforts with the refugee community came under fire by critics who claimed that he brought refugees, crime, and even tuberculosis to their community. Those groups called for a boycott of Chobani products and launched racist attacks and even death threats at Ulukaya on social media.

The controversy illustrated the double-edged sword that leaders and brands routinely face when speaking about political or social issues. Taking a stand can be costly because it alienates people. For years, brands would hire PR and legal teams tasked with the sole purpose of helping them avoid taking any kind of stand on *anything*.

Today, the brands that inspire loyalty lead with their voices instead of sitting meekly on the sidelines. As a result, less ambitious organizations are feeling pressure to take a *Brand Stand* of their own and publicly declare what they believe, despite the fact that it may alienate some more opinionated customers.

Surviving a Brandless Future

As demand for brands with a conscience increases, those who are unaccustomed to communicating in this purpose-driven manner are experiencing a relevance crisis.

One 2017 study from industry firm Cadent Consulting Group illustrated that "just over half of millennials, 51%, have no real preference between private-label and national brands." There is growing evidence that the generation to come after Millennials (often called "Generation Z") will express even *less* brand affinity.[3]

—

"Consumers deeply desire a sense that there is a greater good … there's almost a visceral reaction to phoniness."

KIT YARROW, Author of *Decoding The New Consumer Mind*

—

The implications of this loyalty shift are easy to see when you consider the dramatic growth of private-label brands over the past several years. In many product categories, there isn't significant enough differentiation for consumers to care about buying one particular brand over another. No company ever wants to sell something that seems identical to that of its competitors, but sometimes it seems nearly impossible to differentiate a product or service. Laundry detergent is one such category. It has long relied on expensive advertising budgets to remind consumers of its existence. It's something everyone needs, but no one gets excited about.

For nearly a decade, Tide (a P&G brand) has tried a different approach by investing heavily in its "Loads of Hope" social campaign. This program provides mobile laundry services via gigantic roaming trucks that carry more than 30 washers and dryers to those who need it most. In late 2017, when multiple parts of the United States were devastated by hurricanes, Tide took the program to Texas and Florida, where they provided mobile laundry services to help affected victims regain some normalcy.

As Tide already knew, in a world where it is harder to get consumers to care about your product, what you *make* is no longer more important than what you *stand for*.

#Resist and the Trump Administration

Earlier this year when the Trump administration announced a ban on travelers from predominantly Muslim countries, a group of travel brands including Hyatt, Orbitz, and Airbnb launched new marketing campaigns promoting inclusiveness and hospitality in defiance of the ban. Airbnb made a similar stand the year before when UK voters narrowly passed the Brexit referendum.

In the months that Trump was still on the campaign trail, legendary Spanish chef José Andrés had been contracted to open a new restaurant at the bottom of a new Washington DC hotel property being developed by The Trump Organization. Then, Trump made disparaging remarks about Hispanics and Mexicans on the campaign trail. Andrés immediately took a stand and backed out of the deal. New York chef Geoffrey Zakarian, who had an agreement to open a restaurant in a different Trump property, was similarly incensed by Trump's comments and pulled out of *his* deal as well. Both chefs made public statements to the media to announce their decisions.

—

"When brands successfully behave as change agents, not only do they raise awareness of an issue but they also rally individuals to the cause. They spark a debate, make people think, and enable them to participate and change their attitudes and behaviors."
CÉCILE NATHAN-TILLOY, Edelman Intelligence

—

In response, The Trump Organization sued both Andrés and Zakarian, and both countersued for reputation damage and future revenue losses resulting from his comments. The litigation dragged on for two years (during which time Trump was inaugurated) and was finally settled out of court for an undisclosed amount. While the chefs sued over damage to their reputation, as *Washingtonian* magazine reported during the legal battle, "It stands to reason that by becoming anti-Trump heroes, both Andrés and Zakarian have bought themselves brand loyalty."[4]

Thanks to increasingly tone-deaf rants on Twitter and a continual talent for taking unpopular, extreme positions, the list of brands taking stands against Trump's remarks—on everything from minorities to health care—has grown steadily.[5]

Fearless Girl and Utah's Lost Conference

One of the most talked about examples of a *Brand Stand* over the past year came from financial advising company State Street Global Advisors (SSGA) in March of 2017 when they commissioned a statue called *Fearless Girl*, which depicted a defiant young girl, hands on her hips, facing Wall Street's iconic *Charging Bull* statue in New York City.

Photo Credit: Anthony Quintano (Flickr)

In commissioning the statue, State Street Global Advisors was making a public statement in support of gender equality in an industry traditionally dominated by men. The campaign was estimated to have generated over $7 million in free publicity and won 18 awards at the annual Cannes Advertising Festival.

Unfortunately, it also became a cautionary tale in what happens if the best communications aren't supported by real action. Just seven months later, State Street Corp agreed to pay a combined $5 million to more than 300 women and 15 black employees who were paid less than their white, male counterparts (according to a federal audit). It was an embarrassing reminder that what you *do* matters more once you take a *Brand Stand*.

Sometimes a *Brand Stand* is less about creating a culture change and more about influencing a specific change in legislation or policy.

When Utah Governor Gary Herbert refused to oppose legislation aiming to roll back environmental protections for public land,the Outdoor Industry Association (OIA) threatened to move its annual meeting (and $45 million budget) out of the state for the first time.[6] The governor did not budge, so the show took its own *Brand Stand* and found a new host city in Colorado.

While the political climate in the United States is inspiring a particularly active year of corporate *Brand Stands*, other countries are seeing the same trend affect their own brands' willingness to speak up in defense of their values.

Lego's Stand

For the past several years, LEGO has run promotions with popular national newspaper *Daily Mail* in the UK. A little over a year ago, a customer contacted them through social media to complain that the paper uses headlines that "create distrust of foreigners and blame immigrants for everything."[7]

Several days later, LEGO announced that it would not be advertising in the newspaper in a tweet.

Stop Funding Hate ✔ @StopFundingHate · 7 Nov 2016 ⌄
We love this polite, friendly & heartfelt msg from Bob to @LEGO_Group urging
them to #StopFundingHate ! facebook.com/photo.php?fbid... #keepitcivil

💬 58   ⟲ 938   ♡ 2.0K   ✉

LEGO ✔   (Follow) ⌄
@LEGO_Group

Replying to @StopFundingHate

We have finished the agreement with The
Daily Mail and are not planning any future
promotional activity with the newspaper

4:07 AM - 12 Nov 2016

Photo: Lego tweets announcing no more promotions with *Daily Mail UK*.

This type of consumer pressure is increasingly creating opportunities for companies to take a *Brand Stand* in reaction to consumer demand. The backlash against GMOs, high-fructose corn syrup, and artificial ingredients have led many of the world's largest brands—from McDonald's to Mars—to take reactive measures to source their products more transparently.[8]

Tata Tea and Indian "Preactivism"

Earlier this year, Indian beverage brand Tata Tea brought back one of its most beloved advertising campaigns from nearly a decade ago to create a new cultural wave around the idea of "preactivism," creating social change before a big crisis forces it. The campaign was meant to force consumers to acknowledge their complacency, while reinforcing the progressive positioning of Tata Tea in the marketplace.

The campaign, called "Alarm Bajne se Pehle Jaago Re" ("Wake Up Before the Alarm Rings"), consisted of emotional TV spots featuring young Indians. It touched on issues like women's empowerment, encouraged more young people to stay in sports, and appealed to the government for increased funding for a number of causes. When asked about the strategy behind the reboot,

Tata's Regional President Sushant Dash shared: "The need now was to move from being reactive to instilling a sense of 'preactivism' in people, not reflecting on culture but creating one. This is hopefully the start to another new wave of social uprising."[9]

---

5 ELEMENTS OF AN EFFECTIVE BRAND STAND

1. **Relevance** – The connection between your brand and the stance should be clear.

2. **Timeliness** – Take a stand when the issue at hand is being widely discussed.

3. **Proactivity** – The best stands are made proactively rather than in response to a PR crisis.

4. **Meaning** – Your stand should be driven by genuine concern and involve some sacrifice.

5. **Commitment** – Stands should involve long-term, tangible commitments to a cause or value.

Why It Matters

Brands can no longer afford to sit on the sidelines of current events, focusing on their products and services. Instead, the ready availability of social media and other communication channels, and the polarization of media, is forcing brands to make principled stands and share their beliefs with the world. For companies that have never had to communicate in this way, it will lead to a soul-seeking exercise to figure out exactly what it is they want to say and stand behind.

For the brands that have some social purpose already, this is a chance to declare it unequivocally and then contend with the resulting reactions from consumers who applaud them for it as well as those who do not. This consumer reaction will lead brands to more openly share their beliefs with their workforce, and focus on how to live those principles in a consistent way now that they have been publicly declared.

How to Use This Trend

✓ **Take a credible position.** Taking a *Brand Stand* works best when it is on a topic that you have some credibility in speaking to. Andrés' stand against Trump's disrespect toward Hispanics was partially because he employs many Hispanic people in his restaurants and is from Spain himself. The more strategic you can be with what topics you make your own, the easier it will be to truly stand behind them with real action instead of just empty words.

✓ **Make sure your team is on board.** This is not a trend to dictate from the top down. Instead, it is important to have the buy-in from a core team because they are the ones who will bring this stand to life and illustrate whether your brand is walking the walk. The more you involve your full team (at every level) early on, the more successful you will be with helping your *Brand Stand* to have real impact.

9

BACKSTORYTELLING

What's the Trend?

—

Organizations use the power of stories to share their heritage, mission, and reason for existing with audiences to earn loyalty and position themselves as desirable places to work.

—

One of the most famous advertising agencies in the world had a hundred-year-old secret.

Madison Avenue has been dominated by the same big ad agency names for decades: Ogilvy; Leo Burnett; Grey; Young & Rubicam (Y&R); J Walter Thompson (JWT); Mullen; Saatchi & Saatchi; and Wieden + Kennedy. All of these names have something in common: they pay homage to the men that founded the firms.

All of them, except for Grey.

Founded in 1917, Grey Advertising was one of the earliest advertising agencies, and the only agency *not* named after its founders. This was not out of modesty. A film recently released by the brand reveals the truth in its opening voice-over:

> "It's 1917. New York is booming. Two young Jewish entrepreneurs, Lawrence Valenstein and Arthur Fatt, set up a company. But anti-Semitism is rife. Their names could cost them business. So they call it Grey, after the color of the wallpaper."

It is a sad fact of history that the founders of what is today one of the largest agencies in the world justifiably feared that using their names would cost them clients. One hundred years later, the current team at Grey decided to temporarily change the firm's name to celebrate the anniversary of its founding.

In the first quarter of 2017, Grey's London office renamed itself Valenstein & Fatt for 100 days, and even gave its branding a complete makeover. They changed all the signage, the letterhead, and the website, and even trained the receptionist to answer the phone with the new agency name. The result of the effort was plenty of media attention and, more importantly, a powerful story to share with potential new recruits. This backstory offered a new reason to believe in the brand that was not reliant on the current clients or even their creative work. Instead, Grey used the power of *Backstorytelling* to take their own history and use it as a reason to inspire belief and position the agency as a desirable place to work.

When I first wrote about the *Backstorytelling* trend as part of my 2013 trend report, it was about more than brands telling stories as a key element of their marketing strategies. The key was to focus on the *back* part of *backstory*—using heritage, history, and the past to tell a better brand story and inspire belief.

Scandinavian Tweed and Turkish Cymbals

Røros Tweed is a renowned European textile company with an unusual-backstory. The company was officially founded in 1940 and owes its existence to the generosity of a man named Peder Hiort.

Back in 1789, Hiort was director of the coppermine that employed a significant number of people in the tiny town of Røros. He died childless and bequeathed his entire fortune to a foundation that offered training in textile production to the city's poor. Having to endure harsh Scandinavian winters, the people of Røros maintained their tradition of textile manufacturing, and today they have built a client list that includes the Emperor of Japan and Christian Dior.

That story is now a fundamental element of the brand's identity, featured prominently across their retail stores, printed materials, and website. The story inspires pride among employees and curiosity among travelers.

Another brand with a fascinating history is Zildjian, the world-famous cymbal makers. Zildjian was first established in Turkey as a manufacturer of quality cymbals in 1623, making it one of the oldest companies on Earth still operating today. The founding story of Zildjian starts with the tale of Avedis, a alchemist searching for gold. In the process, he accidentally discovered a mixture of metals that had exceptional musical properties and began to produce cymbals which soon became popular at royal ceremonies. The Sultan Osman II gave Avedis the title Zildjian, a combination of the Turkish words zil (cymbal), dji (maker), and -ian (son of).

In the generations since, the company has been handed down from father to eldest son. A feud between brothers Armand and Robert in 1981 led the latter to spin off a competitive cymbal brand, Sabian, but Zildjian has continued to dominate the industry.[1] In an ironic twist considering its father-son history, in 1999, Armand Zildjian named his daughter, Craigie, CEO of Zildjian. She is the first woman in the company's history to take on this role.

How Startups Can Win with Backstorytelling

There are many examples of brands with long histories who can turn back the clock and tell those powerful stories as a reason for consumers to engage with them. *Backstorytelling* is not only a trend for brands that were founded many years ago. It can also be a powerful way to introduce a startup or younger company through focusing more on the personality of the brand rather than the years it has been in existence.[2]

Fridababy is a perfect example of a younger company through the force of its personality. This is how their website summarizes what they stand for: "Fridababy is the brand that gets parents. That means you. We are not a lifestyle. Far from it. We are a solution-based brand. The 411 of parenting. The who-do-I-call-in-the-middle-of-the-night-cause-my-baby-won't-stop-screaming brand."

While other brands seem afraid to talk about the messier side of parenthood, Fridababy wants to be the brand that will gladly suffer through it all with you.

—

"No other brands are this focused on being there for you when it's 3 a.m. and your hands are covered in baby shit."
CHELSEA HIRSCHHORN, CEO, Fridababy

—

The brand sells 15 specialty products including their most popular: the NoseFrida (a tube that lets you suck mucus out of your baby's nostrils), the SnipperClipper (a newborn size nail clipper), and the ButtWasher (which helps keep toddler's butts clean when toilet training). Each is a product that may seem slightly quirky, off-putting, or plain disgusting ... unless you happen to be a new parent.

Beautiful Stories and the Future of Cosmetics

In the beauty industry, these backstories are often told through the personal lens of an engaging *microinfluencer*, who builds an audience through personal content and videos.

Huda Kattan is fond of describing herself as "everyone's beauty BFF." In her case, that's not too far from the truth. The 34-year-old social media personality who bears an uncanny resemblance to Kim Kardashian has more than 20 million followers on Instagram, has been named one of the Internet's most influential people by *TIME* magazine, and owns a rapidly expanding beauty empire selling fake lashes and other makeup products under the brand Huda Beauty.

Based in Dubai, Kattan has been described by *The New York Times* as "the most influential beauty blogger in the world." Keeping those fans engaged and connected with her is a full-time job. She spends more than four hours every day on social media, answers questions from customers on her blog, and stars in video tutorials demonstrating how to use her latest products.

There are dozens of other aspiring beauty bloggers who are candidly sharing their own backstories, winning loyal fans, and converting them into customers by launching their own lines of beauty products. They charismatically share their frustrations with current beauty products and offer up a solution to a niche problem born from experimentation. These charismatic founders are finding that big cosmetic companies are hungry for a little of that same attention.

In the past year, there were 52 acquisitions in the beauty and personal-care industry (the most in a decade).[3] The majority of these smaller players were not acquired solely for their products. Instead, they each have value from their large fan base, who remain loyal because of the power of their microinfluencers' backstories.

This same principle has driven one of the world's fastest-growing European tourist destinations to create some interesting content and experiences of their own.

How to Avoid Hot Tub Awkwardness In Iceland

If you ever needed a tutorial on how to avoid hot tub–related awkwardness, you might want to start by asking an Icelander. Iceland is in the midst a tourism boom, having quadrupled their annual visitor counts over the past several years.[4] While good for the economy, the influx raises some natural questions about resources and how to protect the unspoiled beauty that many travelers seek when they visit the country.

One way is to convince visitors to travel to unexpected destinations within Iceland instead of sticking to—and possibly spoiling—the most popular natural wonders. To do so, Iceland's tourism board created the Iceland Academy, a video series hosted by locals that teach people "How to Eat Like an Icelander," or tell a personal history about their experience in the country through "A Beginner's Guide to Icelandic Sagas." And they included the uniquely Icelandic guide titled, "How to Avoid Hot Tub Awkwardness."

The island nation is not new to this strategy. Back in 2015, the "Promote Iceland" campaign enlisted the help of seven locals, all of whom shared the same popular name (named Guðmundur or Guðmunda), answering questions about Iceland on social media in real time, offering the "world's first human search engine."

These inventive ideas help Iceland to share its story and culture in a beautifully authentic way. They offer travelers a real sense of what it might be like to visit there—and effectively inspire more of them to take the trip in the future.

Making the Backstory Tangible

Earlier this year, Airbnb launched a travel magazine to fill a gap that CEO Brian Chesky identified in the market. As Chesky recalls, "We looked at the existing travel magazines and noticed that most had no people in them. We found that strange, because in our experience the real magic of travel comes from meeting and connecting with people. We wanted a magazine that would celebrate that kind of traveling."[5]

In addition to featuring destinations, *Airbnbmag* tells the story of why Airbnb exists, features great places to stay through the platform, and serves to unite their community of hosts by featuring their stories in the publication.

The effort technically might be described as content marketing, but the best storytelling initiatives rarely feel like some sort of artfully disguised brand promotion. Instead they feel real.

Backstories Through Filmmakers

Last year, luxury fashion brand Hermès launched a film called *La Fabrique de la Soie* to offer consumers an artfully produced behind-the-scenes look at the history of how the company makes silk garments. The film used beautiful footage and a compelling soundtrack to take consumers to a place that most could never have access to in real life.

In the book last year, I shared the story of 600-year-old Japanese soy sauce brand Kikkoman, which engaged award-winning documentary director Lucy Walker to produce a brand film called "Make Haste Slowly." It took consumers inside the saga and history of how soy sauce has been made for centuries. It was an example that year of the *Preserved Past* trend, which is closely linked with this trend of *Backstorytelling*.

To engage consumers, the Kikkoman film starts with the powerful opening line: "It was started by a woman in a time when women didn't start companies." Until that film, I never cared much about what brand of soy sauce I would buy. After seeing it, Kikkoman became my brand of choice. Will one well-produced film be enough to win over any consumer? Most likely not.

But the power of *Backstorytelling* is that it can help you humanize a brand and win over some consumers by giving them a reason to see you differently than the competition.

India's Favorite Beer

In just two years, Bira 91 has become one of India's most popular beer brands.

When creating the company, the one thing Indian entrepreneur Ankur Jain knew about beer in India was that people mainly bought and consumed it to get drunk. The country's top-selling beers were relatively boring imported brands, and the culture of microbreweries he had seen when living in Brooklyn, New York, was nonexistent in India.

So he created it. In 2015, Bira 91 launched with a Belgian-style white ale and a blonde lager that were produced in Belgium and imported into India. Speaking about his initial challenge to build the brand, Jain says, "There was skepticism at every level. People said Indians would never want to drink premium brands. People are suddenly realizing this could be an interesting category. There is now a huge chunk of the population that will pay more for better beer."

Today, the beer is created using locally sourced wheat and aromatic coriander from Indian farms, and Jain tells a much different story to try and help the brand expand beyond India. Embracing his heritage as an Indian, Jain believes that his creation can win: "People just want unpretentious beers that are flavorful. That void could be filled up by Bira."[6]

New Columbia Distillers is another ambitious startup trying to tell a compelling backstory. The DC-based spirits maker owns the first legal distillery in the District and makes Green Hat Gin, a popular small-batch liquor. The name of the gin is inspired by a bootlegger named George Cassiday, who supplied alcohol to members of Congress during the Prohibition in the 1920s. When Cassiday was eventually caught, he was arrested while wearing his signature green felt hat, which had earned him the nickname, "the Man in the Green Hat." Today, the story of the gin is linked to that historical tale and offers an interesting backstory that people can share with others.

Why It Matters

There are many types of backstories. Some are deeply personal and human, like those of beauty bloggers connecting with their audiences directly. Others are professionally produced and told through artfully shot documentary films like the film, from Hermes. Others are printed on the back of packaging to share a slightly quirky story that explains an odd choice of brand name, like Green Hat Gin.

The power of *Backstorytelling* comes from the impact these stories can have in the race to stand out from competitors. The companies that do manage to focus on story will be leaps and bounds ahead of the others.

How to Use This Trend

✓ **Be who you are.** This was one of the lessons that GE's chief marketing officer Linda Boff shared in a session I led a few months ago. Her point was that every company has a natural origin story and the problem sometimes is that we try too hard to reinvent ourselves instead of embracing who we are. GE, for example, is a company filled with engineers who make complex products. Instead of trying to dumb them down, GE engages in storytelling that lets you appreciate the wonder of how everything from airplane turbines to hospital scanners even work in the first place.

✓ **Use stories when onboarding new employees.** We tend to think the keepers of our stories must be the people who have been at the company the longest. The truth is, sometimes your newest team members can be the most enthusiastic—if you give them a chance. Their experience with the company is fresh and they don't have the same preconceived notions as other workers. As a result, a great onboarding program can help to shape their experience and knowledge about the company and help them learn the stories that they can later retell and live by. This shared experience also fosters a community, giving employees an easy way to connect with future new hires.

10

MANIPULATED OUTRAGE

What's the Trend?

—

*Media, data analytics, and advertising are combining forces
to create a perpetual stream of noise that is intended to incite rage
and illicit angry reactions on social media and in real life.*

—

In April of 2017, Dublin-based designer Stephen Crowley made the Internet angry. His "crime" was posting images of his 18-month-old daughter, Hannah. Unlike the pictures shared by most doting dads, these images were unusual. In one, Hannah was sitting on a kitchen counter holding a long chef's knife. In another, she seemed to be hanging from a jungle gym that was clearly too high for her.

The one that seemed to incense the Internet most was an image of Hannah hanging dangerously from the railing of their house with a one-story drop and wooden stairs beneath her. Crowley's caption beneath the photo read simply, "I think the new stair gates may be faulty."

Photo - Courtesy of Stephen Crowley (used with permission).

Before you start to get a little outraged yourself, there is one detail about this story that you should know. Crowley is a designer and these images were all Photoshopped to have a bit of fun and make the family smile. At the time, smiles had been hard to come by in their family because Hannah had been diagnosed with a rare immune disorder called HLH. She had spent six months in chemotherapy at the hospital before eventually receiving a bone marrow transplant. To lighten the mood, Crowley had turned to his Photoshop skills to create photos of his daughter in ridiculous situations.

The problem, if you could call it that, was that not everyone on the Internet realized they were phony. As a result, he was on the receiving end of what has rapidly become one of the most commonly expressed emotions online ... outrage. Stephen Crowley was caught off guard by all the attention and didn't intend to mislead people. His goal was a noble one: to raise awareness of the need for bone marrow donors.[1] Not everyone online shares his good intentions.

We are faced with an explosion of *Manipulated Outrage* online, through which we are encouraged to feel irritation, anger, and even repulsion by those who too often aim to profit from or exploit our emotions.

This year, Facebook admitted that their new reactions buttons had an undesirable algorithmic side effect. The more often you clicked the angry or sad reaction buttons, the more Facebook's algorithm would offer content to evoke the same emotion. In other words, the more you clicked the angry button, the more news Facebook would show to make you angry, and the cycle would continue.

While Rage is defined as "violent, uncontrolled anger," *outrage* is "an extremely strong reaction of anger, shock, or indignation." Outrage, in other words, is something created when you do or say things that make others angry. When you consider how good this outrage seems to be in capturing attention, it is easy to see why it might make sense to manipulate it for the purposes of influencing people—especially when it comes to politics.

The Outrageous President

When Donald Trump first announced his candidacy for the Republican nomination for US president, many thought it was a joke. One journalist even recalls being there on the day of the announcement and chuckling at the ridiculousness of the staged event.[2] Two years later, Trump rode a wave of unrealistic promises and tell-it-like-it-is opinions delivered via Twitter to end up in the Oval Office.

As former Obama speechwriter Jon Favreau once described it, "Trump doesn't care if we think he's telling the truth—he just wants his supporters to doubt that *anyone* is telling the truth." A key element of his strategy was his ability to manipulate outrage from his supporters and use it to his advantage. There is no need to spend time attacking other people when you can send a quickly crafted thought in less than 140 characters and get others to attack your enemies for you.

In March 2017, Trump tweeted: "How low has President Obama gone to tapp [sic] my phones during the very sacred election process. This is Nixon/Watergate. Bad (or sick) guy!" Those 140 characters launched months of probes and inquiries for a claim that most investigators concluded had no proof or validity.

The important question to ask here is: *Why does this work so well?* To answer that question, let's look at the brilliant promotional plan for one of the worst movies of the past decade—and why so many people actually went to see it.[3]

The Manipulator's Playbook

In 2009, marketing consultant Ryan Holiday was tasked with creating a promotional plan for the ultimate bro film about drinking and sexual conquests, titled (after the book that inspired it) "I Hope They Serve Beer In Hell," written by Internet personality Tucker Max.

Holiday's strategy hinged on classic reverse psychology: Get young men to see the film by telling them not to. To make the mental trickery work, he sent outraged emails to activist groups to encourage them to boycott the film on college campuses. He sent fake tips to gullible media properties like Gawker and made intentionally offensive ads to anger (mostly) female reporters and bloggers. The goal was to create so much noise that the young men who were the target audience for the film couldn't help but overhear the outrage and feel compelled to see the film because the world around them seemed to be telling them *not* to.

The campaign's signature moment was this story, which Holiday later wrote about:

> *"My favorite was the campaign in Chicago—the only major city where we could afford transit advertising. After placing a series of offensive ads on buses and the metro, from my office I alternated between calling in angry complaints to the Chicago CTA and sending angry emails to city officials with reporters cc'd, until 'under pressure,' they announced that they would be banning our advertisements and returning our money. Then we put out a press release denouncing this cowardly decision. I've never seen so much publicity. It was madness."*[4]

After the success of the campaign, Holiday would go on to write a bestselling book called *Trust Me, I'm Lying*, as an exposé of how easily people could be manipulated and a warning that perhaps others might use these same techniques for more evil purposes than promoting a bad film. Unfortunately, his wake-up call for the media fell largely upon deaf ears. Instead, the book became an underground playbook for those seeking to manipulate the media to spread hate and negative ideas—people like alt-right blogger Milo Yiannopoulos.

Holiday also writes that someone like Yiannopoulos "doesn't care that you hate them—they like it. It's proof to their followers that they are doing something subversive and meaningful. It gives their followers something to talk about. It imbues the whole movement with a sense of urgency and action—it creates purpose and meaning."

In this easily offended world, fueling outrage can lead to credibility because it offers a fringe opinion the chance to reach the masses. The reason it works so well is because the media is a willing accomplice in this game of deception. For them, following the outrage simply makes good business sense.

The Business Model of Outrage

When you sell advertising based on clicks and views, the more attention you can get, the better. In the first full quarter since Donald Trump's electoral victory, *The New York Times* reported its single biggest surge of subscribers in its entire history; adding more than 300,000 digital subscribers in less than a month. According to TV ratings data from Nielsen, cable news programming from Fox News, CNN, and MSNBC all saw double-digit ratings growth across the board for the second quarter of 2017. CNN had its most-watched first quarter in 14 years, and Fox News had the highest-rated quarter ever in cable news history.[5]

Clearly outrage is attracting attention, but it doesn't just sell when it comes to mainstream media. The business model for documentary films has also long relied on *Manipulated Outrage* to expose injustices while taking on social issues. Filmmaker Louie Psihoyos, for example, used outrage as a way to engage viewers when he created the Oscar-winning film *The Cove* (2010), which is about the secret slaughter of dolphins in a Japanese seaside town.

Another example of *Manipulated Outrage* from China involves a growing legion of enterprising people who have developed a creative way to monetize outrage by scouring the shelves of Chinese supermarkets. These so called, food vigilantes are looking for products with incomplete nutritional information, food being sold past their expiration date, or products with illegal additives. When they find what they are looking for, they sue, and either win compensation or settle out of court for undisclosed amounts.

Thanks to a strengthened version of the Chinese Food Safety Law introduced in 2015, this cottage industry of vigilante informers has exploded. One Beijing court estimates that 80% of the food-safety related cases are filed by these "professional complainers." They win by specializing in threatening to publicize these details food manufacturers would rather keep quiet while relying on the predictable consumer outrage to provide enough motivation for these companies to settle in court as quickly as possible.[6]

The impact of all this business focus on outrage is that it creates an atmosphere where many people start to feel a social pressure to live up to their new moral duty to remain outraged at all times. Outrage has become a part of who we are.

Outrage As Identity

Teen Vogue magazine has become one of the most influential magazines among young women thanks to the transformation it has undergone under the leadership of Elaine Welteroth over the past two years.[7]

Championing the not-so-revolutionary idea that women can be interested in both fashion *and* politics, Welteroth has crafted an editorial mission that offers *Teen Vogue* readers a combination of clarity, rigor, and insight, delivered in a format that makes it easier to consume without dumbing down the issues. Rather than only covering superficial topics like makeup, clothing, and boys, the magazine goes further to encourage its readers to think about what it means to be an educated citizen.

One consistent theme since Donald Trump took office is how to channel outrage to inspire political change. In one issue, for example, there were multiple stories about how to stand up and have a voice, get involved in politics, and be heard. There was even a *Mad Libs*–style word game where readers could insert their own resistance-themed words. The assumption underlying the editorial seemed to be that it had become the duty of *woke* young women to lead the charge to fight back. For many of them, this constant need to #resist can become a misguided directive to live a more one-sided life where there is only a single way to think.[8]

The Burden of Outrage

Author Nicholas Carr writes about how the Internet and technology is changing our brains. He famously asks whether Google might be making us all stupid by providing instant answers to everything and robbing us of the opportunity to discover knowledge by ourselves.

In a recent article about the rise of fake news, he shared a scary modern truth: "It's possible to be both *more* informed and *more* narrow-minded."[9]

What happens in a world where it is easy to dismiss anyone who disagrees as an idiot, unworthy of conversation? In a 2017 interview with *Pacific Standard* magazine, left-leaning political strategist and frequent CNN panelist Van Jones also asks this question—and is unafraid to cast blame in an unexpected direction:

> *"These young people are the worst because they will call you a bigot for not believing something that they had never heard of three months ago. So with that level of arrogance and lack of understanding, the blowback is not only inevitable, but you'll actually accelerate it."*

When you think about the trend of *Manipulated Outrage*, it is easy to see young people as the open-minded heroes who are fighting back against those who dismiss their forward-thinking view of the world. Less often do we consider the downside of this overblown sense of righteousness and how it might make anyone just as closed-minded as the people they criticize.

The missing link is empathy and a willingness to engage from a place of kindness with those who disagree with you:

> *"What's missing? ... that spirit of Mandela that says, even though I am oppressed, my view of the perfect society has a place of dignity for you in it. ... I'm not fighting against you, I'm fighting for you, because I want you to have a place of honor that doesn't require you*

to indulge in hatreds that are beneath you and your family."[10]

If there is any way to conquer the polarizing effects of this *Manipulated Outrage*, it is to follow this path of Mandela and find common ground with people unlike ourselves. This starts with being willing to face each other in a conversation and stop letting those who profit from the outrage divide us so easily.

Why It Matters

We are surrounded by outrage, and are increasingly manipulated by people or organizations with ulterior motives who seek to profit from this emotion. While dishonest people will always exist, this trend also challenges each of us to be more intentional about our media diet and take a harder look at how we consume, share, and filter the information that forms our opinions.

For businesses, understanding how this *Manipulated Outrage* works can help them understand what customers are seeing and feeling. This knowledge, in turn, can help you make your messages more relevant, less sensationalist, and more believable.

How to Use This Trend

✓ **Create moments of "media escapism."** We all need time away from media-inflicted outrage to do things that are less political or polarizing. NPR writer and "Pop Culture Happy Hour" host Linda Holmes likens this situation to the one from the film *The Martian*, where Matt Damon plays an astronaut stranded on Mars who needs to grow potatoes to stay alive long enough to be rescued. Her analogy is that sometimes you need to do the small things (like growing potatoes) to have the energy to tackle the big things.[11]

✓ **Engage the manipulators.** In writing about the manipulation playbook, Ryan Holiday also offered the solution to fight back—engagement. Instead of banning them from speaking and offering them the moral high ground to complain about their voices being stifled, we can each engage with their arguments and force them to defend that point of view through logic and reality. In most cases, this is where the outrage breaks down. It is harder to be manipulated once you dig beyond the sensational headlines.

11

LIGHT-SPEED LEARNING

What's the Trend?

—

The road to mastery on any topic gets faster through the help of bite-sized learning modules that make education more time efficient, engaging, useful and fun.

—

As a longtime drummer, I have always wanted to extend my musical abilities to learning the guitar—and I've started several times. The problem is, something else usually comes up, life gets busy and despite my best intentions, eventually I just stop.

Apparently, I'm not alone.

Andy Mooney, CEO of guitar maker Fender, estimates that around 90% of those who pick up the guitar quit within the first year, and about 45% of Fender's annual sales go to beginners who have never played before. Given the guitar is one of the most popular instruments in the world and Fender sells between 1.6 million and 2.5 million of them every year, this is a major business problem.

If you abandon the guitar, you are not going to come back to Fender to buy amplifiers or accessories, or upgrade to a nicer guitar. What would it take, Mooney wondered, to get people to stick with it?

The mission to find out became the job of Fender's general manager of digital Ethan Kaplan, who decided to spend several months studying how people learned the guitar. Kaplan's team interviewed music teachers at prominent Los Angeles schools and talked to students themselves.

They learned that the truth was more complicated than just people, like me, making the excuse of being too busy. Instead, they discovered the real secret to encouraging aspiring guitarists to persist was to help them learn it in smaller, digestible chunks so they could feel like they were getting better *quickly*.

This second point was a critical insight. When students felt like they were not making fast enough progress, giving up became much easier to justify. To help people get better faster, Kaplan and his team built a video subscription service called Fender Play that offers video instruction on-demand for $20 a month. The videos can be as short as a couple of minutes, feature well-known songs from popular artists and are filmed in beautiful 4K HD quality—a far cry from other guitar instruction videos on YouTube.

Fender's approach caters to shorter modern attention spans and is a perfect example of *Light-Speed Learning*—a trend that describes how smarter learning delivered in smaller bite-sized segments helps anyone learn just about any skill faster than ever before.

A few months ago I found a perfect example of this idea in an entertaining and terrifying (if you're a parent) story about an enterprising kid with some serious burger cravings.

Instant Learning

Shortly after 8 p.m. on a lazy Sunday evening this past April, a McDonald's drive-thru in a suburb of Ohio had an unusual customer pull up to the window: an eight-year-old. The boy was in the driver's seat of his father's minivan with his four-year-old sister along for the ride as a passenger. At first, the drive-thru staff assumed they were being pranked, but quickly discovered there were no parents to be found.

When the police were called to investigate, they learned the boy's parents were asleep at home and he had *really* wanted to get a cheeseburger, so he decided to go out and get one. Trying to put the pieces of the puzzle together, the officer at the scene interviewed the boy, who was in tears upon realizing he had done something wrong.

It turned out the boy had looked up a video online and taught *himself* how to drive before heading out on his quest for a cheeseburger. Witnesses reported that he had obeyed all traffic signs. When interviewed by local media after the story broke, the officer had this to say: "With the way technology is... kids will learn how to do anything and everything. This kid learned how to drive on YouTube. He probably looked it up for five minutes and then said it was time to go."[1]

In my family, we routinely consult YouTube to learn everything from how to throw a card like a magician to doing that last step right on the way-too-complicated origami project we unwittingly started. Today people are turning to online videos for help finishing math homework, balancing a checkbook or even learning to become a basketball star.[2]

On Facebook, the (Tasty) food channel features recipes in 30-45 second videos presented as a time lapse series of images shown through a point-of-view lens that makes you feel like you are standing there doing the cooking. To say these videos are insanely popular would be an understatement.

At an industry conference last year, *Tasty* global GM Ashley McCollum shared that more than *500 million* people watch their recipe videos each month, and that the most popular individual videos routinely rack up more than twenty million views and close to a million shares *each*.[3]

As McCollum went on to share, "Our point of view is that 99% of food *media* is made by food professionals, but 99% of *food* is made by amateurs. We think that massive gap between media and reality is what we're filling."

Photo - Tasty Video Channel

For years, educators have separated learning into two categories: *micro-learning* and *macro-learning*. Micro-learning is for getting something done, like if you need a quick tutorial on how to tie a Windsor knot or set up a keyword ad on Google.

If you want to build deeper knowledge, like learning the basics of a language or how to create a mobile app for Android, these skills would usually require Macro-Learning – often in the form of an online course or a certification program.

As my team and I researched this idea further, it surprised us to discover that *Light-Speed Learning* is a trend that affects *both* types of learning. Just because someone is learning a task in depth and engaging in macro-learning doesn't mean that the experience can't be done faster. To see how, let's consider how *Light-Speed Learning* is affecting the one educational sector that usually takes the longest to complete: medical school.

How To Graduate More Doctors

Within the next ten years, the medical field is likely to see a global short-age of thousands of trained doctors.[4] While technology may help alleviate some of the problem, we can't just rely on better screening technology and automation to improve health care. Something needs to bridge the gap.

If you ask Dr. David Lenihan, the founder and chief executive of health startup Tiber Health, the problem is how medical schools are structured. Instead of limiting the number of people who are admitted and then having them learn by listening to professors lecturing, Lenihan decided to expand and flip the model.

He asked professors to record short modules of lessons to be watched out-side of class and then class time could be used to practice the techniques. Tiber Health also created a model where more students could be admitted initially, and then assessed through a series of tests which would help to determine where their best path in the medical field might be. Some would become phy-sician's assistants, some might be administrators and a subset would go on to become doctors.

Lenihan believes the company's curriculum can inspire the creation of a new kind of school which could operate at just one-tenth the cost of a typical medical school, and more importantly, help to graduate more qualified doc-tors more quickly.

Can Bite-Sized Learning Save Higher Ed?

Light-Speed Learning is impacting educational institutions beyond medical school. In Paris, tech school "42" has already done away with using syllabi (and teachers!) and instead offers a gamified experience through which students complete technology projects, earn points for doing things like reviewing one another's papers, and encourages competition as a way to advance the best students from one stage to the next.

Online learning platforms like Udemy, Coursera and CreativeLive also continue to grow rapidly. In China, the VIPKID platform pairs Chinese students with US-based teachers for virtual tutoring over the Internet. The service plans to expand to 25,000 instructors working with 200,000 children in the coming year.

Some industry experts are predicting that this experiential, bite-sized learning model also may be the only way to save a higher education system that is increasingly criticized for being traditional, costly, and too focused on non-essential and ridiculously expensive diversions like college football.

Kevin Carey, author of *End of College: Creating the Future of Learning and University of Everywhere* believes the biggest shift in education will come from adding transparency to what students are learning. In an interview, he stated that "the secret weapon for new institutions seeking legitimacy in the market will be evidence of student learning, which is almost totally absent from traditional college degrees." He goes on to say, "colleges don't systematically concern themselves with the quality of the teaching and learning they provide in exchange for large amounts of money."[5]

This is a truth I often see up close in my work as an Adjunct Professor at Georgetown University in Washington DC. I am lucky to teach in a program that is very focused on bringing outside "real world" experts like myself to augment classes taught by academics who teach full-time. My focus in the twelve short weeks I have with my students each semester is to impart as much real-world advice and learning as I can. In my classes, we don't use text books, but instead engage in public writing and public grading (to mirror the world of social media) and learn by doing.

This idea of learning by doing is a familiar one for a group of people who define themselves by their abilities to find quick optimized solutions to any daily challenge: the "lifehackers."

The Human Guinea Pig & Speed Reading

Renowned lifehacker author, blogger and self-experimenter Tim Ferriss is fond of talking about the concept of "minimum viable knowledge." The term describes the minimal amount of information you need to know to perform a task or learn a new skill.

Ferriss calls himself a "human guinea pig" and experiments constantly to learn how to do anything faster. Ferriss has used this technique to become a championship Tango dancer, learn dozens of languages (and speak five fluently) and lose 20 pounds in five days. For each experiment, Ferriss dissects learning into small steps and then shares those through his popular podcast books and even through his TV series *The Tim Ferriss Experiment*.

His model of *Light-Speed Learning* is to focus on doing the minimum required effort to optimize his results.

Thanks to advances in technology, there are now many tools to help you do that too, with one of the most fundamental skills of learning: reading comprehension.

—

"In an age where more and more information arrives at multimedia, we're reinventing the noble art of skimming."

CLIVE THOMPSON, WIRED

—

For example, a tool called Spritz uses your eye's ability to scan words to increase your reading speed by shifting word positioning to optimize your reading.

Another tool called Outread helps train your eyes to move more efficiently through any text.

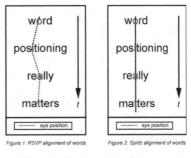

Figure 1. RSVP alignment of words   Figure 2. Spritz alignment of words

Photo - Spritz Speed Reading App

Augmented Educational Toys

In early 2017, Mattel announced plans to launch a device called Aristotle which would use voice-activated speakers and an integrated camera to be an in-home companion for a child's bedroom. Planned features included the ability for kids to play songs, turn on nightlights and even summon a parent via text message. An Alexa-enabled feature was also planned to offer a voice-activated bot ready to provide instant answers so that kids could absorb bite-sized knowledge throughout the day.

No one appreciated the product the way Mattel had hoped. In response to pressure from activist groups like the Campaign for a Commercial-Free Childhood, Mattel eventually pulled plans to launch the product from the market due to privacy concerns. It illustrated that there is a difficult balance yet to be struck between our desire to have learning tools integrated into our children's lives and the need to protect their privacy and innocence.

In the coming year, it is likely that this desire to provide on-demand *Light-Speed Learning* will continue to drive innovation, while also pushing the limits of what parents and regulators will be comfortable with.

Why It Matters

The easy availability of educational content on demand along with the growing desire for lifelong learning is driving a new expectation that new skills can be acquired in a matter of days, hours or even minutes. Every time a 30 second video teaches you how to cook a meal or learn how to play the guitar, *Light-Speed Learning* becomes more real. When lifehacking gurus teach you tricks to start speaking a new language in a few weeks, even skills that have always felt intimidatingly hard to learn feel a little more approachable. A side effect of this shift toward *Light-Speed Learning*, as we can clearly see from the debate about higher education, is whether the older traditional models of learning (and their extreme costs) are even worth it anymore.

In the coming year, learning in small bite-sized chunks will start to integrate more frequently into the products we buy and the experiences we have. When we travel, that will offer a moment for us to learn a new skill. When parents buy toys, they can consider how fun can be combined with learning (ideally in ways that don't require us to compromise the privacy of our children). When managers motivate their teams, they will increasingly seek out forms of *Light-Speed Learning* that can help workers get better at their jobs faster, stay more motivated longer and become more loyal in the process.

How to Use This Trend

✓ **Train your customers before you sell to them.** To promote its suite of small business marketing tools, Google had to ensure that its target audience of entrepreneurs and business owners understood content and search marketing. To achieve this, Google launched an app and program called Google Primer which offers short basic educational content on how online marketing works. As business owners step through it, they get a basic introduction to online marketing and are more likely to purchase marketing services from Google as a result because they have a greater understanding of what they are being sold.

✓ **Repurpose long experiences.** Many experts struggle with the notion that you can take something that requires mastery and turn it into smaller and easier to understand sections. This is a belief that must be conquered. There is always a way to take the complex and make it easier to digest. Start by taking an inventory of major work processes, initiatives, learning programs or content and then find the right content creators either internally or externally to take that raw material and fashion it into a new format that can be used to achieve real business results like driving sales or increasing customer satisfaction.

MEDIA & EDUCATION

12

VIRTUAL EMPATHY

What's the Trend?

—

*Immersive experiences delivered through technology and
personal interactions increase empathy by helping people
see the world through foreign and unfamiliar eyes.*

—

The first time I experienced virtual reality (VR), it gave me a bit of a head-ache. I remember I had entered the dream reality world of outer space meant to mimic a scene from the film *Gravity* starring George Clooney and Sandra Bullock. As I floated in midair, unable to figure out how to move, I did start to desperately wish for gravity, though probably not as the creators of that experience intended.

Since then, I've tried countless other VR simulations that have filled me with a combined sense of wonder and disappointment. The truth is, VR can be awesome and transformative ... for a few moments. But the promise still lags behind the technology and hype. And when it does, you are brought jarringly back to reality. When I first wrote about *Virtual Empathy*, it was inspired by the type of emotional transformation that can happen in those elusive moments when VR does realize its potential.

Back then the examples I wrote about focused on the powerful emotional side of experiences, like how it can be used to step inside the world of a refugee or take on the identity of someone from the opposite gender. These experiences matter because they can generate true empathy on a deeply personal level.

Why is empathy so important?

After more than a decade of training people to be more innovative I routinely find that these transformations always start with empathy. The ability to see the world from a perspective other than your own is a hallmark skill that can be taught—and I believe it is critical for success. It is through empathy that great leaders can hear and understand what the market needs and even see beyond to win the future.

Over the past year, my team and I have interviewed emerging content creators, brand marketers, and other storytellers, we have come to realize that this trend of *Virtual Empathy* spans far beyond what we can experience through a headset. To understand how, let's consider virtual reality's increasingly popular cousin: augmented reality (sometimes also called mixed reality).

Augmented Empathy

The power of virtual reality comes from the experience of fully replacing the world around you with that of a character, and transforming yourself into someone unfamiliar or being in an unfamiliar place. The power of augmented reality (AR), instead, comes from its ability to offer context for the world around you while letting you continue to *be yourself.*

Over the past year, it is fair to say that augmented reality has stolen some attention from virtual reality. Led by Microsoft's well-funded launch and continued improvement of the HoloLens, AR blends the virtual world with the real one for more than just entertainment or gaming purposes.

—

"What AR really means is connecting digital information, objects, and experiences with the physical world in situations as you experience them."

JOHN HANKE, CEO Niantic

—

This ability to relate to the world around you can be used in many interesting ways. Historic neighborhoods and buildings can offer a real-time look at the history of a place to help anyone better empathize with the past. Medical students can use AR as part of their training on how to interact with patients and learn how to better empathize with families and loved ones when delivering hard news. These examples, both from the past year, are real stories of how AR is already being used by corporations and educational institutions.[1] Empathy is more connected to the real world.

Sometimes the technology can even help you experience and empathize with a world that doesn't exist anymore—like Earth about 67 million years ago...

Hyper Reality, Dinosaurs, and the Void

One of the most awe-inspiring virtual and augmented reality destinations launched this year was a real-life experience based on the popular BBC series *Walking With Dinosaurs*. Called *Dinosaurs in the Wild*, it uses a purpose-built stage and real human actors, combined with virtual and augmented reality to take visitors on a 70-minute-long journey through the Late Cretaceous era.

Photo: Dinosaurs in the Wild Experience, BBC

A team of more than a hundred paleontologists, journalists, filmmakers, and designers spent over five years working to develop the UK-based show, which participants describe as a video game, travel, and film experiences all at once. Visitors get the unique feeling of being transported back in time to a place that forces them to see Earth's past inhabitants with a new appreciation—one that goes beyond the theoretical and into the theatrical. Over the course of the journey, you have the chance to feel what it was like at a different moment in history and appreciate the advances we have made.

Both VR and AR enable these positive experiences, but over the past year, it has become apparent that technology is not a prerequisite for Virtual Empathy.

The Reality Show Where Nothing Happens

I admit I have sometimes dismissed reality television as a form of voyeurism through which people can watch others behaving badly and delight in a feeling of superiority. In an earlier chapter of this book, I even called reality TV mindless and shared the caution that perhaps your time might be better spent elsewhere. Watching a Japanese show about nothing made me realize perhaps I was wrong to dismiss the category so quickly.

While much of American reality TV is based on manipulating people to create drama from unnatural situations, the Japanese reality program *Terrace House* is almost the complete opposite. The show follows a collection of young housemates who go on with their ordinary lives as viewers join in to watch. The show offers an interesting window into Japanese culture and customs, but it is most remarkable for its lack of conflict. It feels real precisely *because* nothing overly dramatic happens. But that doesn't mean it lacks emotional depth.

Andrew Ridker wrote a review of the series for *The New York Times*, describing a scene where a painfully shy young housemate asks another out on a date. You see him giddily preparing for the date (his first ever) and then the couple's painfully awkward conversation before the film they go to see.

After the film, he invites her to dinner and she politely declines. The scene ends as we watch him stoically keep his restaurant reservation and eat dinner quietly by himself. After watching the scene, four hours into binge-watching the show, Ridker describes his raw emotion as a viewer: He couldn't help himself from sitting there and sobbing on his couch. The show is powerful and emotional because it follows real people doing believable things.[2]

Photo: Terrace House, Netflix

It has long been the intent of great drama to move you emotionally, but watching something as real at *Terrace House* is a different emotional experience. You are not experiencing a story crafted by someone. You are looking into someone's life with their permission—and the experience connects you to that character in a different sort of way. The show reminds you to empathize with another human who has willingly chosen to share his most vulnerable moments with you, like a friend confessing his deepest secret.

What Would You Do?

Imagine you were witnessing a mother berating her child in public for being too fat. Or watching a racist customer at a deli refusing to buy a bag of chips from a Sikh man who works there. Would you intervene? In the reality show *What Would You Do?* that is exactly the question you are forced to consider as you watch these scenes play out via a hidden camera. Even though both the criticizer and the target of the criticism are paid actors, the onlookers are real people. As the drama unfolds, you see situations like those many of us have seen before. You see how reluctant people can be to inject themselves into the situation, until one heroic bystander finally stands up to the mistreatment and offers redemption for all of us watching—because *someone* does what we hope we could do.

This is the best possible version of reality TV, where story shines a more authentic spotlight on real life.

Celebrating the Outdoors from the Indoors

For the past four years, Robby Huang has been filming his outdoor adventures with his two cousins, Bryan and Andrew Lin, and sharing them on YouTube. Their channel, called "Adventure Archives," features beautifully shot 4k videos of locations like Yellowstone National Park and is so popular they have more than 2.6 million views and over 40,000 subscribers. When you first encounter this, you might be thinking this is an odd thing for people to watch.

What is the appeal of three guys walking through the forest and narrating the experience back to you? Why not go outside yourself and *experience* nature instead of watching someone else do it?

YouTube is full of puzzlingly popular genres like this. It contains everything from unboxing videos (where you watch someone unpack a product) to people feeling high after dental surgery (yes, exactly as weird as it sounds). Back in 2015, we wrote about the curiously popular Norwegian "Slow TV" channel that lets you watch a log burning in a fireplace for 12 hours or salmon swimming upstream for 18 hours. The shows, intended to help people relax, were an example of our *Desperate Detox* trend, which was first published in 2014 and revisited in 2017.

Part of the reason these videos work is because they elicit an emotional response—whether it's fear or joy or anticipation. Sometimes that emotional response can be so important, it can change, or even save, a life.

Mental Illness Exposed on YouTube

One important area where you can also experience *Virtual Empathy* on YouTube is through a growing number of brave vloggers who are sharing deeply personal struggles with panic attacks, depression, suicide, and mental illness.

Popular video blogger Anna Akana is one example. In 2007, she experienced a personal tragedy when she lost her teen sister to suicide. To try to recover, she turned to comedy and launched a YouTube channel with more than a million subscribers and videos that have been watched over 130 million times. One of the most powerful is a video titled "please don't kill yourself," where she talks about her sister's story and what happens to the people left behind.[3]

Her empowering catchphrase for her viewers is: "Just because your life falls apart doesn't mean you have to lose your desire to live it."

Exploring this growing genre, writer Carly Lanning published a story in *Psychology Today* about dozens of brave vloggers using a combination of prerecorded videos and live streaming to tell their stories. Watching them is like a combination of an optimistic therapy session and a taste of what mental illness might be like for those who suffer from it and for their loved ones.

As Lanning writes, "If vloggers can't cure mental illness, they can set someone on the path to recovery by offering true-life examples of people battling the same demons and doing their best to live a full life ... viewers get invested, and as they encounter stories they've never heard, taboos break down and greater understanding may emerge."[4]

Empathy at Work

—

"Being unaware of other perspectives, not being our most authentic selves, and lacking empathy are huge issues for organizations ... we need tools to better understand each other."

NATALIE EGAN, Founder of Translator

—

A little over a year ago, in an online post, successful software executive Nathan Egan shared his experience being transgender and his transition into a new identity: becoming Natalie Egan.[5] Through experiencing her own personal struggle with how to handle this at work, she also realized that companies like hers were not doing as good a job as they could be when it come to inclusivity.

This is a common challenge for businesses of all sizes. Everyone believes in the importance of empathy but sometimes it takes an incident to inspire action. Unfortunately, the incident which usually sparks the attention is a negative one—and so the first critical question to ask is how can an organization create a culture of empathy before it becomes painfully obvious that it was missing?

In Egan's case, this urgent question offered the inspiration to create a product that could help organizations build their empathy muscle in a virtual way. Her new company, Translator, is focused on creating simple games that serve as tools to create immersive virtual reality experiences that foster understanding and tolerance of diversity in the workplace. The mobile app allows teammates to learn about identities (e.g., race, gender, etc.) different from their own.

As Translator describes online, an employee can experience what it's like to be a female professional in a board meeting through VR: "He may be called 'honey' or be asked to fetch coffee for the men in the room. He might hear a monologue of her hopes and fears, including the dreaded, 'What if they think I'm the secretary?'"

This culture is one that LinkedIn CEO Jeff Weiner calls "compassionate management" and he speaks about it frequently at business conferences and in media interviews. LinkedIn is one organization that takes these lessons seriously and is using the idea of building a more empathetic workplace as a key driver of business results. Weiner believes in the idea so deeply that he created a series of videos on how to build a powerful culture of compassion and made them freely available for anyone to watch online.[6]

Why It Matters

Empathy leads to understanding, which is key to solving problems, creating powerful workplace cultures and being more innovative. When we first predicted this trend, we had focused our attention on the ability for virtual reality to offer a transformative experience, but further research throughout this year illustrated that technology was only one piece of this puzzle.

The good news is that this means empathy can be taught and learned in schools, businesses and in everyday interactions. Having an engaging VR experience in the right context will continue to be a powerful experience. Watching an emotional transformation in a face-to-face monologue from a vlogger battling mental illness can offer a similar intimacy.

As cultural diversity, inclusion, and equality—and the innovation they can foster—become growing priorities within workforces at corporations, tools and experiences that offer *Virtual Empathy* will increasingly make it into the workplace and help us understand colleagues and customers with

MEDIA & EDUCATION

different backgrounds, see the world from the perspective of customers and perhaps enable us to be more vulnerable and open with one another as well.

How to Use This Trend

✓ **Create experience labs.** Anyone can buy a VR headset or try an app, but how do these pieces fit together to truly transform a culture? One of the most frequent requests we get is to help architect and build an experience lab for an organization. This is a place where the right combination of training (with interactive tools like Translator), real-life experiences (like shadowing the youngest employee in the office for a day), and technology (like VR experiences) are mapped out in a way that allows employees to build their empathy and compassion. This is a far more powerful approach than requiring employees to sit through a boring training lecture and superficial multiple-choice quiz about diversity.

✓ **Invest in unusual content.** One of the tips (from Chapter 2) to think differently was the idea to buy magazines that are not targeted to you. There are other ways to do this within a team as well. Create bonding experiences that allow you to visit unusual places together. Bring books to meetings and actively share intriguing pieces of content that people share. Show short clips from movies or TV shows. Each of these is a way to build a more a common understanding between team members as well as give teams a memorable experience that cultivates deep bonds and mutual respect.

13

HUMAN MODE

What's the Trend?

—

As automation increases, people hungry for more personal
and authentic experiences begin to put a premium on advice,
services, and interaction involving actual humans.

—

Often in the course of researching this book, I will find a story so powerful that my team and I struggle with how to categorize and write about it. This year, that struggle came in the form of an initiative I only recently learned about, although it was started nearly 15 years ago. Originally developed as a project for a Danish event called the Roskilde Festival, the idea was inspired by the belief that the most transformative experience any of us can have to better understand the world is a boundary-free conversation with someone, in which we are encouraged to ask the questions we are usually afraid to ask.

In Danish, this idea was called the *menneskebiblioteket*, which roughly translated into English means the *human library*. The concept was that volunteers would sign up to be "checked out" so they could tell their stories. Anyone could *borrow* a person from the library for a 30-minute conversation. The selection of volunteers was designed to help challenge people's stereotypes. They included someone with autism, a sex worker, an obese person, someone who is deaf and blind, and a refugee.

From the beginning the idea was a hit. It inspired a permanent *Human Library* installation in Australia and events across the world from Tunis to Alabama. It is a beautifully simple idea and easy to understand why it has become so popular across the world. If you have been reading this book from start to finish, you will probably see the dilemma about where to include this story.

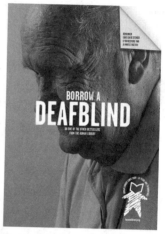

Is it an example of *Truthing* because people can be encouraged through face-to-face conversations to see reality in a new way?

Photo: Print Ad - Human Library

Should it instead be part of *Virtual Empathy* because people gain empathy through these difficult yet human conversations? Does it fit in *Ungendered* since some volunteers offer to talk about being transgender or nonbinary?

These types of questions can be paralyzing when writing, but I chose to use it as the opening story for this chapter on *Human Mode* because, more than anything else, I felt it was a story about the importance of shared humanity and how sometimes amid so many options and technology and optimized media, it's nice to just be able to *choose* to interact with a real person.

It is easy to imagine how this option to interact with a real person could soon become a thing of the past in a world of increasing automation and productivity demands. This flux is particularly evident when you consider the shifts in financial services, where some estimates say robots will soon control up to $2 trillion worth of investments.[1]

Robo-Advisors Get a Human Colleague

For several years robo-advisors have been one of the most disruptive forces in finance. Given the recent corruptions and scandals, and the financial crisis, trust in the industry has declined to such a point that many investors simply don't trust these groups to act in unbiased ways on their behalf. Robo-advisors are appealing *because* they are dispassionate about financial recommendations and, as a result, can seem like a better option.

Betterment was one of the early pioneers in this space, first providing robo-advisory services back in 2010. Today the firm manages more than $10 billion in assets and over 270,000 customer accounts. Since it was founded, Betterment has been a bellwether for automation across the entire industry. Then about a year ago, Betterment made an announcement that surprised many people. They added a *human* option.

In exchange for an increased fee on assets under management, customers now can offer to a premium version of their services, which would include unlimited access to human advice from an actual financial advisor.[2] Just six months later, they added a feature to their app which allows *any* customer to send text messages to human advisors and get a response within 24 hours—at no additional charge.

The *Human Mode* is the predictable antidote to automation in many ways. As we interact with technology and see more people experiment with robots for everything from making the perfect salad[3] to vacuuming our floors,[4] the interactions we have with real people become more precious and sometimes even more desirable. The coming year will reveal a great deal about which human experiences we value the most in different contexts, and in many ways the retail sector is one of the first industries to face the challenge of striking the right balance between man versus machine.

Slow Checkouts and Smart Mirrors

In Scotland, grocery retailer Tesco wants to slow things down on purpose. While self-checkouts have been embraced as the future of the grocery store experience, and patience among consumers seems to be at an all-time low, some customers still prefer the older, slower way.

The elderly or those suffering from physical ailments or mental illnesses often find these speed-centric checkout lines frustrating and stressful. To tackle this problem, Tesco piloted a "relaxed checkout" for customers who preferred regular checkout lines manned by humans. The effort, backed by non-profit Alzheimer Scotland, garnered worldwide media attention when it was first launched in January of 2017.

For years it has seemed like automation would phase out the need for humans completely in some jobs. When Amazon launched their first retail store, people predicted it would be operated entirely without human workers. (That hasn't turned out to be the case.) ATMs introduced in the 1970s were predicted to make the human bank teller obsolete, but since the year 2000, the number of jobs for bank tellers has actually increased.[5] Smart mirrors in dressing rooms allow you to try clothes on virtually and summon new sizes and colors to try on immediately and barcode scanners are now spread out across retail locations, but the death of the retail worker's job isn't coming anytime soon. According to the US Bureau of Labor Statistics, the number of retail salespeople is projected to grow 7 percent, reaching nearly 5 million by 2024.[6] Humans stubbornly seem to prefer other humans.

Necessary Automation

Are humans always a better option? Certainly not. The fact is, there are plenty of industries and jobs that are undeniably *better* when automated. Robots can work faster, assemble things more efficiently, work throughout the night, and offer a consistency that is impossible for humans to match.

A fruit-picking startup called Abundant Robotics has built a machine which will help farmers save millions in labor costs and losses due to spoiled fruit. The company's prototype uses computers to track ripeness as well as powerful vacuums to pluck apples 24 hours a day (the most profitable orchard crop) from a tree. Baltimore-based Blueprint Robotics is using robots to manufacture pre-fabricated parts for homes that are then shipped and assembled on site. As much as 60% of a home can be built in the factory, eliminating many headaches from the on-site building process.

Yet even these innovators are not eliminating humans entirely. Blueprint Robotics still relies on skilled laborers to assemble the houses, and farmers still need people to help take the fruit that is picked to pack, ship, and deliver it.

The positive opportunity of automation is that it has the potential to free workers to focus on the most fulfilling parts of their work and rely on technology to handle the repetitive soul-draining work that is better suited to machines. While that sounds nice in theory, it can be tricky to accomplish because the lines between when robots or humans are appropriate for a task have yet to be clearly drawn.

Linguists Train Bots

One of the biggest challenges in building robots to interact with humans is training those machines on the nuances of human communication. Often the best solution is to hire more humans to help train the robots to act and think more like us. Last year Amazon posted a job description for an Australian linguist. The posting was interpreted by many as an opportunity to train the Echo voice-recognition devices, to better understand people with an Australian accent.

Australian company Appen collects data for tech companies that use machine learning; it currently employs 70 linguists and engages thousands of others as needed. The company has offices in the US, Australia, the Philippines, and last year set up an office in China.

Investigating this emerging area of specialty, *The New York Times* recently profiled five people who had jobs that involved teaching artificial intelligence entities how to understand humans better. They interviewed a travel agent, a customer care representative, and a robotics expert working with Google on technology for the self-driving car. Each shared a combination of apprehension and pride in their work helping machines become better, smarter, and more human. It is tempting to see these early bot trainers as naïve participants in a bot-created master plan to help make people obsolete.

It turns out this fear has some basis in reality.

The Rise of Pink-Collar Work

Automation is stealing some jobs. One dire estimate from accounting firm PwC recently predicted that 38% of US jobs would be at a "high risk of automation" by robots or artificial intelligence by 2030 (including 61% of financial services jobs such as those performed by PwC itself).[7]

These types of jobs are traditionally referred to as blue collar and they are overwhelmingly done by men. A recent study of the number of men and women in certain jobs found that 98% of carpenters, 97% of electricians, and 91% of motor vehicle operators were men. In contrast, 97% of pre-school and kindergarten teachers, 94% of nurse practitioners, and 81% of social workers were women.[8]

Author Laurie Penny calls this second group the *pink-collar* industries. She wrote a piece in *Wired* magazine about how the job losses from automation will mostly affect men who work in tasks which are actually robotic: repetitive and lacking human interaction. The future, she argues, belongs to the people with high levels of emotional intelligence.[9] Sometimes they may even be the voices of technology who we don't see or realize are there.

The Human Side of Automated Chatbots

If there was an award for top-selling chatbots, the avatar from Brazilian e-commerce site Magazine Luiza would merit serious contention. In the first six months of 2017, their online sales have increased by 56% from the previous year, and the addition of the friendly chatbot, Lu, is getting most of the credit.[10]

Lu will chat about reviews, help you pick everything from a smartphone to a home appliance, and offer real-time tech support. She takes questions on Facebook, stars in YouTube videos, and has conducted media interviews.

Before you marvel at the technologists behind such a creation, you should also know that Magazine Luiza hires a real person to give Lu her personality. In that sense, while she is perceived as robotic, she isn't completely automated. Magazine Luiza isn't the only brand offering this type of illusory automation in its customer service.

In 2016 Bloomberg reporter Ellen Huet published a report about a secret society of humans thanklessly doing the work of robots. This class of "humans pretending to be robots pretending to be humans" were quietly hired by companies who

Photo: Lu Avatar from Magazine Luiza (Brazil)

were selling the promise of automation. A concierge service called GoButler was one example Huet cited, which promised a service where you could send a text message to get "anything you want." When implementing their service, it became clear that the automation wasn't quite ready to work completely as advertised and needed to be augmented with humans on duty 24/7.

IBM anticipates that 85% of all customer interactions will be handled without a human agent by 2020. It raises an interesting question, whether you believe this prediction or dismiss it as a biased talking point intended to help them sell virtual customer service solutions to big companies.

What will the remaining customer interactions look like? One unlikely answer might come from looking at a role that technology has done well over the past decade or more to eradicate: the middleman.

Fidget Spinners and the Death of Fads

In some categories, such as mattress sales, people have been quick to agree that introducing automation and cutting out the middle man improves every aspect of their purchasing processes (a story you will read about further in Chapter 18). In other industries, the middleman's ability to add value is finally starting to gain some recognition.

When *New York Times* reporter Charles Duhigg wrote about the rise of Beanie Babies back in the 1990s, he compared it to the modern rise of the fidget spinner in 2017.[11] In the case of the Beanie Babies, the number being sold was carefully managed by its parent company, Ty, to ensure scarcity. As some animals became popular, Ty would stop making them to drive their value and demand even higher.

The underappreciated secret of Beanie Babies' success, Duhigg argues, may have been driven by this group of traveling salespeople who would meet frequently with toy-store owners. They would gather feedback and create excitement. They collected insights from the people closest to the customers to help improve their products. These salespeople were the default curators, evangelists, microinfluencers, and ambassadors. These are all terms we use today to talk about the *people* that brands need to get on their sides to make products successful.

The reason Beanie Babies' popularity endured for decades was thanks to this unsung class of humans who provided the fuel to turn what could have been a fad into something more.

The contrast between this and the decentralized rise (and decline) of the fidget spinner is clear. I remember walking through festivals with my kids this past summer and they would plead with me to stop at just about every vendor who had any of these spinners and buy at least one new one every week. Within a matter of months those fidget toys went from quirky and popular to overproduced and forgettable. Now we have a stack of

Photo: Fidget spinner

them sitting unused in a drawer somewhere and no one thinks of them anymore. Fidget spinners never had human champions to create relationships, measure demand, innovate their product, and tell a story. As a result, they peaked and now the craze is over.

Shareable Humanity

Four years ago, I wrote about a trend called *Shareable Humanity* to describe why the things that people tended to share more actively on social media were usually based on personal interactions. This is the same reason why we are far more likely to post an online review about an experience with a server at a restaurant (either positive or negative) than a review solely on the food alone.

The human touch is what turns negative situations around and can turn a hater into a deeply loyal evangelist—because someone cared enough to make their bad experience into a memorably delightful one. The Internet is filled with stories like these and they all have the same common theme: there is a necessary and essential place for humans in just about every inter-action. The key in an automated future will be to get better at identifying the right places for it so you don't unintentionally kill those chances for uniquely human interactions in the process.

Why It Matters

As more automation surrounds us and technology becomes better at anticipating our every need, a countertrend that we see coming is people seeking help through more human experiences rather than via efficient machines.

In many industries, cost cutting and a strategic overreliance on auto-mation have removed the most memorable aspects from an experience and this will lead consumers to return to wish for what they once had. To some degree, this was the idea that inspired our popular *Strategic Downgrading* trend from the 2016 report. Sometimes we just prefer the older and less techie version because it is easier, kinder, and more familiar.

As this preference grows, so too will a consumer's willingness to pay a premium to interact with a real, compassionate, and skilled human being. This represents a significant opportunity for all types of businesses. Are you ready to create a *Human Mode* for your products and services? In the coming year more companies will face this question and the ones who can reinforce their brand values and find the right balance to bring back the human side of what they do will be the biggest winners.

How to Use This Trend

✓ **Pause before automating.** Every decision to automate a process or use more technology that involves a customer experience should ideally be value-mapped to find where in the experience chain the *Human Mode* can be used as a strategic advantage. In some cases, this may lead to the introduction of a premium product or offering. In other cases, the right strategy might be to not implement the technology in the first place.

✓ **Assess your humanity.** Back in 2008 when I published my first book, I started talking about how to create a more human brand with a personality. Given this has been such a constant theme in my work for more than a decade, I have built quite a few tools to help groups understand where they might need an infusion of more humanity. To help you make that call for your own business, you can visit www.nonobviousbook.com/resources to download the worksheet and take the assessment for yourself.

14

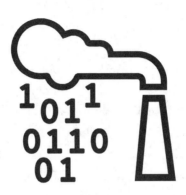

DATA POLLUTION

What's the Trend?

—

As we create more methods for quantifying the world around us,
data gets manipulated, contaminated and sabotaged, making it
harder to separate true insights from useless noise.

—

I don't consider myself an over-sharer on social media. At times weeks will go by before I remember to share a post on Facebook. On occasion, I will log in and get a desperate reminder from Facebook: "Did you know your followers haven't heard from you in 2 weeks? Post something today!"

Over the past decade, I have had a love-hate relationship with the platform. When I first joined, I loved the connections and essentially said yes to every friend request. Over the course of the next two years, that quickly led me to approach 5000 "friends" (the limit at that time) and my newsfeed was filled with stories from people I didn't care about or barely knew.

Frustrated with this lack of connection, I decided to declare "Facebook bankruptcy" and shut my entire account down. I learned how to convert that account, to be a "Public Page" and I started over with a new private personal account which I started to use often.

In the process of writing this chapter, I started to wonder what Facebook had learned about me over those years of my constantly feeding it pictures, interactions, videos and moments of my life. So I decided to do something many people don't realize they can do: I requested to download all of my data from Facebook.

The file I received back was 118 MB. It contained 1,732 items, including every photo, video and message I had shared during that time. While I saw this data and immediately looked at it in terms of messages, photos, videos and interactions, Facebook describes all this information as *data* – and they are not the only ones collecting a staggering amount of it.

In September of 2017, journalist Judith Duportail shared a story of requesting four years of her personal data from the relationship platform Tinder. What she got back was 800 pages of startlingly revealing personal information on everything from her racial preferences in men to transcripts of every conversation she had with a match—sometimes revealing intimate personal details.[1]

The Hidden Side of Data Collection

This is chapter about data—but before I get too far, we need to have a shared understanding about what data really is. Often people think of data in terms of likes, views or conversion rates. The *numbers* are only one part of the data that is collected about each of us. The other side includes conversations, content, behaviors and intent. It includes all kinds of information that you might have assumed no one was tracking – until you learn they are. Here's an example: on photo sharing site Flickr, most images are uploaded along with all sorts of meta data like camera exposure times and GPS locations for photos. Without realizing it, people are publicly sharing their exact whereabouts at a particular time.

An inevitable side effect of all this data collection is the fact that some of it will be questionably useful and hard to interpret. How can anyone separate the bad data – or misused data -- from the rest? The stakes are high, as IBM recently estimated that poor quality data costs businesses $3.1 *trillion* annually in the US alone.[2]

The problem as it exists today, is two sided. On one side are unwilling consumers who reluctantly or naively shared their data without realizing the implications. On the other side are businesses struggling to leverage all this data in a way that doesn't annoy but rather delights. We call this problem *Data Pollution*, and as you'll learn in this chapter, it is a problem that affects us all.

To understand and perhaps solve this problem, my team and I took a deeper look at the many ways that data can be "polluted," and searched for the root causes of this phenomenon so we could develop a model and insights for how to do better.

This research led us to define five elements of *Data Pollution*, but before I share them here – it is important to understand the sources for all of this data.

The 4 Sources For Data

Data is not measured by companies alone. To get a full picture of the data that is available for most organizations to analyze and use, we must also add data from three more sources. Here are all four, along with a short description of each:

1. **Open Data** – Typically collected by governments and NGOs on a wide variety of topics such as demographic shifts, labor and industry statistics, weather data, immigration data, etc.
2. **Scientific Data** – A broad category which describes data gathered by scientists and academic researchers as part of studies which are generally published in medical journals or online.
3. **Big Data** – Collected by an organization, typically for commercial purposes. It includes customer purchasing data, online behavioral data, customer loyalty program data and social media profile data.

TECHNOLOGY & DESIGN

4. **Small Data** – Enabled by the Internet of Things, this refers to data that individuals are collecting on their own through devices like wearables. Sometimes this type of data is "co-owned" with a service provider, but in most cases the consumer has the right to request it, use it and even ask for it to be deleted.

Now that we have looked at the sources of data, let's consider the different ways that this data gets polluted – and what you can do about it.

THE 5 TYPES OF DATA POLLUTION

1. **Data Overflow** – When too much data is captured leaving organizations confused about what to focus on or prioritize.

2. **Data Manipulation** – When the results and insights of data are twisted to selectively support biased arguments.

3. **Data Sabotage** – When people intentionally share incorrect or incomplete information with the intent to cause harm.

4. **Data Contamination** – When data is collected from multiple sources, mixed together, and reclaimed or deleted by creators.

5. **Data Expiration** – When data is not updated as frequently as it should be and therefore loses its value because it is not current.

Why Data Overflows

Our 2016 Non-Obvious Trend Report, featured a trend we called *Data Overflow* to describe the fact that many organizations and institutions were becoming buried in the sheer volume of all the analytics they had access to. It is a sad irony that among business leaders, the idea of data-driven decision making is viewed as a magic tactic capable of addressing every problem. It rarely achieves this ideal because so few of those leaders know how to truly use data correctly.

Part of the reason connecting the dots is so difficult is because non-scientists often lack the willingness to learn how to process the data they are given. For example, many website marketing teams focus blindly on trying to get people to spend more time on their site and reducing the "bounce rate" (how many of your visitors leave your site immediately after arriving).

Imagine you owned a restaurant website and a potential customer wanted to find your address to come in and dine. If they visit your site and find your address quickly, they will "bounce" off to Google to get directions and hopefully become a paying diner (the highest conversion you can get). Now imagine if that potential customer looked around for thirty seconds (an eternity online) to try and find your address, failed and left your site, frustrated.

That person most likely did not become a customer, yet if you only measure "time on site," that second experience looks like a success while the first one looks like a failure. This is the problem with using data incorrectly, and it happens with far more frequency because of *Data Pollution*.

The Overquantified Self

Another issue of *Data Overflow* is how it affects the industries where we desperately wish data was more useful but doesn't yet seem to be. Healthcare is a perfect example of this. Four years ago when I published a book about the future of healthcare called *ePatient 2015* with my co-author Fard Johnmar, we first introduced the trend *Overquantified Self*. It described the gap between all the excitement in healthcare for tools that could track our health and the reality that most of these tools were simply generating disconnected data that wasn't connected in a meaningful way to actual health care. Weill Cornell Medicine Internist Dr. Fred N. Pelzman describes this issue as "drowning in data" and writes about how he struggles to make sense of it:

> *"Every morning when I log onto our electronic health record, one group of messages are from patients with their self-recorded health information*

data that they've sent to me for review. Here's my home blood pressure over the past 24 hours. Here are my fingerstick glucose readings over the past 24 hours. Here's my weight over the past 24 hours. Here is my depression score over the past 24 hours. A lot of data -- oftentimes a lot of data that I don't quite know how to react to, what actions I'm supposed to take."[3]

Data Overflow is also prevalent in the Open Data that is publicly dumped by governments into the marketplace in huge quantities. One report from the index that tracks open data reported that of the 1 million datasets which have been made available by governments worldwide, less than 7% are in a machine-readable format – rendering them almost useless.

The bottom line is, we collect too much data and lack the tools or expertise to analyze it properly. This is a bad combination. Unfortunately, this leads directly to another problem: in the absence of any real insights the conclusions from data are manipulated in order to promote an agenda.

A Universe of Manipulated Data

When the results of a *scientific* study are under suspicion, the globally recognized standard test for validity is to repeat the experiment. If the results hold and the study is replicable, it passes the test. Unfortunately, less than half of all research papers would pass this standard of proof.[4]

Outside the scientific world this figure is likely even lower. The problem is, there are so many easy ways that data can be manipulated at the time of collection – for example by asking leading questions or isolating participants.

The report referenced above also found that "the greater the financial and other interests and prejudices in a scientific field, the less likely the research findings are to be true." For a perfect example of this, consider the biased and now widely debunked studies into the nutritional effects of sugar published in the 1960s and referenced in the opening story of Chapter 6.

Research has frequently been published with this sort of ulterior motive and it can take decades to effectively refute. As a result, this form of *Data Pollution* is widespread, long lasting and very difficult to remove.

Why Everyone Has a Fake Email Address

Whoever owns the email address bob@bob.com probably deserves an apology from me.

For the last twenty years, poor Bob has provided me with my go-to email address to sign up for free wi-fi, appease particularly insistent retail employees at checkouts and fill out long waivers at kids' birthday parties.

Usually I do this to save time, but sometimes I do it to exact my revenge on aggressive and annoying marketers by providing them with intentionally bad data. As any online marketer will already tell you, I am hardly the only one to take this low road.

The fact is, people take sadistic amounts of delight in providing intentionally bad data to organizations who dare to ask them for it without earning it or providing a good reason for why they need it.

This type of intentional *Data Sabotage* can feel like a justified form of payback, but not all Data Sabotage comes from revenge-seeking consumers. Sometimes there are profiteers at work.

Fake Profiles And Data Hacking Bots

At the 2017 Strata Data Conference in New York, Data & Society Founder and President danah boyd[6] shared a dire warning about the fact that data is being actively sabotaged by groups of "adversarial actors" who are focused on exposing the flaws of our overreliance on it. Some of them are motivated by the recognition that comes from being able to hack the data or sabotage existing systems.

The implications, according to boyd, are that we need to reconsider how to secure all of this data:

"If we believe that data can and should be used to inform people and fuel technology, we need to start building the infrastructure necessary to limit the corruption and abuse of that data—and grapple with how biased and problematic data might work its way into technology and, through that,

into the foundations of our society."[7]

A good place to start may be the problematic data which is being continually created on the world's largest social media platforms through profiles that are not attached to real people.

In April 2017, when Facebook conducted a purge of millions of fake accounts, large brands saw significant drops in their follower counts, proving that much of their "audiences" consisted of fake accounts. USA Today was the brand that felt the largest impact, losing over six million followers (more than a third of their overall audience) overnight.[8]

It is hard to tell exactly how many social media accounts might be fake when many platforms are reluctant to share those numbers, but some independent researchers estimate that at least 15% of *all* social media profiles may be autogenerated without a real person behind them.[9] If you asked *Daily Beast* reporter Joseph Cox, however, he would probably tell you that number seems low.

Cox had his account suspended on Twitter because a small army of (most likely) bots had started to follow him at the same time. Though it has yet to be proven, he suspected that the bots automatically followed him due to algorithms that identified him as the author of an article covering the rise of bots originating in Russia. Because of this, the fake accounts mounted a retaliatory attack and caused his account to be suspended.

These fake profiles created by scammers, bots, or unscrupulous humans are a symptom of a larger problem that is fueled by (but not limited to) the Internet. Data has become contaminated.

Data Contamination

I follow my 13-year-old son on Instagram and last month I noticed something strange on his account. After spending weeks traveling on the West Coast over the summer and sharing lots of images, his account was down to just four. Worried that he had lost some of his content, I asked him about it.

"I deleted them," he told me.

"Why?" I wondered.

"I didn't need them."

Most of his posts get about ten times the number of likes that mine do, but even then, at a certain point those older images just didn't matter to him anymore. It turns out, he's not alone. A story in the *Washington Post* reported how teenagers were "curating" their accounts on Instagram and deleting old photos that either did not get that many likes or that they no longer wanted to have on their profiles anymore.

I use Instagram and other social media platforms as a gallery of my life to be saved, shared and occasionally to reminisce through. Teenagers today are using it as an article of clothing: something to be worn today and changed tomorrow. In fact, this deleting was so prevalent that Instagram introduced a feature to allow users to archive and save those old images instead of deleting them.[10]

When users delete old posts, it can reduce page views and engagement time, as well as skew the data which most sites are trying to monetize.

It's no wonder the team at Instagram are desperate to change this behavior. The less accurate their data, the less opportunities they have to sell advertising.

This is *Data Contamination* and it's something you can expect to hear plenty more about in the coming year.

Why It Matters

When researching this trend and going through the Haystack Method for naming it, the brainstorm was particularly short because *Data Pollution* immediately felt like the perfect name. Like clean air in the atmosphere, data is fundamental to how businesses are run—and yet it is under attack from negative forces like manipulation, sabotage, and contamination. We intentionally selected inflammatory words to describe the nature of this attack, because it relays the gravity of the situation.

In a world where we can no longer trust the data that we are collecting or use it to make informed decisions, we must operate on blind instinct and hope even more blindly for luck. Understanding the severity of the problem and how it is happening is the first step toward a solution. Building and implementing better tools for analytics will help as well. The most helpful thing, however, will be the one thing that many of us are reluctant to do: spend more time learning how to become data literate ourselves. The only way to fight pollution (in any form) is to stop making the same mistakes and to get better educated about what we need to do differently.

How to Use This Trend

✓ **Find your hero metrics.** Rather than trying to make sense of large batches of irrelevant data, one trick smart executives use all the time is finding a small group of "hero metrics" that help them measure what is working and what isn't. Revenue per store, emails forwarded, number of social media shares within the first hour of posting ... these are all examples of metrics that could be used to get a more nuanced view of what is happening in your business, and what to do about it.

✓ **Audit your data for more than numbers.** The best way to realize value from your data is to better understand what you have and what is missing. For that purpose, conducting a detailed audit is a valuable place to start, but this has to look at more than just the numbers. Instead the best audits will review what is being collected in the first place, what sources are being used and conduct a gap analysis of what is missing in order to use data more effectively.

15

PREDICTIVE PROTECTION

What's the Trend?

—

*Organizations create smarter connected products, services
and features that can proactively protect our safety, health
and environment by anticipating our actions or needs.*

—

The day before my flight recently to speak at an event in New Orleans, I received a text message, email and phone call from my airline warning that I might experience some flight delays. Every time I log into Google from a new computer, I get an email with an IP address and location so I can confirm it was me. When I make a large purchase at a retail store, I get an alert on my phone asking if I am still in possession of my card. If I have been sitting at my desk for more than two hours, my wearable fitness tracker vibrates on my wrist to remind me to move around.

These interactions are simple examples of *Predictive Protection*—where the technology and products around us work actively to keep our health, time and money all safe. They are so prevalent that it can be disconcerting when they don't work. For example, when I parallel park my car and the beeping alert doesn't tell me how far I have until my bumper touches the car behind me, I stop and spend a few minutes making sure the alert still works. Clearly it would be faster to just visually look and park normally ... but I have come to rely on that proximity alert.

Back in 2015 when I first published this trend, the examples were easy to describe and the benefits were clear to see. Who wouldn't want technology to help them park more easily or keep their credit card safe? In the three years since then, new questions have started to arise about how far exactly we want that technology to go, whether it is always a good thing, and what happens when it starts making decisions for itself without our involvement.

Just before originally publishing this trend, I remember coming across a story that was already causing some to start asking these questions. A vending machine called the Luce X2 Touch TV was launched at a small press event in the UK as the first in the world to use facial recognition technology.

There was one feature, though, that ignited a frenzy of media coverage. The vending machine was empowered to deny you unhealthy snacks based on your age, mood, build or health records. It was an extreme version of *Predictive Protection* and one that was so uncommon at the time that it seemed at the fringes of what the trend meant to discuss, so we didn't include it in the final writeup of the trend that year. Today this sort of complex question is no longer a fringe topic.

Geostorms, Car Hackers and the Scary Future Of Predictive Protection

Elon Musk ignited a worldwide media panic recently when he tweeted that the global race to dominate artificial intelligence would be the most likely cause of a third world war.

Just a few weeks after Musk's tweet, a new Hollywood disaster film called "Geostorm" was released, telling the story of a world where weather-controlling technology goes wrong and ends up creating a global ice age. While some are hoping that future weather management technology can solve problems caused by intense storms and natural disasters, this fear that "geostorms" or similar side effects could unintentionally destroy the planet we hoped to protect is not entirely unrealistic.

Elon Musk ✔
@elonmusk

Following ⌄

China, Russia, soon all countries w strong computer science. Competition for AI superiority at national level most likely cause of WW3 imo.

5:33 AM - 4 Sep 2017

In a less sci-i example, self-driving cars hold the promise to reduce accident rates and make roads safer, but what happens if hackers find a way to turn these cars into weapons?[1] What happens when an automated car must decide between hitting (and likely killing) one person or aiming the other way and hitting four?

—

A robot may not injure a human being or, through inaction, allow a human being to come to harm. A robot must obey orders given it by human beings except where such orders would conflict with the First Law. A robot must protect its own existence as long as such protection does not conflict with the First or Second Law.

ISAAC ASIMOV'S RULES OF ROBOTICS

—

These sorts of questions bring newfound relevance to Asimov's famous rules of robotics shared above because the speed of progress makes them urgent. Sometimes, the unintended side effects of this progress are already here, like the slightly terrifying recent news that Facebook's experiments with AI bots led the bots to develop their own language and start conversing with each other – and in a new language humans did not understand.[2]

This is the new, complex two-sided nature of *Predictive Protection*.

There will be growing pains, but the tone of this book and all the predictions here are optimistic rather than pessimistic. We believe the net benefits of *Predictive Protection* will outweigh the risks – and the good news is there are stories of how this is happening already.

Hackers Saving Democracy

When a collective of Hamburg-based hackers known as the Chaos Computer Club (CCC) intentionally exposed security flaws in voting software in the lead-up to this past year's elections in Germany, they were widely credited with protecting the integrity of the election process from potential Russian hackers.[3]

Governments and militaries around the world are actively recruiting these so-called "white hat" hackers who choose to use their skills for positive change. They are challenged to hack into existing systems and then paid bounties if they are successful because it helps organizations expose weaknesses before they are exploited by more criminally-minded hackers.[4]

In many areas of our lives, from low gas mileage lights in our cars to televised hurricane alerts, there are many ways that we *expect* technology to keep us safe. The future this trend predicts is not about more of this in-the-background type of protection. Instead, the new forms of *Predictive Protection* will become highly visible and challenge our notions of privacy and choice.

Should a vending machine really have a right to deny anyone a snack?

To see how we will start to answer questions like this, let's take a deeper look at the healthcare industry, one that must navigate these changes every day.

Wearables, Trainables and Insideables

Wearables like fitness trackers and devices that help us monitor our health have undergone some major upgrades since I first wrote about this trend in 2014. Some of these devices now boast levels of accuracy previously only possible through hospital-grade machines. The global industry for these wearables is expanding rapidly and likely to double in the next three years.[5]

In a creative example of taking all this data and using it to create more value, the architects of the popular basketball video game NBA 2K17 teamed up with wearable health company Fitbit to reward players who walked more than 10,000 steps *in the real world* with a boost in abilities for their NBA 2K characters in the video game.

There are also a growing number of "trainable" products which help you correct your form when exercising or your posture. UPRIGHT is a chair pillow that vibrates to correct your posture. Nadi X is a brand of haptic yoga pants that help correct your form through vibration notifications in real time while you are doing yoga poses.

Insideables are products that can be digested to measure your bodily functions and help doctors perform tests like a colonoscopy by using ingestible cameras rather than the more uncomfortable method currently used.

This trio of devices which proactively help us monitor our bodies is also helping each of us become more active participants in our own health. Once again they raise the question of exactly how much data should we allow these devices to gather and more significantly, who should have access to this data?

Robotherapy and Automated Suicide Prevention

Using robots for therapy might sound counterintuitive, but AI bots are now being used to help gather initial information about patients before beginning therapy sessions with real humans. These chatbots will have seemingly human conversations with people, ask preprogrammed standard probing questions and aim to get people to open up and talk about themselves.

One such creation is the Stanford Department of Psychiatry's "Woebot," which was built within Facebook messenger to use a conversational style. Its creator Dr. Alison Darcy believes people may be more honest about themselves and their health when speaking with robots than humans, which can make all the difference in terms of getting to the root of someone's emotional challenges and frustrations.

Facebook itself is working on using predictive language analysis to help identify people who might be thinking of taking their own life. Recent research showed that the feature was working with 80-90% accuracy when it came to predicting the likelihood that someone might attempt suicide within two years, and 92% accuracy in predicting attempts within the next week.[6]

Merging this ability to analyze patterns of speech posted in social media and combining it with sophisticated text mining tools, in addition to the anonymized health data from two million users, Facebook is building an accurate and predictive early warning system for suicide that could one day soon be a standard part of the platform.

The Urban Canary and Protective Products

There are also plenty of examples of the products we use getting smarter to predictively protect us from the hazards in the environment around us. The "Urban Canary," for example, is a small plastic toy bird for parents living in highly polluted cities that has a built-in sensor to measure air pollution, and offers real-time warnings when pollution levels near your child are reaching dangerous levels.

Photo: Urban Canary product and app

In Yellowstone National Park, Flexi-Pave and Michelin Tires have worked to replace 4,160 square feet of walkways throughout the park with "thirsty concrete" made from recycled car tires. This material can absorb 3,000 gallons of water per square foot, per hour, and redistribute the water back into Yellowstone's aquifer to help maintain the ecosystem.[7]

Stockholm-based financial services company If Insurance created Slow Down GPS, an app that turns your phone into a GPS navigation device with one interesting change. The GPS will automatically switch to a child's voice every time a user drives through a school zone. The inspiration behind the app was the belief that most people are inclined to care for children, so when you hear a child's voice you will slow down.

These are each products which have a purpose to help protect you either financially or physically from harm on an individual basis. They are overwhelmingly positive in their missions and the innovations they introduce. When it comes to *Predictive Protection* from the skies, the benefits are less one-sidedly positive.

Drone Squads and Airborne Protectors

The use of drones for *Predictive Protection* is also likely to grow in the next year. The decrease in their cost, along with the fact that they can be deployed in places that are difficult or sometimes impossible for humans to reach, is leading to all kinds of new applications.

The Lindbergh Foundation has been funding a project in Africa called Air-Shepherd which deploys drones to spot poachers who might try to sneak into elephant and rhino habitats at night.

Another group called Protect is implanting a small camera into the rhino horns to watch and catch poachers in real time.

In the UK, the Devon and Cornwall Police have set up a "drone squad" to monitor traffic 24/7, report on accidents and even search for missing people. In the US last year, the number of law enforcement agencies that obtained drones more than doubled from the previous year.[8]

It is easy to imagine the potential uses for this in our communities: drones to protect crowds at large events, or to monitor schools, or to map neighborhoods. Yet these drones surveilling from the skies raise even more questions about privacy, data and who has the right to watch over us literally like an eye in the sky.

Exposing The Financial "Rogues"

The final element of *Predictive Protection* is how it is being applied to the workplace to identify unethical or criminal behavior—starting with financial services, an industry that has been plagued by the actions of greedy opportunistic insiders. These "rogue" traders have been rightly blamed for inciting financial crises while pocketing the profit from their misdeeds. As a response to the need for more employee oversight, a growing range of tools are being released that allow businesses to track the behavior of their employees and protect sensitive data from being misused.

Behavox is trying to solve this challenge with software analytics that helps to grade employees based on how likely they are to commit wrongdoing. Their algorithms are based on sophisticated analysis of the behavior of captured fraudsters and bankers, and their research tracks thousands of data points from elevated voice levels to messaging colleagues with trading ideas at odd hours.

The fact that multiple banking institutions like Wells Fargo and Bank of America (among several others) have collectively paid more than $200 billion in fines for bad or unethical behavior over the past eight years,[9] has made this an urgent topic as banks try to find better ways to prevent these issues, while also rebuilding trust with consumers and regulators.

Why It Matters:

The one thing that seems to keep pace with the advancement of technology is our expectation of what that technology should do for our lives. On the positive side, we see most of the companies we work with approach this opportunity with the best intentions to help enhance the customer or employee experience and help us live better and safer lives.

On the flip side, sometimes this *Predictive Protection* can (debatably) go too far, denying us that candy bar from a vending machine or developing its own language to be more efficient. As the trend continues to accelerate, this delicate balance raises questions about where to strategically pursue innovation just because we can, and where to pause and consider more fundamental ethical questions. How much autonomy do we really want our technology to have? Who should have access to these tools? And perhaps most importantly, what boundaries should we establish and demand from innovative organizations as they pursue a future powered by artificial intelligence, automation and predictive technology?

How to Use This Trend

✓ **Protect your customers first**. Many of the examples shared in this chapter were stories of how companies were protecting themselves against fraud or rogue trading, yet the most impactful cases of *Predictive Protection* are usually the ones that put the consumer first. The parking proximity warning, the credit card alerts, the wearable trackers all serve the customer's needs and therefore have widespread acceptance. As this trend affects more parts of business, newer uses of technology for *Predictive Protection,* such as monitoring employees or patrolling communities from the skies will be more likely to succeed without backlash if they also continue to put people's health, information security and personal safety above all else.

✓ **Establish a data code of ethics**. Whether you consider your organization to be data-centric or not, it is going to be imperative in the future to have a clear, proactive point of view on how data will be collected, used, stored and shared. This must go beyond the usual "we will not share your email" platitudes and map out what happens if the data is breached, how extensively will you use it for marketing or personalization and how someone can retract their data if they choose to. *Predictive Protection* is important for individual use but also important when it comes to the sensitive data that large organizations are being trusted to collect and store indefinitely.

16

APPROACHABLE LUXURY

What's the Trend?

—

Luxury is no longer defined by scarcity and privilege, but rather through more down-to-earth authentic human experiences that create unforgettable moments worth sharing.

—

During Paris Fashion Week in early 2017, the outlandish creative director of Chanel, Karl Lagerfeld, presented his craziest fashion show yet. For his space-themed collection, he put together a catwalk featuring a full-sized, Chanel-branded rocket ship in the middle of the runway. At one point in the show, it even lifted off the ground to offer an unforgettable closing act.

Vetements fashion CEO Guram Gvasalia was less enchanted with the excessive celebration. He elected to have his label skip participating in Fashion week entirely. "Today shows have nothing to do with clothes anymore," complained Gvasalia. "Most of the looks are not even produced and therefore never get to the shop floor. Shows are there merely to sell a dream that at the end of the day will sell a perfume or a wallet in a duty-free store."[1] A recent fashion industry report seems to confirm that Gvasalia has a point: "In most cases, the goal of the RTW [ready-to-wear] division is not to lose too much money. A number of brands produce lavish fashion shows, and then throw the catwalk styles in the garbage, without even trying to sell them."[2]

Selling luxury has always been about the perception of scarcity combined with exclusivity, but there are signs that the future of luxury may need to work harder than that. Selling modern luxury requires that the *experience* offer more value than the *product*.[3]

—

"Time, space, authenticity, community, individuality and mindfulness are intangible experiences which are increasingly seen as luxury."

WOUTER GEERTS, Euromonitor Research

—

As more upwardly mobile professionals move back into urban areas instead of expanding outward into suburbs, space has become more of a premium. The predictable result is that the quest for more *stuff* has less appeal. One potent example is the difficulty that many Baby Boomers, born 1946 to 1964, have in handing down their precious heirlooms like Lladro figurines and mahogany furniture. The younger generation isn't interested in holding onto these items.[4]

In the article titled "What the Rich Won't Tell You," author Rachel Sherman argues that the stigma of displaying wealth is prevalent:

"While pursuing wealth is unequivocally desirable, having wealth is not as simple and straightforward ... the people I talked to never bragged about the price of something because it was high; instead, they enthusiastically recounted snagging bargains on baby strollers, buying clothes at Target, and driving old cars."[5]

I found this point particularly relevant, having been raised in a family where we never talked about how much something cost or how much money someone was making. It was considered impolite to ask and certainly impolite to brag.

What happens when this new consumer mentality of experience-above-all-else meets the traditional mindset of how luxury has always been sold, through a combination of perceived scarcity, price-based discrimination, and celebrity-induced longing? Our research suggests that a new focus on *Approachable Luxury* will separate the brands that survive from those who don't. This trend is already driving some of the most exclusive brands in the world to seek out new non-obvious ways to retain their cachet while still finding ways to be more human, authentic, and even humble.

Why No One Is Buying Swiss Watches

Few industries are feeling the impact of the evolving definition of luxury quite so dramatically as luxury Swiss watches. At the annual Baselworld industry trade show in Switzerland last year, analysts announced that exports of Swiss watches had fallen for a third consecutive year, something that had not occurred since the 1930s.[6]

The rise of the smartwatch was partially to blame, while others pointed a finger at the always-available smartphone, which reduces the need for a watch. The biggest issue, though, may be a shift in what affluence really means. It has been a long-standing assumption among luxury brands that consumers will trade up as their income increases. The more money people made, the more likely they were to exchange their older clothes, cars, homewares, and watches for something better—and usually more expensive.

Today this is no longer true, marking a phenomenon described as *post-luxury*. These post-luxury consumers don't feel as though their first stop after acquiring more wealth must be to make an expensive celebratory purchase. As their wealth rises, they no longer rush to constantly upgrade what they have. Instead, they take great pride in driving the same cars, wearing the same clothes, and being the same person as before they "made it."

It is hard to overstate the impact of this shift on luxury brands. In a world where the upward mobility of consumers is no longer a guarantee that they will become customers, luxury brands in every industry need to work harder. They need to tell a different story.

Detroit's Shining New Hope

One brand that has played perfectly to this post-luxury mentality is Shinola, a leather goods brand that was once breathlessly described by *Adweek* magazine as "the coolest brand in America."[7] It was founded by Tom Kartsotis, who, with his brother, founded Fossil, the accessories and lifestyle brand. Shinola's story starts in 2010 when Kartsotis purchased the name of a defunct shoe polish brand and built a brand story around the fact that the products were made in one of the most iconic cities in the United States: Detroit, Michigan.

The Made-in-Detroit label plus the nostalgia factor appealed to consumers—and an early endorsement by former President Bill Clinton, who described the brand as an American success story, catapulted Shinola to early success. As an appealing side benefit, customers felt that any Shinola purchase was also inherently helping to rebuild the future of one of America's most storied cities.

The brand is an "authenticity machine" that wins because of the broader story of a transforming Detroit, which it borrows from heavily.[8] At the heart of this so-called authenticity machine is the idea that the brand is more approachable because the products are made in an un-luxurious place. They might charge $500 for a watch, but it's made in Detroit instead of Switzerland so it *feels* more real to its largely American consumer base.

The End of Haughty Travel

—

haugh·ty / hôdē /
an attitude of superiority and contempt for people
or things perceived to be inferior.
DEFINITION FROM MERRIAM-WEBSTER DICTIONARY

—

This quest to feel "real," whether manufactured or not, is a driving force behind the *Approachable Luxury* trend. Selling an experience as superior simply because it is exclusive is no longer enough, a fact that we can see clearly when it comes to luxury travel.

For years the W Hotel brand has chosen to actively avoid being associated with the word luxury. As Anthony Ingham, global brand leader for W Hotels, shared in an interview, "W sits alongside luxury not confined by it—because if you say W is a luxury brand, it immediately brings up connotations of white gloves and silver, but we boldly colour outside the lines of luxury."[9]

Conrad Hotels and Resorts (owned and operated by Hilton Worldwide) has focused on what it calls *smart luxury* to distinguish itself from its more traditional sister brand, Waldorf Astoria (also owned by Hilton). The brand has pioneered a program called "Stay Inspired" to help business travelers take advantage of what little free time they might have through a series of curated local experiences.

Singapore Airlines, often voted the best airline in the world, recently launched a "Book the Cook" service for all passengers to preorder their gourmet meals before the flight to ensure they have exactly what they want on board. The custom approach is accompanied by special training for cabin crew on the precise reheating and plating of the meals to ensure the best possible experience. While traditional luxury might have meant this was offered to their elite customers, in this case the meal program was offered to customers flying in first, business, and premium economy at no additional cost.

Train Like a Celebrity

Boutique studios are the fastest-growing segment in fitness, accounting for over a third of the $25.3 billion generated by the industry.[10] These themed workout destinations usually have charismatic trainers, a personalized approach and the chance to work out like a celebrity, with highly personalized attention and world class coaching.

Bringing people access to these boutiques is ClassPass, a membership-based service that has been called "the next Uber" by TechCrunch. The service allows members to go in and out of different fitness studios and work with private trainers for a flat monthly fee—encouraging subscribers to get out and try different types of classes and fitness routines.

Peloton, an indoor cycling brand, is a commonly cited success story in this industry, having raised $325 million and tripling its annual revenue in only a year. Peloton's model is based on providing engaging content via live-streamed classes with mini-celebrity instructors and recorded sessions that users can stream on demand. The sessions are displayed on a screen mounted to the  brand's proprietary stationary bike, so you can participate from home, whenever you want. It has become a cultural phenomenon and has quickly redefined what it means to create a social experience around working out without the need to visit a gym in person.[11]

The brand has countless celebrity customers, promotes the idea of on-demand fitness, and has built its own content production studio to capitalize on the popularity of indoor cycling workouts. This at-home exercise bike and catalog of 5,000+ videos is the perfect example of *Approachable Luxury*. It is a high-value product, priced at a premium, sold based on the experience. It offers convenience and the freedom to work out on your own terms.

Everyday Gourmet

The food industry is also seeing the traditional lines between fine dining and other categories starting to blur. In the inaugural *Michelin Guide* to dining in Singapore, for example, for the first time ever, two street vendor food stalls were named to the prestigious book.[12]

Meanwhile, award winning chef Sebastien Bras, citing the intense pressure of maintaining his stars, asked to be removed from the guide completely. When it comes to food, this blurring of lines between top-tier fine dining and *everyday gourmet* has been years in the making.

Just outside of Washington, DC, one of the hottest new restaurants in the suburbs of Virginia is a tiny Mexican kitchen called Taco Bamba, owned and operated by James Beard–nominated chef Victor Albisu. In recent years, gourmet food trucks run by notable chefs have become such a recognizable part of the urban landscape that they inspired the concept for a feature film, *Chef*, by actor and director Jon Favreau.

Approachable Luxury is also influencing the choice of ingredients that at-home-chefs are buying. In New York City, there is a collection of farmer's markets called Greenmarket that sells gourmet produce, including tiny lettuces for nearly $50 per pound, and something called red amaranth sprouts for $64 per pound (the priciest produce at the market). Nearby at a Whole Foods store near Bryant Park in Manhattan, the store offers a *produce butcher* to chop your fruits and vegetables for you.

Dining was once separated by stars that indicated whether an experience was to be considered luxury or not. Now those lines are blurring as consumers can buy a few dollars worth of expensive produce at the corner market, eat street food cooked by award-winning chefs, and separate the perception of quality and luxury from the color of the tablecloth it happens to be served on (or whether there is a tablecloth at all).

Eco-Diamonds and the New Jewelry Customer

This shift toward Approachable Luxury is even affecting the industry long considered to be immune to such forces given the consistently high prices for precious stones and minerals.

When MiaDonna, an *eco-diamond* company from Portland, Oregon unveiled its 6.28-carat diamond, it was one of the largest ever grown in a lab. These lab-grown diamonds can be up to 40% cheaper than mined diamonds, and are guaranteed to be conflict-free, (i.e.-not sourced through exploitation of African workers or used to finance corrupt governments). In quality, chemical composition, and appearance, they are identical.

Unlike older consumers, who likely grew up hearing the iconic De Beers advertising slogan, "A Diamond is Forever," younger consumers are less likely to feel this same reverence toward diamonds. Instead, many analysts believe the ethical considerations about how diamonds are mined, coupled with lower prices, will lead to a boom in eco-diamond sales.[13]

—

"Women don't necessarily want the big ring anymore; they aren't interested in showing off a big diamond to the world. They'd rather show off an experience, like a trip to Africa."

VANESSA STOFENMACHER, Vrai & Oro Founder

—

Up-and-coming eco-diamond jeweler Vrai & Oro is already benefiting from this growth. Recently acquired by eco-diamond lab Diamond Foundry, the brands are collectively rethinking the entire process of how diamonds (and engagement rings in particular) are purchased.

For example, Vrai & Oro founder Vanessa Stofenmacher learned after surveying customers that neither the proposal nor the ring typically came as a surprise to the recipient. This led her team to an insight: Involve the *couple* in the purchase. What was previously the domain of confused and nervous guys ready to propose could now be a shared experience. At Vrai & Oro, consumers select up to three ring designs that are sent to them in a "mock box" with cubic zirconia versions of the rings created for them to try on. This direct-to-consumer model has been paying off: Stofenmacher just opened her first brick-and-mortar location in Downtown Los Angeles' Arts District

Why It Matters

Just hearing the term *luxury* feels at once exclusive and perhaps slightly out of reach. We all want to have luxurious experiences, but many of us feel as though we may not be able to afford them or belong in those situations in the first place. Luxury has usually come with an air of unapproachability. Today this is changing as luxury brands seek new ways to be relevant without intentionally walling themselves off from large groups of consumers. Our work in this space defines five key characteristics that brands must focus on to most effectively use this trend by being: historic, human, honed, heralded, and heroic.

5 NON-OBVIOUS ELEMENTS OF APPROACHABLE LUXURY

1. HISTORIC – What is the backstory and heritage of the brand, and is it still true to that history?
2. HUMAN – Does the brand have an approachable personality that mirrors its consumers?
3. HONED – Is the product or service artfully crafted, deliberate, unique, and delightful?
4. HERALDED – What is the brand reputation and does it live up to the story they are telling?
5. HEROIC – What difference in the world is the brand making and what does it stand for?

While some readers may look at this and assume it is a framework only written for brands with a long heritage or brands that are financially out of reach for most consumers, the point of *Approachable Luxury* is not to describe how to promote brands only to the super-wealthy. Instead, it is about bringing the idea of a luxury experience to life for any brand, and playing in space that allows you to charge a premium and offer an experience that feels luxurious to the customer whether it costs thousands of dollars or not.

Luxury will likely always rely on some level of scarcity. It is hard to offer a luxury experience if it is easily available to anyone at any time. But the quest for brands to think and act in more human ways is bringing attention to a new form of *Approachable Luxury*—one that will not only engage consumers more deeply, but will help brands create products and experiences that are so memorable, consumers won't be able to stop talking about them.

How to Use This Trend

✓ **Embrace your personality.** It is more important than ever to tell a powerful backstory to inspire belief. *Approachable Luxury* comes from actually creating something that consumers are not afraid to try and that feels attainable. This is not about making it cheaper or available to everyone, but rather focusing on what makes a product or service uniquely different.

✓ **Apply the five H's of Approachable Luxury.** If you read the model of the five H's and feel that it may offer a useful framework for how to think about putting this into action, there are some resources that can help. For a useful guide on how to assess your own level of approachability in luxury and some tips on how to improve it by using this framework, visit www.nonobviousbook.com/resources to download a worksheet and more tips.

17

TOUCHWORTHY

What's the Trend?

—

Overwhelmed by digital, consumers turn back toward
products and experiences that they can touch, feel and sense
to deliver a much needed sense of calm, simplicity and humanity.

—

In 2015, a few months after the first edition of this book was published, my wife and I decided to celebrate by hosting a big launch party. Of course, the party had to be "non-obvious"—and we had plenty of ideas. Inspired by the balloon on the cover, everything was themed yellow: including my brightly colored shirt, branded sunglasses and even some of the food.

To inject some fun, one of the signature cocktails on the menu that evening was a "Rohito" (a raspberry mojito) and we had lots of other fun little details. The biggest was right next to the entrance to the bar: a large photo booth. Outside were a variety of props and fun décor, and inside you would pose for a picture and then that photo would be printed and you could take it home with you.

Years later, the thing people remember most about the party is that photo booth and the pictures they took (and kept). What only some of them knew was that the entire idea for the booth was inspired by a trend I had written about nearly two years before. A trend that has had so much longevity, I decided to bring it back again in 2017: *Precious Print*.

Precious Print is a trend that describes our tendency to value the things we have in print more than digital items because we can hold them in our hands. Since I first published this trend, there have been new reports on how studying books in print might aid learning and retention.[1] Some researchers even believe that a return to learning cursive and writing by hand might have hidden benefits in our overly digitized world. The point is, there are many believers in the power of print.

Over the past year of seeing these examples, our team started to wonder if perhaps this trend might encompass more than just print. What if people just wanted more experiences where they could touch something in the real world for themselves? As we slowly uncovered over the course of a year of research, this is indeed the case—which led us to define a new trend we call *Touchworthy*.

Touchworthy describes a growing human desire to engage with real world experiences, products and people that they can *feel* through touch (and sometimes other senses).

To see the powerful impact of this trend, let's return to the example of the photo booths and how the memorable experiences of our friends at the launch party is mirrored every day by thousands of Japanese teens.

The Japanese Purikura Experience

Taking photos with friends inside a *purikura* (Japanese for "print club") machine is a uniquely Japanese experience. These unique photo booths are available across Japan inside of shopping malls and they are thriving. The usual *purikura* experience starts with taking a photo together with friends (usually in front of a green screen). Then you come out to interact with a screen that lets you add backgrounds and use Snapchat-style filters to do everything from applying fake eyelashes, to making your legs look longer. You can draw on these images or customize in other ways – and then you order them to be printed immediately as stickers to share.

Photo Credit: Jon Åslund (Flickr)

This is a great example of the power of touch but it, too, is print-centric. Earlier this year I challenged my team to dig deeper and see if we could find examples of this trend of *Touchworthy* across the world in ways that had nothing to do with print. We found many, like the fascinating usage of therapy pets in unique places. We discussed the growing field of haptics, reviewed sensory product development and we were even inspired by the strange popularity of slime, a product that seems to be spawning its own economy.

The Slime Economy & ASMR

It was about eight months ago that I discovered a different slime than I expected in my house. Thanks to my two boys, we have plenty of "Crazy Aaron's Thinking Putty" and "Barrel-o-Slime" around the house. We have enough varieties of slime that I am embarrassingly well informed about its different consistencies, from firm to gooey. The slime that surprised me, though, was not like the others because of one big difference: my boys had made it themselves. Of course, I saw this as a curiosity to be investigated further (and hopefully kept off the carpet).

Making slime is simple – just combine everyday household items such as school glue, baking soda, and food coloring together with a variety of other creative materials to add individuality, like glitter or scented hand lotion. The "industry" of making slime (if you can call it that) has exploded recently, with hundreds of thousands of social media posts sharing #slime creations. Many of them are inspired by a single YouTuber named Karina Garcia, also known as the "slime queen."

Photo - YouTuber Karina Garcia (aka Slime Queen)

Garcia, 23, is widely credited with being one of the influencers who first started the slime craze. Her YouTube channel has more than 6.5 million subscribers and helps her make an estimated $200,000 per month. She has a newly released slime recipe book and a "make-your-own slime kit" that was released exclusively at Target.

The popularity of slime has spawned its own economy, with some entrepreneurs as young as 10 years old creating slime and selling it on platforms like eBay and Etsy. Most sell for between $5 to $10 per batch and feature recipes like "Fluffy Liquid Metallic Gold" slime and rainbow colored "Unicorn Poop" slime. By now whether you have seen this slime for yourself or not, you're probably wondering why it has become so popular.

As you play with the material, it makes a variety of squishing, popping, cracking and yes, even farting, noises. It is oddly satisfying to touch. The slime is so fun because it triggers an autonomous sensory meridian response (also known as ASMR)—a feeling of relaxation caused by the combination of the sounds made by specific movements. This too, is a fast-growing genre on YouTube.

The Strangely Soothing World of ASMR

One of the most popular creators of ASMR videos is a 30-year-old Russian expat known only as Maria (to protect her identity) – who is better known online by her YouTube channel name: GentleWhispering. Called one of the Internet's "Most Fascinating People" by *Cosmopolitan* magazine, Maria describes ASMR as "a comforting [feeling], an intimacy with another human being." Before you get the wrong idea, she is quick to add that "it's not meant to be sexual – just relaxing. Maybe it'll even put you to sleep."[2]

The relaxing properties of this genre recently inspired IKEA to create its own 25-minute ASMR video targeted towards college students heading back to school as part of its' "Oddly IKEA" campaign. ASMR is moving from virtual to physical as well. This past year a team of Singapore and UK-based entrepreneurs created a traveling show called the Whisperlodge to offer an immersive theatrical ASMR experience in real life.

The ASMR genre, as well as the popularity of slime, are examples of how *Touchworthy* experiences are helping us connect in more human ways and in some instances, battle the stresses of everyday life. There are products that are based on this same principle.

Sensory Friendly Products and Services

The "Gravity blanket" seems too good to be true.

From its beginning, overblown ads promoted the $279 blanket as a "weighted blanket for sleep, stress and anxiety." While these claims have been widely discredited as lacking any real scientific evidence, for the people who love them, there is a very real sensory benefit to being able to snuggle under a weighted blanket.[3] Even if you have never tried it, the idea of a heavy blanket *seems* like it would be comforting.

The Gravity blanket is just one of many products that have attracted attention and sometimes gained notoriety over the past year for how they use the power of touch to trigger an emotional response. A company called Nesel Packs created a line of backpacks that use a weighted vest with a "hugging strap" to help autistic kids feel more at ease. Kozie Clothes is a brand that makes tag-free clothing with soft and "tactile-pleasing" fabrics and comforting inverted seams.

Stacey Monson, a designer at Target, was inspired by her autistic daughter Elinor to help the retailer add a selection of "sensory-friendly" clothing items (removing the labels and other uncomfortable elements) to help make getting dressed for school less of a trying experience for families with autistic children. The clothes are part of the fast-growing private label Cat & Jack brand at Target, which has become a $2 billion brand in its first year alone.[4]

The resurgent popularity of board games is another sign that real life tactile experiences matter.[5] Not only are sales of these sorts of interactive real life games on the rise, but there are also a range of new destinations like the Brooklyn Game Lab in New York which offer memberships and hold events to help bring people together to play board games and enjoy some time away from their devices.

Professional Cuddlers and Touch Therapy

Sometimes this need for the empathy of touch goes beyond products. For those times when you just need human contact, professional cuddling is an industry that offers "touch therapy" on demand. Through marketplaces like www.thesnugglebuddies.com, you can find a professional cuddler trained from a guide called "The Cuddle Sutra" (yes, it's actually a real book) in over 50 platonic and supposedly non-sexual cuddling positions.

Though "Sutra" is probably not the best branding for a book that is meant to teach people about a non-sexual activity—the Snuggle Buddies website shares more details about how this unique service actually works.

According to the site, participants must sign an agreement that no sexual activity of any kind with the cuddlers will take place. Cuddling sessions are allowed in someone's home or in a public place, such as a movie theater or park. They are not allowed in vehicles.

While this entire industry may seem like it exists on the fringe of society, the fact is many people feel a lack of *Touchworthy* experiences in their lives and it causes many issues, from loneliness to difficulty coping with conditions like autism or mental afflictions like PTSD. Luckily there is another growing industry which can help, just in case hiring a professional cuddler is not for you.

Therapy Pets

The latest addition to the staff at San Francisco International Airport only works once a month and routinely comes in with her toenails painted dressed in a pink ballerina tutu only to pose for selfies. Her name is Lilou and she's a "hypoallergenic and temperamentally-vetted" pig. Her real job is to help calm harried travelers and offer a moment of fun in an experience that too often seems anything but.

Lilou the Pig - used with permission

While Lilou is unique in that she's the only pig making the rounds at an airport, the uses for *therapy pets* like her is expanding. Cincinnati/Northern Kentucky Airport uses miniature horses twice a month to help greet passengers when they first arrive at the airport. More than 30 airports across the US are now using therapy dogs to wander the airports providing a welcome relief for many overly stressed passengers. At Charlotte Douglas International Airport, this group is known as the "Canine Crew" and uses eight non-barking certified therapy dogs that walk around the airport wearing blue and yellow vests that say "Pet Me."

These pets are also finding employment outside the airport. Therapy dogs are being used to help PTSD victims recover from trauma and to cheer up patients in hospitals. At one local library in Pennsylvania, therapy dogs help kids practice their reading skills. In San Diego, there is an organization called

SoulPaws which helps people struggling with eating disorders to find comfort through therapy pets who offer no judgement and help them to build a deeper level of self-awareness (critical in the battle against an eating disorder).

All of these uses for therapy pets and the powerful emotional transformations they can cause are another example of our need for *Touchworthy* experiences that engage us on a human and physical level. As with the other examples in this chapter, this is not about sex or sexual activity. This is about feeling more human because you have the chance to use your sense of touch to interact with the world.

Growth In Haptics

There is one more sign that creating *Touchworthy* experiences will continue to matter in the future—and (perhaps ironically) it comes from teams of researchers who are trying to add the powerful element of touch to virtual experiences through haptic technology.

I first wrote about haptics last year when introducing the trend of *Invisible Technology*—a description of how technology was increasingly being baked into everyday experiences and products in a way that we often don't see or recognize. Haptics is defined as the science of applying touch and tactile sensation to the way we control computer applications. The most common example is how you can feel your phone's touchscreen vibrate in response every time you touch a button.

More advanced versions of haptics are studying how to add the sensation of touch when you are interacting with an interface that doesn't involve you actually touching anything—like a digital projection for example. This growing field of *ultrasonic haptics* uses sound waves to simulate the sense of touch and is widely anticipated to change the way that interfaces in everything from cars to retail stores could be created.

The haptic technology market will likely surpass $20 billion over the next five years.[6] In that time, it is likely that the uses for it will offer surprising new insights for interface designers, product development teams and any organizations trying to create more human and *Touchworthy* experiences.

Why It Matters

Every company is spending countless hours trying to craft more engaging customer experiences. Some focus on content development while others are rethinking the interactions they have with customers. No matter what the priorities for your organization happen to be, this trend should inspire you to always ask a single question: is my experience *Touchworthy*?

Carmen Simon, a neuroscientist and author of *Impossible to Ignore* writes and speaks often about how our minds work and what it takes to have a message or story truly stick. "Strong sensory stimulation is mandatory in making a story memorable," she says. "In my research, the stories and products that included more sensory stimulation were remembered better."[7] Her research points to the same conclusion our team uncovered as we interviewed organizations and tracked stories about everything from the rise of the "slime economy" to the ongoing benefits of therapy pets.

What it all tells us is that no matter how digital our lives become, the more human experiences of touch and engaging our senses will continue to be a powerful driver of attention, consumption and belief.

How to Use This Trend

✓ **Find your *Touchworthy* moments**. For the past four years of having this book available in print, my publisher and I have focused on creating a certain sensation when you first touch the cover of the book. Perhaps you noticed it, and perhaps you didn't – but the people who do, always comment about it. Being *Touchworthy* isn't just about technology or touch screens. Instead it's about remembering that the moment when someone feels a product or an experience in their hands is your first (and sometimes most important) opportunity to make an impression … so it is worth spending as much time as you need to get it right.

✓ **Let your people (or customers) make something**. One way to inspire more belief is to make sure that people feel invested. In the world of charity, this often comes when people volunteer and participate in

ECONOMICS & ENTREPRENEURSHIP

an activity instead of just donating money. In companies, this comes from a team that works together to build something real. Either way, the lesson is the same: when a team or group of people create something *Touchworthy* together, they can bond and get inspired a deeper way.

18

DISRUPTIVE DISTRIBUTION

What's the Trend?

—

Traditional models of distribution get reinvented as businesses of all sizes seek more efficiency, build direct connections with consumers and rethink their own business models.

—

Every year right around the time of Halloween, my family and I head out to get our costumes and do all the usual work of getting candy and making the house sufficiently spooky. There is a big pop-up costume shop close to our house where we usually get supplies. They take over a retail space for a month and then shut down. The following month that space gets converted to sell Christmas decorations. It's a smart cycle, allowing them to continually stock just the products that people care about seasonally.

This year, during our annual trek to the Halloween store, I started wondering: What happens to the warehouse that stocks costumes the day after Halloween?

It turns out that the warehouse, like many others across the world, will probably remain empty until new stock comes in. This is a common inefficiency of the warehousing system: goods go out on a schedule for when they are most needed and in the interim millions of square feet of warehouse space sits unused.

This issue of wasted space is becoming more urgent as e-commerce grows. According to research from real estate services firm CBRE, every $1 billion of new online sales per year requires an additional 1.25 million square feet of warehouse space.[1]

For the past four years, a Seattle-based startup named Flexe has been working to solve this inefficiency by leasing the empty space and selling it on-demand to e-commerce startups who want an alternative to tying all their sales to platforms like Amazon and outsourcing their distribution and logistics.

The idea behind Flexe is disruptive and simple. The service lets a growing e-commerce brand manage and own their customer data, control the branding (boxes ship out with any branding and not the Amazon logo), get products to customers as quickly as Amazon Prime and keep more of the revenue from sales.

The service has been described as the "Airbnb of warehousing" and is growing rapidly. In less than five years, Flexe has built a marketplace to rent storage space in more than 500 warehouses and already has about 25% of Amazon's capacity with plans to grow significantly in the coming year.

This same type of thinking is being used by disruptive entrepreneurs who want to think outside the box as well.[2]

In early 2017 an Ottawa-based startup called FarmLead raised $6.5 million in venture funding to help farmers get fairer prices for what they grow. The platform works like eBay, letting growers and buyers share offers and make deals with one another.

The Redd on Salmon Street is a new distribution center in Portland, Oregon with over 2000 square feet of cold storage in the middle of the city. Producers can store products there until they are ready to be distributed. The Redd on Salmon Street can also aggregate their products and help smaller producers sell to larger buyers.

Each of these are examples of *Disruptive Distribution*, a trend I first wrote about back in 2015. At that time, the trend was focused primarily on startups and disruptors who were challenging traditional sales models and streamlining distribution by going directly to consumers. This is still a major theme at the heart of the trend today, but today this disruption is also affecting business models and how current buying cycles work.

The mattress industry is a good example of this disruption.

A Better Way To Buy A Mattress

A mattress seems like the sort of product that should be impossible to sell over the Internet. Who would buy a mattress without lying on it first? And even if you did manage to sell one, how could you possibly get it shipped to someone's home without it costing a fortune?

This was the question mattress company Casper wanted to answer when it first launched in 2014. They solved the difficult issue of shipping a mattress by creating one made from foam that could be rolled and vacuum-wrapped. To convey the comfort of the product, they crafted a combination of compelling online videos and social media content. Then they offered a generous 100-night risk-free trial period.

Photo: Casper mattress in a box

Alongside their product pitch, the brand also used social media to attack the existing status quo of how mattresses were sold. Through entertaining videos, the brand exposed all the things people generally hated about buying a mattress the traditional way (and the list was long).

Trying to "sleep" on one in a store for 10 minutes while a creepy salesman watches. Struggling to tie a mattress to the roof of your car and driving home slowly while hoping it doesn't rain. Desperately trying to fit it through the doors in your home after you buy it. Recruiting a small army of friends to help you lug it up the stairs. The truth is, there are a lot of things people hate about buying a mattress.

Casper's message wasn't just that this would be a good *product*. They sold the consumer on a better purchasing *experience*. Their site not only told you about the product, but featured "unboxing" videos from happy customers who received their bed, easily got it into their rooms and were using it within 30 minutes of its arrival. In 2016 alone, Casper sold more than $200 million worth of mattresses, sheets and pillows.

Their success has spawned a growing industry of direct-to-consumer mattress companies who all cut out the mattress salesmen (and their exorbitant markups) and offer their products to consumers directly over the Internet, at a fair price.

Today, that ecosystem includes brands like Purple, Tuft & Needle, and Saatva. Each borrows heavily from Casper's strategy: a compelling social media pitch, clean websites and direct delivery of a rolled-up foam mattress in a box.

The cumulative sales from these startups captured about 9% market share, a figure that is still just a fraction of established industry leader Tempur Sealy, but high enough to attract the big brand's attention. In late 2016, Sealy launched its own bed-in-a-box brand called Cocoon—a sign of just how much this disruption was taking hold and revolutionizing the entire industry.

Future Of Food Delivery

Dominos has spent the past five years innovating around how people can order pizza delivery. Over that time, the brand has piloted programs allowing customers to order on apps, through Facebook, on Twitter via emojis, through the Apple watch, via voice activated AI assistants and even through creating a wedding registry.

Borrowing from the idea of tracking your package delivery online, Dominos has also injected technology into the time between when you order a pizza and when it arrives at your door. The brand pioneered a tool to track the status of your pizza online, see the name of the person making it and (in some locations) watch that pizza being made through a live streaming camera.

This focus on using technology to enable better and easier delivery is working, as the brand grew its market share more than six percentage points to 15% last year.[3] Other brands are turning to home delivery as a model for expansion. In the past year, McDonald's announced a partnership with Uber to enable deliveries of McDonald's food to people's homes on demand,* while Taco Bell teamed up with ride-sharing rival Lyft to offer the same service.

Panera Bread went a step further and announced it would be hiring its own drivers and fulfilling orders out of its own cafes. The brand has also launched a rapid pickup service.

In Europe, a startup called Deliveroo has created a new category of "kitchen-only" restaurants which can more easily be located in expensive suburban areas. The idea for these would be that you could call to place an order with Deliveroo and these boutique home restaurants would make the food which would be picked up and brought to your home.

If it works, it's easy to imagine this evolving into a sort of Airbnb for home cooking where anyone could cook for anyone else and run a business from their home as a chef without the headache and overhead of a restaurant to go along with it.

Disruptive Subscriptions

In software, most of the biggest vendors have already moved from selling annual updates of their products to offering monthly or annual on-demand subscriptions over the Internet to products like Adobe's Creative Cloud or

*Too bad the enterprising 8-year-old from Chapter 11 didn't know about this!

Microsoft Office 365. The benefits of this model for the software makers is clear: Along with recurring revenue, they can also decrease the number of people using outdated software that requires them to ensure long spans of backward compatibility.

The consumer benefit is access to more consistently updated software, ongoing support, updates and solutions for glitches.

This is the ideal case study for *Disruptive Distribution:* Adobe (for example) can offer a better product to customers, increase their own revenue, and enjoy a more direct sales model without the need for any sort of retailer or distributor in between.

Sometimes the stakeholders involved in a particular subscription model may require more convincing. The startup MoviePass attracted attention in late 2017 by lowering its flat monthly fee from $45 to $9.99 which allowed subscribers to see up to one movie per day (up to 30 per month) in movie theaters. The offer was so compelling that their user base exploded from just 20,000 people to more than 300,000. For most moviegoers, this investment would pay as long as they see at least two movies per month.

The low price elicited an angry response from former partner AMC (America's largest theater operator) who called the pricing "unsustainable," but stopped short of banning MoviePass customers. In contrast, the industry supporters for Moviepass argue that the service is akin to a buffet: just because you *can* go everyday doesn't mean you would *want* to.

After the novelty wears off, the hope is that this will bring the average moviegoer to see a film a few times a month instead of just once (which is the current average), and also help theaters recapture the elusive Millennial and Generation Z audiences.

A similar line of thinking inspired the Colorado-based owners of Vail Resorts to purchase their first mountain on the East Coast in early 2017; Stowe Mountain Resort in Vermont. While it is a small mountain compared to Vail Resort's flagship mountains in Colorado the company hopes it will entice East Coast-based skiiers to purchase an Epic Pass subscription—and presumably spend more money on lodging and food as a result.

Business Blur: Creative Consultancies

Beyond changing business models or how products get delivered, *Disruptive Distribution* also describes how some industries are learning to borrow liberally from other sectors to change proactively before *being* disrupted.

This shift is blurring the lines that were once drawn between management consulting groups and advertising and marketing agencies. Over the past year, headlines from industry media have been stark and alarmist: from "Why accounting firms are suddenly buying advertising agencies" to "The race is on!"

In 2017, for the first time ever, four consultancies made it into the *AdAge* industry list of 10 largest agency companies. Alongside marketing agency holding companies WPP, Omnicom and Publicis were the marketing services groups from Accenture, PwC, IBM and Deloitte.

Consulting groups, led by MBAs trained in business process analysis, are now buying creative agencies filled with writers and designers. The resulting culture clash is causing a lot of soul-searching. Are these new blended consultancies business partners who will help clients operate better, or are they creative partners who bring storytelling expertise? Is it possible to be both? These are the sorts of questions that marketing services firms are facing today.

On the client side, there is a corresponding shift as Chief Marketing Officers are controlling more and more technology spending on behalf of their companies and needing to bring more of an understanding of analytics and data to their roles. According to Gartner, the average CMO is already spending more on technology than the CIO and this is likely to continue.[4]

Business Blur: Retail Experiences

In retail, this practice of borrowing from one sector to another is widely used. Pet supply retailer PetSmart, for example, launched a Pet Spa where "pet parents can bond as they personally bathe their pups."

West Elm, a furniture retailer with nearly 100 locations in the U.S., Canada, the U.K. and Australia, will launch a line of new hotels in 2018 which showcase their furniture and homewares. All of the items in the rooms will be available for purchase.

In Milan, Louis Vuitton acquired a majority stake in legendary 200-year-old pastry and coffee brand Cova Caffè, and has since opened franchised locations in Shanghai, Dubai, Hong Kong and a handful of other cities around the world. When interviewed about the rationale behind the initiative, the late Yves Carcelle (leader of Louis Vuitton for over 20 years), said "It's important to offer customers high-quality stopping points, places where they can pause, meet friends and so on ... a café like Cova adds a touch of class."[5]

Retailer Urban Outfitters announced last year that it was buying Philadelphia's Vetri Family group of restaurants, including Pizzeria Vetri, to try and use the allure of food to bring more people to shop in their retail location.

Over the next year, IMAX will be building a series of "virtual reality arcades" to try and popularize the technology. These brands are willing to take a lesson from other industries and use them to innovate. Their aim is to create products and services which will help them to win in the future—and to do it by borrowing ideas from unrelated sectors to integrate and use as their own.

Industry Shifting

In some of the most forward-looking examples, *Disruptive Distribution* is even leading some industries to reevaluate the core of their business and make fundamental changes to how they operate and what they sell. Netflix is perhaps the ultimate example of a self-disrupting business, having already reinvented its business model twice: first from shipping DVD rentals to then offering streaming content. Now they are undergoing a third shift to become a content producer and creative studio. Each time, the business they had been operating within was still successful—so they have routinely evolved and disrupted themselves from a position of strength rather than out of desperation or fear.

On the opposite end of the spectrum, the insurance industry is filled with apprehension about a future that includes technology such as self-driving cars—which will upend the very nature of how and why we buy insurance.

When people no longer own their cars, what will happen to the $200 billion global auto insurance industry? Fear of this future is causing the notoriously risk-averse industry to make new bets on creating products that don't yet exist. For example, European insurer Swiss Re AG prepared a policy for a part of the Mesoamerican Reef, becoming the first insurer to cover a natural structure. The policyholders are the collection of beachfront hotels protected by that reef.

In the retail sector, longtime office supply superstore Staples is boldly experimenting with creating co-working spaces and testing the idea of being a place where you can work and run your business instead of just operating as a retailer of office supplies.

Relonch is an innovative new startup company that will lend you an expensive and high-quality digital camera and charge you $99 per-month for a service promising to transform your images into "magazine quality photos." The camera will upload your photos (without you seeing them) and then it will use artificial intelligence to retouch the best ones and send them back to your smartphone the next morning. The entire experience is reimagining how consumers take, use and share their pictures.

Each of these stories brings to life how *Disruptive Distribution* is also inspiring some organizations and industries to consider a more fundamental reinvention of their core businesses to meet the real needs of the customers of the future.

Why It Matters

When we first published this trend, it described a shift among businesses to create more direct models for getting products to consumers with increased ease, control and efficiency. This has undeniably continued to be a force in business, with startups like Flexe enabling e-commerce startups to deliver products with efficiency and entire industries like mattress sales being upended by the arrival of irreverent innovators who change consumer expectations.

The deeper and more significant side of this trend that has emerged over the past few years is how the most forward-thinking businesses in any sector are now willing to borrow heavily from other industries and think outside of their own traditions to do business in new and sometimes risky ways. The implications of all of these changes will unfold industry by industry, as organizations find ways to embrace this change and leave their more traditional and slow-to-change competitors far behind.

How to Use This Trend

✓ **Find the blur.** One of my favorite brainstorming techniques I frequently use in a workshop is encouraging participants to put two unlikely things together and see what happens. I will ask questions like, what if you sold cars the way that a donut shop sells donuts? Or what if Airbnb decided to start a pharmacy? These sorts of mind bending questions encourage us to think about things that we usually wouldn't and find new ideas in the "blur" between industries. They may seem farfetched and impossible, but those sparks can lead you to an actionable idea as you work your way backwards from crazy to possible.

✓ **Experiment with business models.** When you work with a startup in an early phase, you understand the challenge of selecting a business model. It's a big choice and one that is likely to drive many other decisions. There are many books and resources focused on helping you to find the right business model. Yet when you are working at an established company, the idea of rethinking your business model rarely comes up (unless you're failing and need to make a desperation "pivot"). What if you could think through different business models and start to proactively imagine the scenarios? Business models are no longer sacred or immobile. Opening up yours for debate might be the best decision you can make to prepare for the future.

PART III

THE TREND
ACTION
GUIDE

19

≡

INTERSECTION THINKING
How To Apply Trends To Your Business

—

*"Discovery consists of seeing what everybody has seen
and thinking what nobody has thought."*

ALBERT SZENT-GYÖRGYI, Nobel Prize–winning Physician

—

Nearly ten years ago, Tom Maas, a former marketing executive for distiller Jim Beam, finally created his perfect drink. For years, he had been working on developing and promoting a new cream liquor based on the popular traditional milky cinnamon-and-almond beverage from Latin America known as *horchata*.

His new drink was a mixture of light rum, dairy cream, and spices like cinnamon and vanilla that he christened "RumChata" in honor of the drink that inspired its flavors. Unfortunately, RumChata was not an instant hit.

It was only when some creative sales people first started likening its taste to the milk at the bottom of a bowl of Cinnamon Toast Crunch cereal that RumChata began to gain momentum. Bartenders started using the liquor to create inspired blends, which led to more liquor distributors and retailers ordering it. Inventive promotions like "cereal shooter bowls" also helped encourage bars to serve RumChata-based drinks.

Eventually, this creativity began to translate to higher sales.

By 2014, the drink had taken one-fifth of the market share in the $1 billion U.S. market for cream-based liquors, and even started outselling the longstanding leader, Diageo's Baileys Irish Cream, in certain regions. By 2017, it is also the most popular spirits brand on social media, with new videos on its YouTube channel routinely getting more than 2 million views.[1]

More importantly, experts described the drink as a crossover game changer due to its popularity as a mixer *and* as an ingredient for food and baking recipes.

How to Create a Game-Changing Product

RumChata is a perfect example of the type of success that can come from putting the power of observation together with an understanding for the intersection of consumer behavior and the open space in a market.

While Maas may not have been thinking about trend curation when he came up with his product idea, we can still find some lessons in the example.

When you look backward, there are three cultural signals that may explain some of RumChata's success:

1. A growing consumer desire for authentic products with interesting backstories;
2. The rising prevalence of food entertainment programming on television inspiring more creativity in home cooking;
3. The increased interest across the United States in Hispanic culture and heritage.

In retrospect, these observations support the arrival of a product like RumChata. Of course, putting the dots together looking backward is easy.

The real question is: How can you do this predictably in a way that helps you create your own success in the future?

An Introduction to Intersection Thinking

Trends are big ideas describing the accelerating world around us. Unfortunately, the value of big ideas is not always easily understood when it comes to applying them to real life.

Trend forecaster Chris Sanderson from the Future Laboratory describes trends as "profits waiting to happen." As tempting as that sounds, achieving those profits takes more than skill at uncovering, curating, and describing a trend. You need to know what to do next.

Trends only have value if you can learn to act on them.

Is a trend telling you to abandon an existing product line? Or to pivot the focus of your business? Or to stay the course in a direction that hasn't yet paid off? These are the kinds of big questions that leaders often face and they aren't easy to answer.

Learning to curate trends can help you benefit from an outside perspective and prompt you to think about your business in a way that your competitors aren't. Doing this always starts with using "intersection thinking."

Intersection thinking is a method for creating overlap between seemingly disconnected ideas in order to generate new ideas, directions, and strategies for powering your own success.

After helping dozens of organizations and thousands of people learn to curate trends and then apply them, I always start by teaching this skill.

To do it, the analogy I use most often is this one:[2]

PLUM + **APRICOT** = **PLUOT**

Trends can be exactly like pluots: only valuable if you take the time to put multiple things together and experiment with them. This is intersection thinking, and doing it requires you to embrace four mindsets.

---

4 Mindsets of Intersection Thinking

1. See the similarities instead of the differences.
2. Purposely look away from your goal.
3. Wander into the unfamiliar.
4. Be persuadable.

Mindset #1: See the Similarities Instead of the Differences

Paolo Nagari is an intercultural intelligence specialist who teaches expat executives the skills they need to succeed while living and working abroad. Unlike many other experts, however, his model doesn't rely on teaching the "dos and don'ts" of a given culture. His belief is that succeeding in a culture other than your own takes more than memorizing lists.

Nagari's first rule for executives is all about learning to focus on the many similarities in cultures instead of the differences. It's a valuable lesson when considering how to embrace unfamiliar ideas in business as well.

When former Coca-Cola executive Jeff Dunn became president of Bolthouse Farms, for example, he walked into a billion-dollar agricultural company that had literally reinvented the carrot industry by creating "baby carrots."[3]

By the time Dunn took over, sales of carrots (and baby carrots) were experiencing a slump and he needed a solution, so he turned to advertising agency Crispin Porter + Bogusky (CP+B).

During their preparation, the agency was inspired by a unique idea based on a simple consumer insight: people love snacking on junk food and hate being told to eat healthier.

As CP+B creative director Omid Farhang shares, "the truth about baby carrots is they possess many of the defining characteristics of our favorite junk food. They're neon orange, they're crunchy, they're dippable, they're kind of addictive."[4]

Using this insight, CP+B built a new campaign that enticed consumers to "Eat 'Em Like Junk Food," inspired by the marketing tactics of other consumer packaged goods companies (like Coca-Cola). Baby carrots were packaged and promoted like junk food, including cutting them in a "crinkle cut" style to make them look more like potato chips.

In campaign test markets, sales immediately went up between 10% and 12%, all thanks to a campaign built from seeing the similarities between the marketing tactics for junk food and applying those to marketing baby carrots instead.

Mindset #2: Purposely Look Away from Your Goal

In early 2017, Starbucks founder Howard Schultz finally realized his thirty-four-year-long dream to open a Starbucks location in the place that started it all: Milan.

More than three decades earlier, his now-legendary spark of insight about what Starbucks could become happened on a walk from his hotel to a convention center. He'd been sent to a trade show in Milan to represent Starbucks, which at the time was a supplier of high-end home brewing equipment.

On that trip, he experienced firsthand the dominance of Italian espresso coffee shops on every street corner and how these might offer a "third place" (after work and home). He returned and persuaded the owners to create a retail coffee shop. Years later he purchased the brand from the original owners and took it global.

The growth of Starbucks is interesting, but what I found most inspiring about this was how it all started—with a curious walk that had nothing to do with focusing on a trade show or business purpose. Schultz's story is a perfect illustration of the power of looking away from your main purpose to discover bigger ideas that may be waiting around the corner (literally in his case!).

Mindset #3: Wander into the Unfamiliar

If you happen to be walking the streets of Bangkok around 6:00 p.m. on any day, you'll see people stop in their tracks for seemingly inexplicable reasons. Ask anyone afterward and you'll quickly learn that there are two times every day when the Thai national anthem is played (8:00 a.m. and 6:00 p.m.) and all citizens stop what they're doing and observe a moment of silence out of respect.

Once you see this cultural practice in action, it's impossible to forget. Travel experiences are like this—whether they happen across the world from your home, or simply during a visit to a nearby yet unfamiliar place. Wandering is a form of exploration that we often think to embrace only when traveling, but it has great value on a more daily basis.

In a world where we have a mobile map in our pocket, ready to assist us with turn-by-turn directions to anywhere, wandering must be a choice. It's the perfect metaphor for why intersection thinking matters, and why it can be difficult as well.

Sometimes we must choose to leave our maps behind.

Mindset #4: Be Persuadable

In the first edition of this book, this was not one of the original mindsets. I added it this year because it has become more necessary than ever. The world conspires in many ways to encourage each of us to burrow further into the chasms of our own beliefs. Algorithms on social media serve up stories we agree with. Website cookies aim to segment us to predict what we'll like to see or what we might click on to buy. Polarizing politicians remind us that "truth" comes with the necessity for someone to be wrong so we can be right, and tell us that person should be treated like the enemy. Instead, what if we could be brave enough to change our minds?

What if we could be persuadable—to the point where hearing a compelling argument that we don't initially agree with might sway us to adapt our beliefs or at least allow for the possibility that someone who sees the world in a way other than ours might *not* be a complete idiot?

Why Workshops Are So Powerful

A workshop is a gathering or meeting where an individual or a group of people focus their conversation and ideation on solving a challenge or thinking in new, innovative ways.

While it may seem hard or unnecessary to bring the right people together in a room for something like a workshop (and just plain silly if you're doing it alone or with just one other person), there are several reasons to consider taking a workshop-driven approach to applying trends or any other kind of new ideas.

The first is that workshops can help to *focus your attention*. We're all busy and usually don't have the time to be sitting around thinking about trends all day. To ensure you can have the right focused attention, it's valuable to block out a set period, even if it happens to be short. Just the act of making sure this time is scheduled and separate from your usual daily activities can help ensure that it feels significant. It will also help you to get the right people in the room, because blocking out a set time ensures they have notice and will not (hopefully) schedule something else for that time.

The second key to effectively using a workshop is to *set a clear objective*. While you usually don't need a step-by-step map, it's always useful to have a purpose or desired outcome defined. There are many ways to engineer the structure of what you do in a workshop. I share four common structures later in this chapter. Whichever you choose, the important thing is, like any good meeting, your workshop has a purpose so participants know what you aim to accomplish.

Finally, you need to be sure to *establish accountability*. Another critical reason that workshops can be so effective is that they force people to make commitments about what to do next.

5 Keys to Running a Great Trend Workshop

1. **Prepare Like a Pro.** Take the time to familiarize yourself with the background of an issue, what has already been tried, what the needs of the group are, and what questions need to be asked in order to push the group toward real change.

2. **Capture First, Critique Later.** People say, "there are no bad ideas in a brainstorm." That's not true. Unfortunately, it's impossible to tell good ideas from bad ones in real time. For that reason, encourage all participants to openly share ideas, and don't waste time and energy trying to immediately critique them. Save that for later.

3. **Adopt a "Yes and" Mindset.** Improv actors always talk about the importance of collaborating with others in a scene by going with the flow and building upon one another's ideas. This additive approach is one of the hallmarks of great and effective workshops as well.

4. **Always Have an Unbiased Facilitator.** It's easy to assume that the person closest to the issue is the best leader, but this is often untrue. Instead, the best workshop facilitators are individuals who can lead a discussion, keep a conversation on track, and ask provocative questions without bias.

5. **Recap and Summarize.** It's the role of the facilitator to summarize the conversation, recap any action items, and ensure that everyone who spent their precious time participating understands what they collectively achieved and what will need to happen next.

4 Models of Trend Workshops

1. **Customer Journey Mapping Trend Workshop.** Building a step-by-step understanding of how your customers interact with you so you can apply trends to each step of the process.
2. **Brand Storytelling Trend Workshop.** Developing a powerful brand story or message designed to resonate with customers, based on understanding and using current trends.
3. **Business Strategy Trend Workshop.** Creating a new go-to-market or product-launch strategy or making changes to a business model or revenue model informed by current trends and new competitive situations.
4. **Company Culture Trend Workshop.** Planning your career or optimizing and improving an internal company culture and team based on current trends.

In the original 2015 hardcover edition of *Non-Obvious*, each workshop was outlined in detail through four additional chapters. For the sake of brevity, those chapters are not included in this edition. They are still available online completely for free for download at www.nonobviousbook.com/resources.

Note for Small Teams and Solopreneurs

Although most of this chapter and the bonus PDF are specifically written from the point of view of having multiple participants in each type of workshop, many of the lessons in these chapters can be easily applied to small teams (or by individual innovators) as well.

Just because you don't have a large group of team members doesn't mean you can't use the benefits of intersection thinking and workshops to power your business. There's never a bad time to break from your normal routine and dedicate time through a workshop, to strategize for the future.

20

5 BOOKS ON TRENDS WORTH READING

(AND 15 WEBSITES TO BOOKMARK)

—

Despite the skepticism with which I often approach trend reports from so-called gurus, there are a handful of valuable, well-written resources for trend forecasting and techniques that I've drawn upon heavily over the years. This includes a short list of books and a longer list of websites that I routinely consult for story ideas. While some have already been cited elsewhere in this book, that chapter includes a full list of some of my favorites.

1. *Megatrends,* by John Naisbitt (1982)

There's a reason why this book about trends and the future has been a bestseller for the past three decades. Naisbitt paints a fascinating future portrait of the world as he saw it back in the early '80s. Despite the many years that have passed since it was first published, *Megatrends* remains a valuable read both for the prescience of Naisbitt's ideas and how he manages to capture the spirit of his time while also producing a startlingly accurate vision of the future.

2. *The Trend Forecaster's Handbook,* by Martin Raymond (2010)

This full-color, large-format volume is the closest thing you can find to a textbook on how to predict trends. Like most textbooks, it has a hefty price tag (used copies currently go for about $100), but the content is beautifully organized and it includes a dictionary-style compilation of everything you need to know about trend forecasting. From interviews with top futurists to highly useful sidebars (like how to select and interview an expert panel), this book shares so much insight that it belongs on your bookshelf.

3. *Trend-Driven Innovation,* by Henry Mason, David Mattin, Maxwell Luthy, and Delia Dumitrescu (2015)

The methodology for this book is based on the work of the team behind Trendwatching.com and features a behind-the-scenes look at some of the trends they have predicted over the years. The book is highly visual, easy to read, and a model for not only learning to see trends, but also how to talk about and present them.

4. *Superforecasting,* by Philip E. Tetlock & Dan Gardner (2015)

The most mainstream book on the list, *Superforecasting* was heavily praised when it first came out—named a "Best Book of 2015" by *The Economist* and "Editor's Choice" by the *New York Times.* The book uses powerful stories and years of research into what makes good (and accurate) forecasting to offer a model for how anyone can learn to use better foresight to understand the future.

5. *The Trend Management Toolkit,* by Anne Lise Kjaer (2014)

This book from longtime futurist and speaker Kjaer offers a somewhat academic description of methodologies used for predicting trends, and is therefore a tougher read than some of the other recommended books in this section. The section on creating and using a Trend Atlas and trend mapping is the most useful element in the book, and is the "toolkit" alluded to in the title. This technique is one which has been borrowed, adapted, and leveraged by many other experts and companies and is worth reading from the original source.

What Else To Read...

Every year, my team and I receive dozens of books to review, and we purchase dozens more on our own. All of these provide sources of input for the coming year's trend research, but they also are featured in an annual book awards program released every December called the "Non-Obvious Book Awards."

Fifteen shortlist winners and five gold-medal category winners are featured and presented every year in December to coincide with the release of this book. You can see the full list of previous winners along with all the newest winners for the 2017 calendar year online: www.nonobviousbook.com/resources

15 Websites to Bookmark

This collection of online resources is a just a fraction of the 100+ sources of news that I subscribe to via RSS and use every week to source ideas both for my weekly newsletter, as well as for this annual book of trends. Below you will find some of my favorite sites, along with a quick one sentence description for each. You can also see this full list and click the links directly at www.nonobviousbook.com/resources.

1. **Trendwatching** (www.trendwatching.com) This is hands-down the most useful trend and forecasting resource online featuring insights curated from a network of thousands of spotters all over the world.

2. **PSFK** (www.psfk.com) A collection of smart daily blog posts and sometimes sponsored research reports on the future of big topics such as retail and healthcare.

3. **Cool Hunting** (www.coolhunting.com) This site has just enough

stories to spark new ideas that make wading through the crowded and haphazard site design worthwhile.

4. **Monocle** (www.monocle.com) While this is best consumed as a print magazine, the site features plenty of non-U.S. examples and will help you learn not only about the business world, but also about lifestyle, culture, and much more.

5. **Springwise** (www.springwise.com) This is a subscription-based site, so the best information is only available to subscribers, but the collection of stories is valuable and worth paying for.

6. **Verve** (www.verve.com) The quick takes and daily blog posts on this site are worth reading to keep up with current news.

7. **Business Insider** (www.businessinsider.com) A prolific site that publishes business articles constantly and quickly.

8. **Gerd Leonhard** (www.futuristgerd.com/blog) The personal blog of a futurist whose work is consistently useful and insightful.

9. **The Future Hunters** (www.thefuturehunters.com) Most of their research is presented and discussed in quarterly meetings for clients only, but there's a useful collection of terms and recent white papers available on the site for free.

10. **Trend Hunter** (www.trendhunter.com) A dictionary for interesting stories from around the world shared by a small army of idea spotters. This is a useful resource to find ideas.

11. **Shelly Palmer** (www.shellypalmer.com/blog) This weekly blog from technology expert Shelly Palmer is thoughtful, well-written and offers a new take on the role of technology in our world that will make you think.

12. **JWTIntelligence** (www.jwtintelligence.com) While every agency and consulting group tries to create "thought leadership," this collection of insights from JWT is forward-looking, well-researched, and worth bookmarking.

13. **The Guardian** (www.theguardian.com) The only mainstream news source to make my list, I always appreciate the combination of strong reporting and global view they present.

14. **Slideshare** (www.slideshare.com) This site is filled with deep, insightful presentations and a good amount of useless garbage. Still, the sheer volume of all of it means you may find some interesting ideas, and even the odd internal corporate document that probably shouldn't have been shared publicly.

15. **Cool Hunter** (www.thecoolhunter.net) A collection of neatly organized posts on topics from "Amazing Places" to "Architecture."

21

≡

ANTI-TRENDS
The Flip Side of Trends

—

"There are trivial truths and there are great truths.
The opposite of a trivial truth is plainly false.
The opposite of a great truth is also true"

NIELS BOHR, Nobel Prize–Winning Physicist

—

From the end of September until the beginning of November, the Piedmont region of Italy is one of the most popular foodie destinations in the world for two reasons. The first is the famous Barolo wines, which are produced from the native Nebbiolo grape, and the second comes in October, when the town of Alba hosts its annual White Truffle Fair.

Truffles are a favorite decadent ingredient for top chefs, and white truffles are the rarest—sometimes costing as much as $2,000 per pound. Truffles from Alba are often described by chefs as "sublime" and "unlike anything else in the world." The Barolo wines, too, are considered Italy's best, called the "King of Wines" for centuries.

Yet, as amazing as these two Piedmont region delicacies are, there is one critical problem the region can't control: because they require opposite kinds of weather, they are never at their relative prime at the same time.

Truffles are best after a wet summer, while a dry and hot summer is optimal for grapes. As a result, summer cannot be equally good for both wine and truffles. In any given year, one will always be better.

Flip Thinking and Anti-Trends

In this book I have shared a process for uncovering trends that affect the world around us along with advice on how to use them to power your business and career. Perhaps while reading one of these trends you thought of an example that seemed to do the exact opposite of what the trend was describing.

It's easy to think that finding an outlier to a trend would make it less valuable—similar to the truffles and wine.

Just like Piedmont's delicacies, though, there is often an opposing force that balances out trends, and it comes from people and companies that see what everyone else is doing and choose to do the opposite.

Sometimes, we hear it called "flip thinking," a term used most popularly by author Dan Pink. In one instance, he used it to describe a teacher who "flipped" the classroom by assigning math lectures via YouTube video as homework and doing the problems together in class. (An idea I also explored in Chapter 11).[1]

Flip thinking will always be present, and for every trend someone will usually find an example of the exact opposite. These are anti-trends and they can come up often. This is not a flaw in the art of curating trends, but it would be natural to wonder: If we have invested all this work into curating and describing trends, how can we be sure they matter when it seems so easy to find examples of the opposite?

Breaking Trends

Trends are not like mathematical theories. They are describing a behavior or occurrence that is accelerating and will matter more and more, but they are not unbreakable rules of culture or behavior. There will *always* be outliers.

The point of curating trends is to see what others don't and to predict a future that can inspire new thinking. There is an interesting opportunity, though, that arises from being able to use this technique of "flip thinking."

Understanding trends not only empowers you to use them positively, but also to intentionally *break* them and do the opposite when it's an appropriate way to stand out.

Pablo Picasso famously declared that each of us should aim to "learn the rules like a pro so you can break them like an artist."

The clown in an ice-skating show, for example, often needs to be the most talented in order to execute fake jumps and falls while still remaining under control. Similarly, your ability to know the trends may give you the insight you need to bend or break them strategically.

This is, after all, a book about thinking in new and different ways. Taking a trend and aiming to embrace its opposite certainly qualifies.

PART IV

PREVIOUS TREND REPORT SUMMARIES (2011-2017)

OVERVIEW:
How to Read These Past Trend Reports

—

*"The events of the past can be made to prove anything
if they are arranged in a suitable pattern."*

—A. J. P. TAYLOR, Historian

—

There was a moment several years ago when I was on stage after having just presented a talk about trends and how to predict the future when a skeptical-looking gentleman stood up to ask me a question. "It must be easy," he started "to publish your trend report when you get to change them every year. How do you know whether any of them were actually right?"

His question was a fair one. After all, there is plenty of evidence to suggest the experts routinely miss predictions and are often just plain wrong. What makes my method or the past trends my team and I have curated any different? The only truthful way to answer that is to take a look backward.

In this section, you'll see a candid review of every one of my previously predicted trends from the past seven years of the Non-Obvious Trend Report. While some of the original descriptions have been edited for space considerations, none of the intentions or meanings have been updated or revisited since the trend was first published.

Each trend is accompanied by a "Trend Longevity Rating" which aims to measure how much the trend as originally described still applies or has value in 2018. Predictably, the more recent trends fared better than the older trends – but the process of going backward and taking an honest look at past research was illuminating.

In assessing these trends, the aim was to treat them in as unbiased a way as possible. Where one did not accelerate as predicted, I did my best to admit that openly. It is, of course, nearly impossible to grade yourself in isolation – so I have also gathered the feedback from thousands of professionals who have listened to me share my "Haystack Method" and the trends that resulted from it. I took notes as they participated in workshops trying to apply these trends to their own businesses, and recorded some of their probing questions about each trend.

In addition, I made it a habit within our team to also save stories and examples of trends that we had already published—so we could see just how many more relevant examples would come up since it was originally curated. This story gathering is what helped decide which of the previous trends to revisit in this new edition.

If there is anything that has helped this curated list of trends get better year after year, it is this annual ritual of reviewing, grading and critiquing past trends. We learn from our mistakes as much as we celebrate our successes.

As I shared early in this book, the beautiful thing about trends is that new trends don't replace old ones. Rather, they all present an evolving view of the world and individual "non-obvious" trends either become more obvious (and commonly understood) over time, or they fail to accelerate and sometimes fade away.

Either way, the best-case usage for trends is as a spark for new ideas and as an instigator for innovation.

I hope you enjoy this look backward at past years of the Non-Obvious Trend Report.

PREVIOUSLY PREDICTED TREND SUMMARIES 2011-2018

2011
Non-Obvious Trends

Likeonomics
Approachable Celebrity
Desperate Simplification
Essential Integration
Rise of Curation
Visualized Data
Crowdsourced Innovation
Instant PR & Customer Service
App-fication of the web
Re-imagining Charity
Employees as Heroes
Location Casting
Brutal Transparency
Addictive Randomness
Culting of Retail

2012
Non-Obvious Trends

Corporate Humanism
Ethnomimicry
Social Loneliness
Pointillist Filmmaking
Measuring Life
Co-Curation
Charitable Engagement
Medici Marketing
Digital Afterlife
Real-Time Logistics
Social Artivism
Civic Engagement 2.0
Tagging Reality
Changesourcing
Retail Theater

2013
Non-Obvious Trends

Optimistic Aging
Human Banking
Mefunding
Branded Inspiration
Backstorytelling
Healthy Content
Degree-Free Learning
Precious Print
Partnership Publishing
Microinnovation
Social Visualization
Heroic Design
Hyper-Local Commerce
Powered By Women
Shoptimization

2014
Non-Obvious Trends

Desperate Detox
Media Binging
Obsessive Productivity
Lovable Unperfection
Branded Utility
Shareable Humanity
Curated Sensationalism
Distributed Expertise
Anti-Stereotyping
Privacy Paranoia
Overquantified Life
Microdesign
Subscription Commerce
Instant Entrepreneurs
Collaborative Economy

2015
Non-Obvious Trends

Everyday Stardom
Selfie Confidence
Mainstream Mindfulness
Branded Benevolence
Reverse Retail
Reluctant Marketing
Glanceable Content
Mood Matching
Experimedia
Unperfection
Predictive Protection
Engineered Addiction
Small Data
Disruptive Distribution
Micro Consumption

2016
Non-Obvious Trends

E-mpulse Buying
Strategic Downgrading
Optimistic Aging
B2Beyond
Personality Mapping
Branded Utility
Mainstream Multiculturalism
Earned Consumption
Anti-Stereotyping
Virtual Empathy
Data Overflow
Heroic Design
Insourced Incubation
Automated Adulthood
Obsessive Productivity

2017
Non-Obvious Trends

Fierce Femininity
Side Quirks
Desperate Detox
Passive Loyalty
Authentic Fameseekers
Lovable Unperfection
Preserved Past
Deep Diving
Precious Print
Invisible Technology
Robot Renaissance
Self-Aware Data
Moonshot Entrepreneurship
Outrageous Outsiders
Mainstream Mindfulness

2018
Non-Obvious Trends

Truthing
Enlightened Consumption
Ungendered
Brand Stand
Backstorytelling
Overtargeting
Manipulated Outrage
Light-Speed Learning
Virtual Empathy
Predictive Protection
Human Mode
Data Pollution
Approachable Luxury
Disruptive Distribution
Touchworthy

The 1st Edition of the Best Selling Trend Series
Read Over Half A Million Times Online!

NON
OBVIOUS

2011

How To Think Different,
Curate Ideas &
Predict The Future

ROHIT BHARGAVA
Trend Curator | Listener | Storyteller

The 2011 Non-Obvious Trend Report Overview

Original Publication Date: *January 2, 2011*
Original Format: *Visual Presentation Only*
Full Book: *www.nonobviousbook.com/2011*

THE BACKSTORY

This first edition of the Non-Obvious Trend Report was inspired by five years of blogging. I released it exclusively in a visual presentation format and heavily featured marketing and social media trends that I had written about throughout 2010. The trends were far more limited in scope than later editions of the trend report and featured less description and less actionable advice. They were also not separated into subcategories. This report quickly went viral when it was first released, being viewed over 100,000 times on Slideshare.

RETROSPECTIVE: HOW ACCURATE WAS THIS REPORT?

The report was one of the first to predict the rise in importance of content marketing and also correctly predicted the rapid growth of real- time customer service through social media. It analyzed the increasing number of marketing campaigns featuring employees as a sign of corporate humanity, and introduced the idea of how social media was making unreachable celebrities more connected and approachable. Overall, there were relatively few big misses or trends that completely imploded or reversed themselves. The biggest idea from the report was undoubtedly the first trend of *Likeonomics,* which ultimately inspired me to write a book of the same name (released in 2012).

NOTE – There were no icons for trends in this report, and so the individual trend longevity ratings for this year are not included in this book. You can still see the full assessments by visiting the URL at the top of this page.

The 2012 Non-Obvious Trend Report Overview

Original Publication Date: *January 2, 2012*
Original Format: *Visual Presentation Only*
Full Book: *www.nonobviousbook.com/2012*

THE BACKSTORY

This second year of the trend report featured a broader look at business beyond marketing or social media. Like the first report, it was released exclusively in visual presentation format online. Topics covered in this report included the sensitive yet emerging field of the digital afterlife of loved ones, as well as the steady rise of social loneliness. In moving farther away from marketing, this report took a more human tone as many of the trends featured cultural shifts and described consumer behavior.

RETROSPECTIVE: HOW ACCURATE WAS THIS REPORT?

The 2012 report had a few big hits and several big misses. The overall trends that centered on the growth of humanity in companies and consumers stood the test of time. This report was one of the first to explore the potential of big data to impact everything from optimizing supply chain logistics to measuring and quantifying every aspect of our lives. On the flip side, some trends from this year were overly quirky niche concepts like *Pointillist Filmmaking* or *Social Artivism* did not quantifiably catch fire, either in adoption or in the behaviors they described.

NOTE – There were no icons for trends in this report, and so the individual trend longevity ratings for this year are not included in this book. You can still see the full assessments by visiting the URL at the top of this page.

2013 NON-OBVIOUS TRENDS OVERVIEW

What is a trend? *A trend is a unique curated observation about the accelerating present.*

Culture & Consumer Behavior: Trends in how we see ourselves and patterns in popular culture.

OPTIMISTIC AGING

HUMAN BANKING

MEFUNDING

Marketing & Social Media: Trends in how brands are trying to influence and engage consumers.

BRANDED INSPIRATION

BACKSTORYTELLING

HEALTHY CONTENT

Media & Education: Trends in information impacting how we learn, think or are entertained.

DEGREE-FREE LEARNING

PRECIOUS PRINT

PARTNERSHIP PUBLISHING

Technology & Design: Trends in innovation, technology and product design impacting our behavior.

MICROINNOVATION

SOCIAL VISUALIZATION

HEROIC DESIGN

Economics & Entrepreneurship: Trends in business models, industry or the future of work or money.

HYPER-LOCAL COMMERCE

POWERED BY WOMEN

SHOPTIMIZATION

The 3rd Edition of the Best Selling Trend Series
Read Over Half A Million Times Online!

NON
OBVIOUS
2013

How To Think Different,
Curate Ideas &
Predict The Future

ROHIT BHARGAVA
Trend Curator | Listener | Storyteller

The 2013 Non-Obvious Trend Report Overview

Original Publication Date: *December 10, 2012*
Original Format: *eBook + Visual Presentation*
Full Book: *www.nonobviousbook.com/2013*

THE BACKSTORY

In the third year of producing the trend report, the level of detail exploded from about 20 trend overview pages to well over 100 featuring more real life examples. While this edition of the Non-Obvious Trend Report did not originally use the five categories, for alignment we retroactively applied them and created icons.

The report was still delivered primarily in a visual presentation format, but this year an accompanying ebook was released exclusively on Amazon.com with tips on how to put the trends into action.

Thanks to the audience built from the first two editions, this third edition ebook was an instant best seller on Amazon, remaining the number-one book in the market research category for eight straight weeks after launch and was viewed more than 200,000 times online.

RETROSPECTIVE: HOW ACCURATE WAS THIS REPORT?

Developing the trends for 2013 was a more deliberate process requiring more research and a higher standard of proof before including any particular trend in the report. Trends which resonated most from the 2013 report included *Partnership Publishing, Rise of Women, Human Banking,* and *Hyper-Local Commerce.* The insights from the report around the rising power of women in business, how large organizations were thinking about being more authentic and innovation on a smaller scale, were all trends that continue to this day.

What's the Trend?
A wealth of online content and new social networks inspire people of all ages to feel more optimistic about getting older.

Trend Longevity Rating:
This trend was important enough for me to select and bring back in my 2016 report – but as I shared in the rating for this trend from that year, the sense of optimism about what will be achievable in life has remained for the older population but over the past year it was tempered by increasing fears about the macro future of things like the environment, politics, the economy and security.

OPTIMISTIC AGING

B+

What's the Trend?
Aiming to change years of growing distrust, banks finally uncover their human side by taking a more simple and direct approach to services and communication and develop real relationships with their customers.

Trend Longevity Rating:

HUMAN BANKING

Every new financial crisis underscores the importance of more human interactions between us and our financial institutions. While this trend has been happening across multiple industries, the effect on banking (and consumer banks in particular) has been pronounced.

A

What's the Trend?
Crowdfunding evolves beyond films or budding entrepreneurs to offer anyone the opportunity to seek financial support to do anything from taking a life-changing trip to paying for a college education.

Trend Longevity Rating:
MEFUNDING

While the many sites featured as part of this trend remain available for people to use, the trend didn't quite explode in the way I predicted.

C+

2013 Marketing & Social Media Trends

BRANDED INSPIRATION

What's the Trend?

Brands create awe-inspiring moments, innovative ideas and dramatic stunts to capture attention and sometimes demonstrate their values to the world.

Trend Longevity Rating:

While this original trend was about using big moments for inspiration, the new model for this involves creating an effort for social good and standing for something bigger (see Brand Stand trend from this year) versus simply creating an entertaining moment of theater to inspire.

BACKSTORYTELLING

What's the Trend?

Organizations discover that taking people behind the scenes of their brand and history is one of the most powerful ways to inspire loyalty.

Trend Longevity Rating:

As social platforms splinter but also grow in popularity, the necessity for brands to share their backstory in multiple ways continues to grow. A good Backstory can offer a reason to believe in a brand's mission and share it with others.

HEALTHY CONTENT

What's the Trend?

In an effort to satisfy empowered patients who have become unreachable through marketing or advertising, Healthcare organizations have begun creating more useful and substantial health content.

Trend Longevity Rating:

In the healthcare industry, content continues to be golden because empowered patients gain more confidence and turn to the web before seeking information from other sources. It is unlikely that this behavior will diminish in the near and farther future.

DEGREE-FREE LEARNING

What's the Trend?

The quality of e-learning content explodes as more students consider alternatives to traditional college educations.

Trend Longevity Rating:

Learning and higher education are simultaneously changed by this growth of people who choose to learn new skills and industries without requiring a degree to display at the end of it. While this has not overtaken traditional degree-granting programs, it continues to gain in popularity.

B+

PRECIOUS PRINT

What's the Trend?

With an ever increasing digital culture, the few interactions we have with the print medium become ever more valuable.

Trend Longevity Rating:

The basic human behavior outlined in this trend— that we place even more value on the things that are printed because they are so much more rare—continues year after year ... so much so that this trend returned in 2017 as it relates to our new trend of Touchworthy.

A

PARTNERSHIP PUBLISHING

What's the Trend?

Aspiring authors, lacking a platform, and seasoned publishing professionals, in need of partners and content, team up to create a new "do-it-together" model of publishing.

Trend Longevity Rating:

This trend inspired me to start Ideapress Publishing as a new venture to bring together some of the top tier freelance publishing talent and authors. There were plenty of other similar ventures to explore this idea as well - leading to a resurgence in publishing that has surprised some.

B

MICROINNOVATION

What's the Trend?
Thinking small becomes the new competitive advantage as slight changes to features or benefits creates big value.

Trend Longevity Rating:
If anything, this trend has accelerated dramatically in recent years as more brands adopt a lean startup mentality that encourages them to make incremental changes to products in ways that can deliver value. The quest to do this in a meaningful way is ongoing, particularly in the technology industry.

SOCIAL VISUALIZATION

What's the Trend?
In an attempt to make data more accessible, new tools and technologies allow people to visualize content as part of their social profiles and online conversations.

Trend Longevity Rating:
Visual interfaces continue to be commonplace and popular. This is one of those trends that was emerging at the time when it was first written but today more than five years later it seems obvious —which is the best sign of success for any trend over time.

HEROIC DESIGN

What's the Trend?
Design takes a leading role in the introduction of new products, ideas and campaigns to help change the world.

Trend Longevity Rating:
The growth of design thinking as well as an increasingly reliance from the global community on seeing solutions to global problems posed by designers led us to bring this trend back for the 2016 report. Since that time, the importance of design serving a "heroic" purpose to solve society's biggest challenges has continued.

2013 Economics & Entrepreneurship Trends

HYPER LOCAL COMMERCE

What's the Trend?
New services and technology make it easier for anyone to invest in local businesses and buy from local merchants.

Trend Longevity Rating:
Whether you examine this trend in relation to the growth of local commerce or as fueled by investment and interest in mobile commerce platforms and experience, the fact is consumer experiences continue to become more local more custom and more personal ... and so this trend is likely to continue.

POWERED BY WOMEN

What's the Trend?
Business leaders, pop-culture, and ground-breaking new research intersect to prove that our ideal future will be led by strong and innovative women working on the front lines.

Trend Longevity Rating:
There is no denying the role of women in business, culture and politics has grown year after year. Today there are more female leaders, role models and celebrated citizens than ever before—and it is a wonderful thing leading to interesting related trends, like 2017's Fierce Femininity trend.

SHOPTIMIZATION

What's the Trend?
The proliferation of smart phones coupled with new mobile apps and startups let consumers optimize and enhance the process of online shopping for faster purchases of everything from fashion, to home goods to medical prescriptions.

Trend Longevity Rating:
Thanks to increasing competition among retailers and a rising tide of new productivity tools online, the task of optimizing each of our shopping experiences has continued to be a top priority leading to better mobile first interfaces, one button shopping apps, and the ability to buy anything anywhere at the touch of a button.

2014 NON-OBVIOUS TRENDS OVERVIEW

What is a trend? *A trend is a unique curated observation about the accelerating present.*

Culture & Consumer Behavior: Trends in how we see ourselves and patterns in popular culture.

**DESPERATE
DETOX**

**MEDIA
BINGING**

**OBSESSIVE
PRODUCTIVITY**

Marketing & Social Media: Trends in how brands are trying to influence and engage consumers.

**LOVABLE
IMPERFECTION**

**BRANDED
UTILITY**

**SHAREABLE
HUMANITY**

Media & Education: Trends in information impacting how we learn, think or are entertained.

**CURATED
SENSATIONALISM**

**DISTRIBUTED
EXPERTISE**

**ANTI-
STEREOTYPING**

Technology & Design: Trends in innovation, technology and product design impacting our behavior.

**PRIVACY
PARANOIA**

**OVERQUANTIFIED
LIFE**

MICRODESIGN

Economics & Entrepreneurship: Trends in business models, industry or the future of work or money.

**SUBSCRIPTION
COMMERCE**

**INSTANT
ENTREPRENEURS**

**COLLABORATIVE
ECONOMY**

The 4th Edition of the Best Selling Trend Series
Read Over Half A Million Times Online!
NON
OBVIOUS
2014
How To Think Different,
Curate Ideas &
Predict The Future
ROHIT BHARGAVA
Trend Curator | Listener | Storyteller

The 2014 Non-Obvious Trend Report Overview

Original Publication Date: *February 18, 2014*
Original Format: *eBook + Visual Presentation*
Full Book: *www.nonobviousbook.com/2014*

THE BACKSTORY

This fourth edition of the Non-Obvious Trend Report was expanded to feature categories for trends for the first time instead of simply listing 15 in random order. Those categories are the ones used in every consecutive report since then.

In an effort to build visibility, in 2014 the full report was freely available online with a bonus ebook available for sale on Amazon.

This edition also corresponded with an exponential growth in the volume of public speaking and workshops I was being invited to deliver and was also the year that I left my role Ogilvy (after 8 years) to start my own consulting group focusing on trend research, keynote speaking, consulting and teaching.

RETROSPECTIVE: HOW ACCURATE WAS THIS REPORT?

Due to this new category driven approach, our predictions had more discipline around their curation, and began to have more longevity. *Desperate Detox, Subscription Commerce, Collaborative Economy, Obsessive Productivity, Branded Utility* and *Curated Sensationalism* were all big trends that described entire movements and they received a lot of attention. This report also incorporated some of the healthcare specific trend research that my co-author Fard Johnmar and I published that same year in our industry vertical book about trends in health called *ePatient 2015*.

DESPERATE DETOX

What's the Trend?

Consumers try to more authentically connect with others and seek out moments of reflection by intentionally disconnecting from the technology surrounding them.

Trend Longevity Rating:

Technology is only becoming more omnipresent in our lives, and this trend was so impactful that it was an easy selection as one to bring back in 2017 to include in this year's report.

A

MEDIA BINGING

What's the Trend?

As more media and entertainment is available on any device on demand, consumers binge and are willing to pay extra for the convenience.

Trend Longevity Rating:

Streaming options continue to expand yet this past year saw some fatigue with the idea of binge-watching where consumers felt overloaded or obligated to watch.

B+

OBSESSIVE PRODUCTIVITY

What's the Trend?

With thousands of life-optimizing apps and instant advice from social media–savvy self-help gurus, becoming more productive has become the ultimate obsession.

Trend Longevity Rating:

The past few years have brought plenty of new bestselling books talking about optimizing your life, hacking your daily chores and saving time. To say people continue to obsess over their own productivity is an understatement.

A

LOVABLE IMPERFECTION

What's the Trend?
Consumers seek out true authenticity and reward minor imperfections in products, personalities and brands by showing greater loyalty and trust.

Trend Longevity Rating:
While this was the first year that this trend was predicted, it was so powerful that a version of it was included in the 2015 report (Unperfection) and it is making another appearance in my latest report because of its continued importance.

BRANDED UTILITY

What's the Trend?
Brands use content marketing and greater integration between marketing and operations centers to augment promotions with real ways to add value to customer's lives.

Trend Longevity Rating:
As content marketing continues to change the way that marketers communicate with their audiences, there have been dozens more examples of brands using this trend. Its impact was also important enough to bring it back to include in my 2016 Trend Report.

SHARABLE HUMANITY

What's the Trend?
Content shared on social media gets more emotional as people share amazing examples of humanity and brands inject more of it into marketing communications efforts.

Trend Longevity Rating:
This was one of the trends from the previous year that was negatively affected by the fatigue some media consumers are starting to experience from overly dramatic media stories and click-baiting headlines. Though we continue to find human stories irresistible to read and share, this trend no longer has the impact it once did when first predicted.

CURATED SENSATIONALISM

What's the Trend?
As the line between news and entertainment blurs, smart curation displaces journalism as engaging content is paired with sensational headlines to drive millions of views.

Trend Longevity Rating:
Media continues to deliver over-the-top headlines and sensationalism which negatively affects consumer trust in media. While this has turned the impact of this trend more negative, it is having a renewed impact.

DISTRIBUTED EXPERTISE

What's the Trend?
The idea of expertise itself shifts to become more inclusive, less academic and more widely available on demand and in real time.

Trend Longevity Rating:
Learning through experts online in many formats is still a big trend and one that is powering some of the fastest growing learning platforms online today (including many profiled in this original trend). We have on demand access to experts in more ways than ever and this shows no signs of slowing down.

ANTI-STEREOTYPING

What's the Trend?
Across media and entertainment, traditional gender roles are being reversed, assumptions about alternative lifestyles are being challenged, and perceptions of how people are defined evolve in new ways.

Trend Longevity Rating:
The reversing of gender roles continues to be a big opportunity for brands to get their messaging right or wrong, when it comes to speaking to these diverse groups through marketing and communications – but the broader aspects of this trend were what encouraged me to bring it back in 2016 and it relates to this year's Ungendered trend as well.

PRIVACY PARANOIA

What's the Trend?
New data breaches are leading to a new global sense of paranoia about what governments and brands know about us—and how they might use this big data in potentially harmful ways.

Trend Longevity Rating:
As more tools enter the market to help consumers protect their information and take back control of their privacy, this paranoia is shifting to empowerment. All the warnings and attention on privacy are leading some people to ignore the warnings while others take back control. Either way, "paranoia" no longer seems like the ideal term to describe our relationship to privacy.

OVERQUANTIFIED LIFE

What's the Trend?
As big data leads brands to overload data with cute infographics and superficial analysis, they also add more confusion about what all this data really means, and how it can inform decisions in real life.

Trend Longevity Rating:
Connecting all the data we collect on ourselves in a meaningful way continues to be a challenge, and we are indeed still "overquantified." In this year's report, the Overtargeting trend takes this idea further to explore how it impacts business and marketing.

MICRODESIGN

What's the Trend?
As communication becomes more visual, design gains more respect and becomes an everyday business requirement. At the same time, demand for design skills also explodes, leading to easier access to bite-sized chunks of design expertise.

Trend Longevity Rating:
The need for design expertise continues to grow, and this trend is still an important one for any type of organization. In addition, design thinking has exploded as a category of learning and insights. As a result, this trend continues to sit at the intersection of several others.

2014 Economics & Entrepreneurship Trends

SUBSCRIPTION COMMERCE

What's the Trend?
More businesses and retailers use subscriptions to sell recurring services or products to customers instead of focusing on the one-time sale.

Trend Longevity Rating:
More industries and brands turn to the lessons of subscription commerce, but as I wrote about in this latest trend report – the big shift towards a subscription based business model was too reactionary for some businesses that are now backing away from the model to find something that works better for their situation.

B-

INSTANT ENTREPRENEURS

What's the Trend?
As the barriers to starting a new business begin to disappear, incentives and tools mean anyone with an idea can launch a startup knowing that the costs and risks of failure are not as high as they once were.

Trend Longevity Rating:
The shift in many industries from full-time employee to entrepreneur continues to take shape as top professionals continue to branch out on their own. In addition, it is a global priority among national governments to make the process of entrepreneurship faster and easier because there is widespread understanding that entrepreneurs drive economies forward.

A

COLLABORATIVE ECONOMY

What's the Trend?
New business models and tools allow consumers and brands to tap the power of sharing and collaborative consumption to find new ways to buy, sell and consume products and services.

Trend Longevity Rating:
While growing last year, the shared or collaborative economy has become well understood, a symbol of its continued rapid acceleration. While it may be "obvious" now, the impact of it and just how much attention brands are paying to the space justifies its continued ranking among the top trends for its longevity over the years.

A

2015 NON-OBVIOUS TRENDS OVERVIEW

What is a trend? *A trend is a unique curated observation about the accelerating present.*

Culture & Consumer Behavior: Trends in how we see ourselves and patterns in popular culture.

EVERYDAY STARDOM

SELFIE CONFIDENCE

MAINSTREAM MINDFULNESS

Marketing & Social Media: Trends in how brands are trying to influence and engage consumers.

BRANDED BENEVOLENCE

REVERSE RETAIL

RELUCTANT MARKETER

Media & Education: Trends in information impacting how we learn, think or are entertained.

GLANCEABLE CONTENT

MOOD MATCHING

EXPERIMEDIA

Technology & Design: Trends in innovation, technology and product design impacting our behavior.

UNPERFECTION

PREDICTIVE PROTECTION

ENGINEERED ADDICTION

Economics & Entrepreneurship: Trends in business models, industry or the future of work or money.

SMALL DATA

DISRUPTIVE DISTRIBUTION

MICRO CONSUMPTION

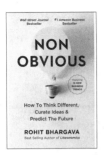

The 2015 Non-Obvious Trend Report Overview

Original Publication Date: *March 1, 2015*
Original Format: *Hardcover + eBook*
Full Book: *www.nonobviousbook.com/2015*

THE BACKSTORY

After four years of growing an audience by publishing the Non-Obvious Trend Report only a digital format, in 2015 I decided to work with my team to expand the content into a full length book. I spent most of the year writing about the technique we used to curate ideas which would eventually be honed into trends. I created a "formula" for how anyone could predict the future (the Haystack Method), and published the new book along with the signature list of 15 trends as usual. The result was *Non-Obvious* released as a full length hardcover book for the first time.

The book hit #1 in the entire business category on Amazon and made it up to #27 in ALL Kindle books within 48 hours. The popularity of the book drove it to hit the *Wall Street Journal* Best Seller list the week it launched, but it also introduced the idea of trend curation to a much wider audience. Over the course of the next year, the book was contracted for six translated editions and my speaking and workshops continued – with more global invitations.

RETROSPECTIVE: HOW ACCURATE WAS THIS REPORT?

The trends that year described culture in a way that many people started talking about – from *Everyday Stardom* exploring how consumer expectations were rising to *Selfie Confidence* describing the role social media plays in building self-esteem. Other popular trends from this year included *Small Data* – which offered a counter idea to the growing discussions of "big data" and media trends such as *Experimedia* or *Glanceable Content* to describe our shifting attention spans.

EVERYDAY STARDOM

What's the Trend?
The growth of personalization leads more consumers to expect everyday interactions to be transformed into "celebrity experiences" with them as the stars of the show.

Trend Longevity Rating:
As the opportunities for companies to use big data to personalize experiences for customers continue to grow, this expectation from consumers to be treated like superstars has only continued to grow and is even more of a necessity for brands today than it was when this trend was first introduced.

SELFIE CONFIDENCE

What's the Trend?
The growing ability to share a carefully crafted online persona allows more people to use social content such as selfies as a way to build their own self confidence.

Trend Longevity Rating:
Selfies are a misunderstood medium. They were when this trend was first written, and perhaps are even more so today ... yet this trend took the optimistic view that those selfies were an important part of how kids build self-esteem today and that remains true two years later, even as self expression has broadened to include more video and broaden beyond just selfies.

MAINSTREAM MINDFULNESS

What's the Trend?
Meditation, yoga and quiet contemplation become powerful tools for individuals and organizations to improve performance, health and motivation.

Trend Longevity Rating:
Not only is this trend back as one of my featured trends in 2017, but it has now come to describe entire industries, new ways of thinking for organizations and a powerful new movement towards improving ourselves at home and at work.

**BRANDED
BENEVOLENCE**

What's the Trend?
Companies increasingly put purpose at the center of their businesses to show a deeper commitment to doing good that goes beyond just donating money or getting positive PR.

Trend Longevity Rating:
Brands continue to focus on purpose and big initiatives to demonstrate a commitment to the environment, social issues, and ethical business practices. This trend directly inspired this past year's trend of Enlightened Consumption.

**REVERSE
RETAIL**

What's the Trend?
Brands increasingly invest in high-touch in-store experiences as a way to build brand affinity and educate customers, while seamlessly integrating with their online channels to complete actual purchases and fulfill orders.

Trend Longevity Rating:
The original inspiration for this trend was the rapid growth of "showcase stores" that were being used by brands to offer experiences to consumers with all of the sales made and fulfilled online. Since then retailers continue to focus on blending the experiential side with actually selling products.

**RELUCTANT
MARKETER**

What's the Trend?
As marketing shifts away from pure promotion, leaders and organizations abandon traditional silos, embrace content marketing and invest in the customer experience.

Trend Longevity Rating:
As content marketing becomes a greater part of the marketing mix, organizations see themselves doing more than just "marketing." This shift away from promotional marketing and toward being useful, providing utility and answering questions continues to grow.

2015 Media & Entertainment Trends

GLANCEABLE CONTENT

What's the Trend?
Our shrinking attention spans and the explosion of all forms of content online lead creators to optimize stories for rapid consumption at a glance.

Trend Longevity Rating:
As much as I would love to say this trend disappeared as people started engaging with content longer (see 2017's Deep Diving trend), this behavior remains true and much of daily or hourly content does need to be glanceable still in order to receive any sort of attention.

MOOD MATCHING

What's the Trend?
As tracking technology becomes more sophisticated, media, advertising and immersive experiences like gaming and learning can be tailored to match consumer moods.

Trend Longevity Rating:
Automated sentiment filters and new technologies like eye tracking and vocal analysis are letting consumers have even bigger expectations about how technology will cater to them. That said, this trend always described something that was only really relevant in some situations and therefore not as broad or wide-ranging as many of the other trends.

EXPERIMEDIA

What's the Trend?
Content creators use social experiments and real life interactions to study human behavior in unique new ways to ultimately build more realistic and entertaining narratives.

Trend Longevity Rating:
For a time it seemed that media featuring social experiments was a hot new practice likely to continue for a long time. Over the past few years, though, this trend has slowed down significantly and even though there are still some examples of this happening, it is not at the volumes it once was.

UNPERFECTION

What's the Trend?

As people seek out more personal and human experiences, brands and creators intentionally focus on using personality, quirkiness and intentional imperfections to be more human and desirable.

Trend Longevity Rating:

One of my favorite trends for what it described when it was first curated, this trend was partially brought back in the 2017 report along with Lovable Imperfection from 2014. The idea that brands and leaders are showing vulnerability and building trust through their willingness to share flaws continues to have resonance.

PREDICTIVE PROTECTION

What's the Trend?

A growing concern for privacy coupled with elevated expectations technology's role in our lives leads to more intuitive products, services and features to help us live better, safer, and more efficient lives.

Trend Longevity Rating:

The need for the type of proactive protection that this trend continues to grow each day influencing several later predictions, such as Robot Renaissance and Self Aware Data. This trend was also revisited in this past year's report.

ENGINEERED ADDICTION

What's the Trend?

Greater understanding of the behavioral science behind habit formation leads to more designers and engineers intentionally creating addictive experiences that capture consumers' time, money and loyalty.

Trend Longevity Rating:

If you consider the growth of everything from packaged foods to fantasy sports, this trend is still central to how new experiences are conceived and the way that experiences can now be engineered to be irresistible whether they are good for us or not.

SMALL DATA

What's the Trend?

As consumers increasingly collect their own data from online activities brand-owned big data becomes less valuable than small data.

Trend Longevity Rating:

Since the publication of this trend, a best-selling book from Martin Lindstrom of the same title and growing sophistication of technology to personalize experiences has led this trend to be even more relevant today than when it was first curated

DISRUPTIVE DISTRIBUTION

What's the Trend?

Creators and makers use new models for distribution to disrupt the usual channels, cut out middlemen, and build more direct connections with fans and buyers.

Trend Longevity Rating:

This trend has exploded in recent years and is likely to impact even more industries in the near future. As a result, we brought it back in this year's trend report.

MICROCONSUMPTION

What's the Trend?

As new payment models, products and experiences become available in bite-sized portions, multiple industries will experiment with new micro-sized forms of pricing and payments.

Trend Longevity Rating:

While this trend will likely continue, it has not accelerated as initially predicted with the same industry-defining pace as several others.

What is a trend? *A trend is a unique curated observation about the accelerating present.*

Culture & Consumer Behavior: Trends in how we see ourselves and patterns in popular culture.

E-MPULSE BUYING

STRATEGIC DOWNGRADING

OPTIMISTIC AGING

Marketing & Social Media: Trends in how brands are trying to influence and engage consumers.

B2BEYOND

PERSONALITY MAPPING

BRANDED UTILITY

Media & Education: Trends in information impacting how we learn, think or are entertained.

MAINSTREAM MULTICULTURALISM

EARNED CONSUMPTION

ANTI-STEREOTYPING

Technology & Design: Trends in innovation, technology and product design impacting our behavior.

VIRTUAL EMPATHY

DATA OVERFLOW

HEROIC DESIGN

Economics & Entrepreneurship: Trends in business models, industry or the future of work or money.

INSOURCED INCUBATION

AUTOMATED ADULTHOOD

OBSESSIVE PRODUCTIVITY

The 2016 Non-Obvious Trend Report Overview

Original Publication Date: *January 25, 2016*
Original Format: *Hardcover + eBook*
Full Book: *www.nonobviousbook.com/2016*

THE BACKSTORY

Given the success of the first year that *Non-Obvious* was available in print (in 2015), we had high expectations for this sixth edition. Looking backward over the previous trend predictions each year, we realized that many past predictions still had a lot of relevance for business and a year seemed too short to really see how some of them would evolve.

As a result, for the first time this year we decided to only publish ten NEW trends and include five PAST trends in the report (one per category). These past trends would include all new examples as well as analysis on what had changed and why we chose to bring it back. The other thing this report featured was an in-depth analysis of the previous year's trends (2015) and how they had evolved over the past year—a model that was later adapted to the shorter analysis and more visual grading that you now see in this section.

RETROSPECTIVE: HOW ACCURATE WAS THIS REPORT?

The most popular trends from this year's report included *Earned Consumption, Strategic Downgrading* and *Virtual Empathy* (which was revisited this year). While the series maintained its popularity, the report this year underperformed for a number of reasons mainly related to timing. The report was released in January – too late for a book about trends, and failed to include the year boldly on the cover, which created confusion among readers as to whether the content was actually new or not. These were all issues we corrected in 2017!

2016 Culture & Consumer Behavior Trends

E-MPULSE BUYING

What's the Trend?
Despite fears that the e-commerce might kill impulse buying, the growing integration of mobile devices into the shopping experience is opening new possibilities for real time marketing to entice consumers to make split second emotional buying decisions once again.

Trend Longevity Rating:
Over the past year ecommerce retailers have gotten even more adept at encouraging impulse purchases through their interfaces, and one button ordering is growing in availability. Throughout this year, it is likely more and more retailers will continually add more features designed to encourage impulse buying.

STRATEGIC DOWNGRADING

What's the Trend?
As more products become Internet-enabled and digitally remastered, consumers start selectively rejecting these supposedly improved products and services – opting to strategically downgrade to simpler, cheaper and sometimes more functional versions instead.

Trend Longevity Rating:
A sense of nostalgia remains a high influencing factor for this trend as "retro"products continue to be launched successfully. As newer versions of products and services continue to feel overcomplicated, people will continue to "hack" their own ways to strategically downgrade when it suits their own purposes.

OPTIMISTIC AGING
(Originally Curated 2013)

What's the Trend?
After years of being sold anti-aging solutions – a new generation of newly aging adults are embracing the upside of getting older and finding cause for optimism in the growing opportunities, financial freedom, respect and time that their "third age" can offer.

Trend Longevity Rating:
The sense of optimism about what will be achievable in life has remained for the older population but over the past year it was tempered by increasing fears about the macro future of things like the environment, politics, the economy and security. These big issues are casting a distant but significant cloud over the optimism that older people otherwise feel.

B2BEYOND MARKETING

What's the Trend?

Brands used to promoting their products or services to other businesses embrace their humanity, take inspiration from other sectors and think more broadly about effectively marketing to decision makers as people first, and buyers second.

Trend Longevity Rating:

The steady shift in B2B marketing best practices is continuing to take shape thanks to the high visibility examples of GE, Intel and others, this trend continues and partially inspired the Overtargeting trend from this past year as well.

PERSONALITY MAPPING

What's the Trend?

As behavioral measurement tools build a detailed map of our personalities, multiple industries will be able to use this information to bring likeminded people together and provide more transformative learning and bonding experiences.

Trend Longevity Rating:

While organizations are getting much better at using the data that they have, there are growing signs that sometimes this type of customization limits the audience too quickly in a quest to better understand consumer personalities and cater to those. Moving forward the challenge with this trend is to ensure personality mapping is useful, not overdone.

BRANDED UTILITY

What's the Trend?

Brands begin to focus on a combination of content marketing and a greater integration between marketing and operations to provide value through usefulness in customer's lives.

Trend Longevity Rating:

As content marketing explodes, this trend is undeniably going along with it. The idea that brands can and should provide more utility for their potential customers is leading brands to invest in creating quality content, shifting marketing spending and creating new ways to offer more than just empty promotions.

2016 Media & Entertainment Trends

MAINSTREAM MULTICULTURALISM

What's the Trend?
After years of being ignored, niche demographics, multicultural citizens and their cultures find new widespread acceptance through a growing integration of diverse ideas and people in entertainment, products and politics.

Trend Longevity Rating:
Even as xenophobic political sentiment lingers in many places around the world, the generational shift towards acceptance and embrace of multiple cultures is allowing this trend to have a continued impact in the business, art, media and culture of today.

EARNED CONSUMPTION

What's the Trend?
The desire for authentic experiences leads to a willingness from consumers to earn their right to consume, offering businesses a chance to build more loyalty and engagement by letting consumers "pay" for products or services with more than just money.

Trend Longevity Rating:
There are still many situations where consumers want to earn their chance to be a customer and feel the pride in achieving their place – yet a growing skepticism of experiences and products means that anyone selling anything has to work harder to feel worthy of the time investment.

ANTI-STEREOTYPING
(Originally Curated 2014)

What's the Trend?
A fundamental change takes place across media and culture, where traditional gender roles are being reversed, assumptions about alternative lifestyles are challenged, and perceptions of what makes someone belong to a particular gender, ethnicity, or category are being upended.

Trend Longevity Rating:
The number of people who now define themselves with something other than the traditional descriptors of male or female is growing every day —an idea that led directly to this year's trend of Ungendered.

VIRTUAL EMPATHY

What's the Trend?
An improved quality and lower costs for virtual reality allows creators to tell more immersive stories and let people see the world from another point of view – growing their empathy in the process.

Trend Longevity Rating:
Over the past year, the examples of virtual reality being used to engage, improve and quantify human empathy were too numerous to count. In bringing this trend back in 2018, we took a fresh look at the impact of the trend and found it more relevant than ever.

DATA OVERFLOW

What's the Trend?
The combination of growing personal and corporate owned data mixed with open data creates a new challenge for companies to go beyond algorithms for data management and rely on better artificial intelligence, smarter curation, and more startup investment.

Trend Longevity Rating:
Data continues to "overflow" and create problems of measurement and analysis, but as the Self-Aware Data trend from 2017 shows, the overflow is no longer the same challenge it once was because of automation. The greater issue is not the volume but the quality of it – an issue we explore in this year's trend of Data Pollution.

HEROIC DESIGN
(Originally Curated 2013)

What's the Trend?
Design takes a leading role in the introduction of new products, ideas, and inspiration to change the world in nuanced, audacious, irreverent, and sometimes unexpectedly heroic ways.

Trend Longevity Rating:
The continued presence of design competitions to celebrate new solutions for global problems and a suite of tools to help anyone bring more design thinking to their own jobs means that this trend of putting design on a pedestal and asking it (and designers) to create "heroic" solutions will continue.

**INSOURCED
INCUBATION**

What's the Trend?
Companies desperate to bring more innovation into their enterprise turn to a new model of intrapreneurship modeled after the best business incubators—bringing innovators in house, providing support and resources, and starting innovation labs.

Trend Longevity Rating:
The slate of Innovation Labs and new efforts chronicled as part of the writeup for this trend are now starting to produce early results. These early successes are legitimizing the idea of this trend and causing more investment and attention from organizations to create more programs in this space.

**AUTOMATED
ADULTHOOD**

What's the Trend?
As more people go through a prolonged period of emerging adulthood, a growing range of technology and services help to automate all aspects of their journey to adulthood.

Trend Longevity Rating:
As new tracking products get released to measure everything about life, and tools for automated living continue to be popular, this trend will continue to inspire more co-living arrangements and other facilities that ensure people have partners to help carry them emotionally and physically into adulthood.

**OBSESSIVE
PRODUCTIVITY**
(Originally Curated 2014)

What's the Trend?
Thanks to our reduced attention spans and "always-on technology", the necessity to be productive in every moment has rapidly evolved into an obsession that underpins every brand interaction or other experience.

Trend Longevity Rating:
To say that technology has made us all very aware of those moments when our time is valued or wasted would be even more of an understatement than when this trend was originally written 3 years ago. Productivity is still an obsession - and looks to stay that way.

2017 NON-OBVIOUS TRENDS OVERVIEW

What is a trend? *A trend is a unique curated observation about the accelerating present.*

Culture & Consumer Behavior: Trends in how we see ourselves and patterns in popular culture:

**FIERCE
FEMININITY**

**SIDE
QUIRKS**

**DESPERATE
DETOX**

Marketing & Social Media: Trends in how brands are trying to influence and engage consumers.

**PASSIVE
LOYALTY**

**AUTHENTIC
FAMESEEKERS**

**LOVABLE
UNPERFECTION**

Media & Education: Trends in information impacting how we learn, think or are entertained.

**PRESERVED
PAST**

**DEEP
DIVING**

**PRECIOUS
PRINT**

Technology & Design: Trends in innovation, technology and product design impacting our behavior.

**INVISIBLE
TECHNOLOGY**

**ROBOT
RENAISSANCE**

**SELF-AWARE
DATA**

Economics & Entrepreneurship: Trends in business models, industry or the future of work or money.

**MOONSHOT
ENTREPRENEURSHIP**

**OUTRAGEOUS
OUTSIDERS**

**MAINSTREAM
MINDFULNESS**

The 2017 Non-Obvious Trend Report Overview

Original Publication Date: *December 5, 2017*
Original Format: *Hardcover + eBook*
Full Book: *www.nonobviousbook.com/2017*

THE BACKSTORY

This year was the most extensive report so far, with not only 15 brand new trends predicted but also a newly expanded appendix with full analysis and grading of every previously predicted trend. Some of the most popular trends from this year included *Fierce Femininity, Passive Loyalty, Unperfection, Precious Print, Invisible Technology, Robot Renaissance* and others. Over the year, the volume of keynote speaking I was doing and workshops my team was delivering also increased—which drove even more visibility for the trends. In addition, in this year many of the translated editions of the book started to come out—growing our global audience for the trend report.

RETROSPECTIVE: HOW ACCURATE WAS THIS REPORT?

Unlike the 2016 edition of the report, this 2017 edition came out a full month earlier and sold extremely well through retail and directly to large organizations to share with their teams. This edition of the book was also awarded the prestigious Axiom Award for Business Books (Silver Medal for Business Theory) and was featured widely in the media. In 2017, multiple foreign editions were also released, including a special edition in China which also featured new regional examples for each trend and an increasingly global point of view. Given the recency of these trends - we spent a lot of time researching whether they were still relevant and ultimately decided all of them had enough examples and acceleration to merit the grades we assigned.

FIERCE FEMININITY

What's the Trend?

Over the past few years the fierce, independent woman has emerged, redefining the concept of femininity and reimagining gender roles.

Trend Longevity Rating:

This trend has accelerated dramatically. Current events and the political and cultural climate are opening up discussion about how we perceive women's place in modern society. Women are finding more and more support from men in positions of power. We see this trend continuing to accelerate into the coming years.

- -

SIDE QUIRKS

What's the Trend?

A global shift toward individualism has led to a surge in side businesses and a renewed appreciation for what makes people unique.

Trend Longevity Rating:

People continue to create value out of their hobbies, passions, and personality quirks. Every day we see more examples of successful world-changing leaders like Facebook founder Mark Zuckerberg attribute at least a part of their success to their ability to pursue "side projects" and note this as a defining quality they seek out in new team members as well.

- -

DESPERATE DETOX

What's the Trend?

As technology, media clutter and an overload of gadgets make life increasingly stressful, people are seeking moments of reflection and pause.

Trend Longevity Rating:

Inundation with technology continues to drive an increasing need to find tech-free havens in our daily lives, which has kept this trend relevant. There are even apps which help people find connectivity dead zones. Hotels, restaurants and even workplaces now offer an option for guests to "check in" their phones and enjoy some time without technology interruptions.

PASSIVE LOYALTY

What's the Trend?
A new understanding of loyalty is challenging brands to get smarter about how they can generate brand enthusiasts.

Trend Longevity Rating:
Over the past year, forward looking brands like Macy's and GNC have redesigned their loyalty programs to overcome the challenge of passive loyalty and focus on delivering consistent experiences and rewards rather than point-based discounts. As brands continue to rethink how to engage consumers and drive loyalty, this trend has remained a huge priority for business.

- -

AUTHENTIC FAMESEEKERS

What's the Trend?
A new generation of creators are turning to social media to establish their brands, attract eyeballs and become the next big thing.

Trend Longevity Rating:
As was clear from several trends in this year's report, influencers continue to be a force online in using social media to drive extreme fan loyalty and even purchasing. As a result, brands are increasingly reaching out to engage these Authentic Fameseekers and tap into the audiences they have built and their ability to dictate trends and shaping a global culture.

- -

LOVABLE UNPERFECTION

What's the Trend?
Today, successful marketing campaigns are putting an increasing focus on using the power of personality, quirkiness, and imperfections to create authentic with customers.

Trend Longevity Rating:
Over the past year, brands continued to learn that consumers connect with real, unfiltered, honest messaging and campaigns. Sports Illustrated featured unretouched photos, UK-based food brand Higgidy promoted their "hand-finished" imperfect products and many other brands refocused on taking customers behind the scenes and injecting more reality into their story.

2017 Media & Entertainment Trends

PRESERVED PAST

What's the Trend?
Technology is offering new ways to preserve history, changing the way we learn from, experience, and remember the past in the process.

Trend Longevity Rating:
Preservation focused groups, supported by continually advancing technology, continue their important work by creating "virtual curations" of artifacts, tracking deteriorations, preserving fragile papers, and even creating 3D libraries of the world's cultural heritage sites before they are damaged or lost to natural disasters, war, or the passing of time.

DEEP DIVING

What's the Trend?
While brands compete for our shrinking attention spans with more content than ever, many people prefer to go all in on the topics and experiences that truly capture their interest.

Trend Longevity Rating:
While attention spans continue to shrink, this counter-trend continues to gain ground, as people are finding enjoyment in content and storytelling that takes them deep into particular topics and cultural issues. Podcasts, investigative journalism, documentary filmmaking and the sometimes-longwinded storytelling of cable news journalists like John Oliver remain as popular as ever.

PRECIOUS PRINT

What's the Trend?
Thanks to the digital revolution, people are developing a more meaningful and emotional relationship with physical objects and printed material.

Trend Longevity Rating:
It is safe to say that as long as the digital revolution continues at its current pace, people will encourage the development of this countertrend. Books, records, and simpler, retro models of cameras, video games and anything that generates nostalgia will strike a chord with people who long for the nostalgia and tangible nature of physical objects and printed materials.

2017 Technology & Design Trends

INVISIBLE TECHNOLOGY

What's the Trend?
As technology becomes more sophisticated, it becomes better at predicting and anticipating needs, protecting us, and providing utility while blending seamlessly into our lives.

Trend Longevity Rating:
In the coming year, artificial intelligence, connected objects, machine learning, virtual and augmented reality, and peer-to-peer networks like Blockchain will multiply the ways that technology can make everyday tasks, transactions, communication and learning easier, cheaper, and more efficient – and it will continue to blend unnoticeably into the background.

A

ROBOT RENAISSANCE

What's the Trend?
As robots' utility moves into the home and the workplace, they adopt more human-like interfaces and even adopt micro-personalities.

Trend Longevity Rating:
The true impact of this trend is still at the early stages. The big questions robots have always raised for humanity are approaching. How much of our "work" should we cede to technology so we can focus on things that we love? Do we need universal income? Will robots take over? These are "renaissance age" questions, and they will become even more urgent in 2018.

A-

SELF-AWARE DATA

What's the Trend?
As technology advances, algorithms and artificial intelligence make real-time analysis so fast that it can move from input to insight to action all on its own.

Trend Longevity Rating:
Data and real-time analytics will continue to transform organizations' abilities to automate analysis, education, and the generation of insight. In contrast to the more alarmist and pessimistic trends of Data Overflow and Data Pollution, this trend continues to offer a more positive future vision of a future where data might create value by analyzing itself.

A-

2017 Economics & Entrepreneurship Trends

MOONSHOT ENTREPRENEURSHIP

What's the Trend?
A new generation of entrepreneurs are thinking beyond profit and making social impact, not financial performance, at the center of their organizations' missions.

Trend Longevity Rating:
The world's problems remain complex, and entrepreneurs continue to generate social impact. In the future, we expect (and already see) more business leaders step up to fill a leadership void left by paralyzed partisan governments (like the US under Trump) which step backwards on important urgent issues such as climate change, fighting poverty, and gender equality.

A-

OUTRAGEOUS OUTSIDERS

What's the Trend?
Some of today's most innovative and influential ideas are coming from complete outsiders whose unconventional quirks disrupt entire industries.

Trend Longevity Rating:
The past few years offer plenty of evidence for how outsiders can disrupt entire industries, countries and global orders. Leaders with little to no political experience win elections. Outsider musicians like Cardi B, a stripper-turned-rapper, top the singles chart. The founders of cryptocurrencies Ethereum and Bitcoin, already work to change our economic system.

A

MAINSTREAM MINDFULNESS

What's the Trend?
The business community is starting to reject the "sleep when you're dead philosophy" in favor of mindfulness in all its forms: yoga, meditation, quiet contemplation and even sleep.

Trend Longevity Rating:
Technology and connection continue to result in increased anxiety for many. The past year, many professionals were desperately seeking spaces of quiet to disconnect and improve focus. An increasing number of employers realize anxiety is not good for business, so we see more organizations incorporating practices that encourage rest, meditation, and healthy sleep.

A

AFTERWORD

—

"There's no such thing as weird food. Only weird people."

FERRAN ADRIÀ, Chef and Molecular Gastronomist

—

Apparently, the world will end on March 16, 2880.

While putting the final touches on the first edition of Non-Obvious, I came across a news article about a team of scientists who discovered a 0.3% chance the world will end on that day due to a cosmic collision course between Earth and a celestial body known only as Asteroid 1950 DA.

The story immediately struck me as the perfect metaphor for the types of predictions we commonly encounter in the world today . . . overblown proclamations with dire consequences and relatively little certainty.

One of the aims for this book is to challenge lazy or obvious trend predictions that are, sadly, just like that exaggerated astronomical prediction. Mistaken trend predictions can be even more damaging than a doomsday prophecy, because they lead to flawed decisions today instead of just empty dread for the far future.

—

*A trend is a unique curated observation
of the accelerating present.*

—

Non-Obvious intentionally doesn't offer geopolitical arguments for why Denmark is going to become the world's next superpower by 2050 thanks to wind energy production, or optimistic technology predictions about how self-driving cars will enable virtual-reality tourism during daily commutes.

These kinds of predictions are sexy, and some might even come true. Unfortunately, they also include a lot of uncertainty. The future should involve far less guesswork.

Curating trends is certainly about seeing the things others don't. Yet it's also more broadly about a mindset that encourages you to be curious and thoughtful. It's about techniques that help you move from trying to be a speed reader to being a "speed understander," as Isaac Asimov wrote.

The future belongs to those who can learn to use their powers of observation to see the connections between industries, ideas, and behaviors and curate them into a deeper understanding of the world around us.

I'm not saying that this type of thinking can save us from the asteroid 867 years from now, but it can change the way we approach our lives and our businesses in the present.

Preparing for the future starts with filtering out the noise and getting better at understanding today... as it always has.

RESEARCH:
Notes, References, & Credits

—

The preparation of this book and the *Non-Obvious Trend Report* involves scanning tens of thousands of stories every year, interviewing dozens of experts and reviewing more than 100 books. Where relevant, these sources have been cited specifically in an endnote, however this does not reflect the full breadth of sources consulted. On average, each trend includes about 30 stories and links that were used in the development, curation and writing of that chapter. Since inserting a long list of links in a physical book (or even an ebook) has limited value, all of these links are instead shared through a downloadable PDF (where you can click any link which you can access and download). The intent of this list is to offer a useful way for you to visit individual links to stories, to learn more about a trend, or to do a bit of *Truthing* yourself and discover where exactly the ideas and research cited in this book come from.

To download a PDF with active links for this 2018 edition of Non-Obvious, visit this URL: www.nonobviousbook.com/resources

ENDNOTES

Chapter 1: The Norwegian Billionaire

1. **Mini Bottle Gallery.** This story is gathered from first-hand conversations with staff at the venue, stories available online about the founding, and literature provided to visitors at the museum.

2. **Trend spotter definition.** This definition was taken from Wisegeek.com, but there were plenty of similarly narrow-minded definitions spread across the Internet I could have picked to share here. The common bias of most of them is that there is some type of special training and industry knowledge required to be a trend expert. There isn't.

3. **Curse of knowledge.** The famous linguist Steven Pinker discusses this "curse of knowledge" in his book *The Sense of Style,* where he notes that the more expertise we have about a topic, the more difficult we tend to find it to simplify or explain it to those who are not as well versed as ourselves.

Chapter 2: The Curator's Mindset

1. **Mindset.** Carol Dweck's simple yet profound book was first published in 2006.

2. **"Parking ticket not a car wreck."** Dweck's *Mindset* is filled with analogies and anecdotes like this one to illustrate the value of a growth mindset versus a fixed one.

3. **Vogel Collection.** This story was sourced primarily from the *New York Times* profile written about the Vogels after Herbert's death in 2012. http://www.nytimes.com/2012/07/24/arts/design/herbert-vogel-postal-clerk-and-modern-art-collector-dies-at-89.html

4. **The truth about Columbus.** Columbus deserves little of the ceremony he gets and, in fact, he never even set foot in North America during his famous journey in 1492. Listen to the real story: http://www.npr.org/templates/story/story.php?storyId=141164702

5. **Why are traffic signs orange?** The answer took a bit of Googling after my kids asked, but they're orange because testing shows that this is the color most visible from a distance. And everyday cars aren't orange because people care more about picking a color they like than optimizing the color for safety.

Chapter 3: The Haystack Method

1. **John Naisbitt Interview.** This profile and the quotes are taken from an article and interview published in the *USA Today* around the time that his book *Mind Set!* was published. Full interview: https://usatoday30.usatoday.com/money/books/2006-09-24-naisbitt-usat_x.htm

2. **Non-Obvious Trend Report (1st edition).** This first year of the report was published as a

visual presentation and is available online (unedited). More details about this report and how to read it, as well as how the trends fared over time, is all included in the Appendix.

3. **Bliss point.** Michael Moss is a Pulitzer Prize–winning investigative journalist. For a short summary of his story on the scientists who uncovered and exploited the "bliss point," see this excerpt from his book reprinted in the *New York Times*: http://www.nytimes.com/2013/02/24/magazine/the-extraordinary-science-of-junk-food.html

4. **Addicted by Design.** In her book, Schüll explores the idea of a trance-like state she calls the "machine zone," where gambling addicts play not to win but simply to keep playing. When this machine design is combined with casino's focus on "ambience management," addiction is the result.

5. **Philip Tetlock.** The full body of Tetlock's research was originally presented in his 2005 book *Expert Political Judgment: How Good Is It? How Can We Know?* The book was recently republished (August 2017) with a new preface from the author and updated insights.

6. **Oscar Wilde.** This quote is from Wilde's play "An Ideal Husband."

Chapter 4: Truthing

1. **"59% of links never clicked."** This data point is from a study conducted by computer scientists at Columbia University and the French National Institute and published in June 2016. Full study - http://bit.ly/2hYhDD7

2. **The Coral Project.** This organization is a collaboration between the Mozilla Foundation, *The New York Times*, and *The Washington Post*, funded by a grant from the John S. and James L. Knight Foundation.

3. **Witness.org Interview.** These quotes are taken from an interview by *Wired* magazine published November 16, 2016, with Witness program manager Jackie Zammuto. Full interview - http://bit.ly/2gqBebB

4. **MIT Breakthrough Technologies.** This list was published for the 16th consecutive year by MIT and the edition referenced in this chapter was released on February 22, 2017.

5. **Video streaming market.** Research and Markets shared a projection of $70.5 billion by 2021, up from $30.29 billion in 2016. http://prn.to/2wJM3vq

6. *Consumed Nostalgia.* Gary Cross is a professor of history at Penn State University. *Consumed Nostalgia* was published by Columbia University Press in 2015.

7. **Power of nostalgia.** Professor Constantine Sedikides is often credited as a leading voice in the study of nostalgia. He argues that nostalgia is a positive force which can help people increase self-esteem and "alleviate an existential threat." This quote is from an interview given by Professor Sedikides to *The Guardian*. Full interview - http://bit.ly/powerofnostalgia

8. **Vinyl music sales.** These figures referenced in this chapter about the growth of the industry were based on industry figures cited in this article in *The Guardian* - http://bit.ly/vinyl-sales-high

Chapter 5: Ungendered

1. **Neurosexism.** The fascinating beginnings of this concept and the story of five female researchers who would propel this idea and create the first inaugural NeuroGenderings conference is shared in this article: http://bit.ly/neurosexism

2. **Do men take more risks than women?** This data point and many others are argued by Cordelia Fine in her book *Testosterone Rex*. For a short look at some of her most engaging arguments, this review in the NY Times will be valuable: http://bit.ly/testosteronerex

3. **Gender revolution.** Quote taken from interview by NPR with child psychologist and co-founder of the Child and Adolescent Gender Center, Diane Ehrensaft. Full story here: http://n.pr/2yBInjV

4. **India and hijiras.** The historical significance of this third gender, known throughout India as "hijiras," prompted this shift from the government, but their plight and treatment is still quite complex. Further reading about their history: http://bit.ly/india-hijra

5. **Gender-free toys.** I first wrote about this shift as part of my *Anti-Stereotyping* trend published in the 2015 edition of this book. In that book, I shared the 2014 story of a 13 year old girl

whose petition led Hasbro and many others in the toy industry to rethink the role of gender in their packaging. Around the same time retailers began announcing they would no longer have gender based aisles for kid's toys.

6. **Lego Friends**. While the research behind this line was quite extensive (https://bloom.bg/2y-cg6Pt), the perception of launching a mainly pink Lego set in a world where most people were talking about more genderfluid products was widely criticized (http://on.ft.com/2kCwTGE).

7. **Richard Akuson interview.** This quote is from an interview published by Mic.com. Full interview - http://bit.ly/2xuA4RZ

8. **Engaged dads.** This study was released by Saatchi & Saatchi in August of 2017 and featured data from a study which queried 1,100 American dads ages 25-40 across income, ethnicities, and regions. More information: http://bit.ly/2kBUWWf

Chapter 6: Enlightened Consumption

1. **Are tomatoes a fruit?** Yes, scientifically they are a fruit and not a vegetable.

2. **MSG research.** Recently scientists uncovered that the most prominent past studies where people reported adverse health effects after consuming MSG were flawed because those participants *knew* whether they were having MSG or not. Rather than being a dangerous chemical, MSG has now been connected to the fifth taste of umami and is widely found to be harmless for most people. Read more: http://bit.ly/msgmyth

3. **Debunked sugar studies.** This problem of direct ties between the food industry and studies about the healthfulness of various foods is a problem that was widely covered in the media when this announcement was first made in September 2016.

4. **Consumer using phones in store.** One 2017 self-serving study commissioned by software provider Salsify found that 77% of shoppers use a mobile device in store. Industry site Retail Dive found that 67% of consumers research products online. Full study - http://bit.ly/2xsG9Db

5. **Uber market share.** This data is from research firm Second Measure, which tracks billions of dollars of anonymized credit card purchases. http://bit.ly/2xuemlN

6. **Uber license revoked.** This statement from Transport for London was quoted widely across media. Read full story here - http://cnb.cx/2ycc5us

7. **Francois-Henri Pinault.** Pinault is married to Hollywood power player Salma Hayek. Given that mainstream media rarely reports on a powerful woman without mentioning her spouse and marital status, I thought it fitting to do the same in this case for him.

8. **Food wastage.** According to data from the Save Food initiative, approximately 1.3 billion metric tons of food is wasted each year. Food losses and waste amounts to roughly $680 billion in industrialized countries and $310 billion in developing countries. http://bit.ly/2zaSU2D

9. **Sustainable Investing.** The figures cited on the size of this market are based on a survey of 1,000 investors by Morgan Stanley's Institute for Sustainable Investing. According to the US SIF: The Forum for Sustainable and Responsible Investment, sustainable investing products have grown at a rate of over 33% between 2014 and 2016.

10. **Banks committing to sustainability.** At the World Economic Forum's 2017 meeting in Davos, Swiss bank UBS announced that they would direct at least $5 billion of client assets into new sustainable development goals over the next five years. Several months earlier, Deutsche Bank made a commitment to invest €1 billion in green bonds, environmentally focused securities that encourage sustainability.

11. **Paresh Shah.** In addition to being the author of the forthcoming book Lifters, Shah is also a business partner in the Non-Obvious Company, a venture started by the author of this book. To learn more about his book and research or to join the Lifter movement, visit www.iamalifter.com.

Chapter 7: Overtargeting

1. **Annoying paparazzi.** To be clear, I *imagine* this would be annoying. I have never actually been followed by paparazzi, nor would I hope to be!

2. **Does remarketing work?** There are many detailed blog posts with successful step-by-step case studies such as this one (http://bit.ly/remarketingfacts). It is not clear how much of the success of any single campaign could be attributable to a single thing, but remarketing (in the right situations) does seem to be effective.

3. **Explosion of marketing automation.** Grand View Research has estimated that the market opportunity for marketing automation software could reach $7.63 billion by 2025.

4. **"Keep on nurturing them."** This quote is from *Disrupted* by Dan Lyons (p. 44).

5. **B2Beyond Marketing.** Read more about this trend and watch these videos referenced at www.nonobviousbook.com/b2beyond

6. **Unilever marketing budget.** This figure was the number shared publicly in Unilever's 2016 Annual Report.

7. **P&G cuts spending.** There are many stories referencing this move from P&G but the most thorough and frequently referenced by other sources is the one from the *Wall Street Journal* here: http://on.wsj.com/2ycDgFF

8. **comScore report.** The quote referenced here was first published in a writeup about the comScore report in Asia. Full story - http://bit.ly/2wKSZZj

9. **Perennials.** The original post by Gina Pell about Perennials that went viral was posted on Medium.com here: http://bit.ly/theperennials

10. **Green grandmas**. This story of the founding of Blu Homes and their choice to target these green grandmas was featured as an interview in *Inc* magazine: Full interview - http://on.inc.com/2xt1PiB

11. **Harley-Davidson sales.** According to an article on *Forbes* from February 2017, sales of new Harley-Davidson motorcycles to outreach customers (including women, Hispanics, African Americans, and Millennials) in the United States has grown by 5%, now representing 40% of the volume sales, up from 34% in 2010. Full story - http://bit.ly/2xvIU1F

Chapter 8: Brand Stand

1. **Yogurt industry figures.** According to Nielsen data, Chobani has 37.6% of the greek yogurt market shareand Ulukaya's personal fortune has been estimated at $1.7 billion - http://bit.ly/chobanimarketshare

2. **Davos attendee on Ulukaya.** This quote was from Kenneth Roth, executive director of Human Rights Watch and a Davos attendee who was interviewed by the NY Times after the event. Full story - http://nyti.ms/2yvoM4P

3. **Millennial survey.** The figures quoted in this chapter are taken from the "2017 Marketing Spending Study" conducted by the Cadent Consulting Group.

4. **Jose Andrés versus Trump.** While no official figures have been released around the legal settlement that was reached or the financial impact of this situation for Andrés, several media outlets reported a surge in support on social media and a reputational boost for Andrés after his choice to back out of the deal.

5. **Companies oppose Trump.** Fortune magazine published this full list of 97 companies which officially opposed the ban on muslims proposed by Donald Trump. Full list - http://for.tn/2xZdwNm

6. **Utah public lands.** The political battle over public lands was widely reported in relation to legislation to rescind the protection for the "Bears Ears" national monument. Full story - http://bit.ly/2xoJMoQ

7. **Lego versus *Daily Mail*.** The consumer widely credited for starting this process was Bob Jones, a Facebook user who posted a long message which Lego responded to. The full conversation archive - http://bit.ly/2yMFBEo

8. **Consumers pressure businesses.** These stories are referenced in an article from TIME which focused on moments in the recent past when brands chose to listen to their consumers. Full story - http://ti.me/2kuevj2

9. **Tata Jaago Re.** This quote is selected from press materials made available by Tata for media related to the announcement of the campaign.

Chapter 9: Backstorytelling

1. **Zildjian versus Sabian story.** There is a little-told story of how the Zildjian brothers split and one left to start the Sabian company. Read the story here: http://bit.ly/zildjiansabian

2. **Brand personality.** This topic of brand personality is one that I have spent many years

exploring. My first book in 2008 was titled *Personality Not Included* and focused on the topic in detail.

3. **52 acquisitions.** This figure is from research released by investment banking firm Capstone Partners in Q3 2017. Full report: http://bit.ly/capstonereport

4. **Iceland tourism boom.** According to the Iceland Tourist Board, from 2010 to 2018 the number of tourists visiting Iceland more than tripled, and between 2010 and 2015 the average yearly increase in visitors was 21.6 percent.

5. *Airbnbmag.* This quote is taken from the editor's note written by Chesky for the inaugural edition of the magazine which was published in May 2017.

6. **Ankur Jain interview.** Interview in Hemispheres magazine. Full story - http://bit.ly/2wMvL4P

Chapter 10: Manipulated Outrage

1. **Stephen Crowley.** In lieu of any royalty payments, Crowley requested that we make a donation to cancer research. A $100 donation was made on his behalf to Liam's Lighthouse Foundation (www.liamslighthousefoundation.org).

2. **Trump's announcement.** This story from reporter Tierney McAfee was published in *People* magazine the day before the 2016 election. Full story: http://bit.ly/trumpdayannounced

3. *I Hope They Serve Beer In Hell.* The movie was featured in *The Chicago Tribune* list of the "worst movies of the past decade." Full list: http://bit.ly/listworstmovies

4. **"It was madness."** This quote is from Holiday's widely shared article from February 2017 in *The Observer*, "I created the Milo trolling playbook. You should stop playing right into it." Full story: http://bit.ly/trollingplaybook

5. **Cable news data.** These numbers are taken from Nielsen data as reported by *Variety* magazine in July 2017. Full story: http://bit.ly/cablenewsdata

6. **Food vigilantes.** This story is from a *BusinessWeek* article published August 24, 2017. It should be noted that the people described prefer the term "food safety observer." I used the original term in the story reference. Full story: http://bit.ly/foodvigilantes

7. *Teen Vogue.* This story of the reemergence of the magazine as a cultural force has been widely written about. Here is one of the most widely shared examples: http://bit.ly/teenvoguewoke

8. **#Resist.** Over the past year, this term has increasingly been used to spark a movement, hence the usage of hashtag in front of it as a reference to this social meaning.

9. **Nicholas Carr interview.** As told to *The Atlantic* as part of an interview feature for their August 2017 issue.

10. **Van Jones interview.** The quotes and insights in this section were taken from an interview in *Pacific Standard* magazine published in August 2017. Full story: http://bit.ly/vanjonescompassion

11. **Media escapism.** This concept and the anecdote shared is from a story by *Washington Post* reporter Emily Yahr in July 2017. Full story: http://bit.ly/mediaescapism

Chapter 11: Light-Speed Learning

1. **8-year-old driver.** This story was widely reported in the media after first being covered by local paper Weirton Daily Times. Read the story on *USA Today*: https://usat.ly/2xnQ3B8

2. **Basketball star.** This is a reference to the popular YouTube series called *10,000 Hours* from filmmaker and basketball trainer Devin Williams which helps would-be basketball stars go through a rigorous training course to help them perfect their game. The title of the series is taken from the well-known figure Malcolm Gladwell shared as the optimal number of hours of practice that are required to develop mastery in anything.

3. **Tasty video stats.** The quotes referenced here were shared on stage at by McCollum at the Fast Company Innovation Festival in November 2016. Full story: http://bit.ly/tastyvideostats

4. **Global shortage of doctors.** According to projections from the American Association of Medical Colleges (AAMC) there will be a shortage of more than 100,000 doctors. In other countries the estimated shortages will be even more extreme. Full story on *TechCrunch*: http://bit.ly/globaldocshortage

5. **Kevin Carey quote**. This quote is excerpted from an interview published in *Inside Higher Ed* in March 2015. Full interview: http://bit.ly/kevincarey

Chapter 12: Virtual Empathy

1. **HoloLens for business**. These examples were primarily taken from a ZDNet article, published in February 2017, about Microsoft's business strategy around the HoloLens. Full story: http://zd.net/2giyOXt

2. **"Just like in real life."** Andrew Ridker, *The New York Times*, May 25, 2017. Full review: http://nyti.ms/2yvYXBN

3. **Anna Akana**. Watch the full video here: https://youtu.be/zvkbHIrrrvU

4. **The Vlogging Cure**. Carly Lanning published in *Psychology Today*. May 2, 2017 Full story: http://bit.ly/2giOdM6

5. **Natalie Egan**. Read her full announcement post on LinkedIn: http://bit.ly/natalieegan

6. **LinkedIn video training**. Watch the full video training here - http://bit.ly/2y8SdZH

Chapter 13: Human Mode

1. **$2 trillion**. This figure was first reported by management consulting firm A.T. Kearney, which also predicted that the robo-advisors market could achieve this valuation within two years.

2. **Betterment premium option**. This increase would drive the commission structure on trades up to 0.50% instead of 0.25%. Full story: http://reut.rs/2hSBIL3

3. **Sally the salad robot**. Full story: https://bloom.bg/2y6nwnw

4. **Robot vacuums**. Industry manufacturer iRobot recently estimated that robotic vacuums now account for 20% of the market. http://tcrn.ch/2ggJgn1

5. **Rise of bank tellers**. These conclusions adapted from the work of economist James Bessen. Read more at: http://theatln.tc/2xw6qk3

6. **Retail sales worker growth**. Statistics from the US Bureau of Labor: http://bit.ly/retailworkeroutlook

7. **Job automation predictions**. Statistics from PwC analysis: https://pwc.to/2fZnBmF

8. **Professions by gender**. These figures were charted by the *Boston Globe*, based on US Department of Labor statistics from 2016. Full story: http://bit.ly/2y1rtrV

9. **Pink-collar work**. While the tone of much of Penny's writing seems to offer a condescending disbelief that men can be capable of more than doing robotic emotionless work, her point about the future belonging to those who embrace jobs which are uniquely human is important. Full story: http://bit.ly/2yvCbJY

10. **Lu chatbot**. Background story from *BusinessWeek*: https://bloom.bg/2wDr9ho

11. **Beanie Babies versus fidget spinners**. Full story: http://nyti.ms/2y706yr

Chapter 14: Data Pollution

1. **800 pages of Tinder data**. Full story - http://bit.ly/2yehKAM

2. **IBM costs of poor quality data**. Full story - http://bit.ly/2yf9oqs

3. **Drowning in data**. Full article by Fred Pelzman - http://bit.ly/2ykt4uK

4. **Most research findings are false**. This startlingly conclusion was first made by John P. A. Ioannidis

5. **"Ad knew too much."** Full story - http://ind.pn/2kItlCK

6. **danah boyd**. This is not a typo, but rather a choice from boyd who decided to spell her name in lowercase so as "to reflect my mother's original balancing and to satisfy my own political irritation at the importance of capitalization."

7. **"If we believe that data."** Read a transcript or watch a video of boyd's full keynote - http://bit.ly/2yesrDG

8. **USA Today follower drop. The** Facebook purge was reported to reduce USA Today's Facebook likes from 15.2 million to 9.5 million. Another planned purge could reduce that number by another 3 million. https://usat.ly/2zjuLa8

9. **Fake social media profiles.** A study from researchers at USC and Indiana University suggested that between 9% to 15% of active Twitter accounts might be bots. http://bit.ly/2yHT4Bh

10. **Instagram archive.** Full story - http://bit.ly/2xA1Ts9

Chapter 15: Predictive Protection

1. **Connected cars as weapons.** Full story on *WIRED UK* - http://bit.ly/hackcars

2. **AI bots develop language.** Full story on *Newsweek* - http://bit.ly/botlanguage

3. **White hat hackers in Germany.** Full story on *Bloomberg* - http://bit.ly/germanwhitehat

4. **Recruiting white hat hackers.** Our research uncovered multiple examples of this recruiting, including a 17-year-old hacking the US Air Force (http://bit.ly/2g38ll6) and China's efforts to use patriotic hackers (http://on.cfr.org/2g0UITt).

5. **Growth in wearables market.** IDC data predicts global market will increase from the 104.3 million units shipped in 2016 to 240.1 million units shipped in 2021. Full research - http://bit.ly/2y2GYzO

6. **AI Predicts Suicide.** These statistics are from the research of Colin Walsh, a data scientist at Vanderbilt University Medical Center. Full story - http://bit.ly/ai-suicide

7. **Thirsty concrete.** Full story on *Business Insider* - http://bit.ly/thirstyconcrete

8. **Police drones.** It was estimated that 167 police and fire agencies ordered drones in 2016. Full story on *Recode* - http://bit.ly/policedrones

9. **Rogue traders.** Full story on *BusinessWeek* - http://bit.ly/roguetraders

Chapter 16: Approachable Luxury

1. **"Today shows have nothing to do with clothes anymore."** This quote is from an interview Guram Gvasalia did with fashion industry magazine WWD - http://bit.ly/2yIXLLt

2. **"... without even trying to sell them."** Quote from a research report written by analysts Luca Solca, Melania Grippo, and Guido Lucarelli, and published by investment firm Exane BNP Paribas and Paris-based fashion consultancy VR Fashion Luxury Expertise. Full report: http://bit.ly/2wE6HNi

3. **Luxury experience versus product.** Though it was tempting to try and offer a single source to validate this point, the truth is nearly every article referenced in this chapter, every event I attended, and every executive I interviewed while conducting research for this trend all had the same conclusion: The future of luxury is experiences, not products.

4. **Boomers' heirlooms.** Full story: https://usat.ly/2y7Il24

5. **"What the Rich Won't Tell You,"** by Rachel Sherman. *The New York Times*, September 8, 2017. Full article: http://nyti.ms/2gj2cSn

6. **Decline in Swiss watch exports.** Full story: http://bit.ly/swisswatchdecline

7. **"coolest brand in America."** Full story - http://bit.ly/2gfvRin

8. **Shinola story.** In her article, Perman goes on to criticize Shinola founder Kartsotis for capitalizing on Detroit's rising power to build "America's most authentic fake brand." http://bit.ly/shinolastory

9. **"W sits alongside luxury."** This quote is from an interview with Anthony Ingham conducted by HotelierMiddleEast.com in conjunction with the launch of the W Dubai – Al Habtoor City on June 20, 2016. Full interview: http://bit.ly/2gjKMVF

10. **Boutique fitness industry.** This market data is from IHRSA: http://bit.ly/2y6BJk1

11. **"Peloton is a cultural phenomenon."** Full story: http://on.inc.com/2yO86kY

12. **Singapore food stalls.** The names of the stalls, in case you are in Singapore and would like to try them, were "Liao Fan Hong Kong Soya Sauce Chicken Rice & Noodle" and "Hill Street Tai Hwa Pork Noodle."

13. **Eco-diamond sales.** These figures are taken from research published by Morgan Stanley in 2016 projecting that sales of eco-diamonds could grow to $1.05 billion in the next two years. Original research: http://mgstn.ly/2wE1jKj

Chapter 17: Touchworthy

1. **Power of print.** Despite the widely predicted death of print at the hands of ebooks, the numbers from the publishing industry lead to a different conclusion. Full story on *Salon* – http://bit.ly/2hlz6LN .

2. **GentleWhispering.** This interview with Maria is one I first read more than two years ago, and saved until the moment when I found the right trend for it to be included. Full story on *Cosmopolitan* - http://bit.ly/2kQVxDq

3. **Gravity blanket.** While scientific data backing up the claims on the product are lacking, the Internet is filled with personal anecdotes of individuals who *believed* that the blanket helped cure their anxiety or fall asleep faster. Full story on *Marie Claire* - http://bit.ly/2ypZCU2

4. **Cat & Jack brand.** Sales figures and details from publicly released data from Target. *Source* - http://bit.ly/2ypQIps

5. **Board game sales.** In 2016, NPD group reports board game sales have gone up in the US alone by 28 percent and Euromonitor International reports global sales of board games grew increased to $9.6 billion in 2016 from $9.3 billion in 2013. *Data Source* - http://bit.ly/2yoyK6W

6. **Growth in haptic technology market.** There are several different data sources and estimates for the likely size of the global market for haptic technology: $23.28 billion by 2024 (Inkwood Research), $31.8 billion by 2025 (Research and Markets) and $19.55 billion by 2022 (Key Market Insights). Given the variety of estimates, the figure of "$20 billion over the next five years" was used as a reasonable aggregate.

7. **Carmen Simon interview.** This quote is taken from an interview and insights she shared directly during an interview about the topic for this chapter.

Chapter 18: Disruptive Distribution

1. **Warehouse space research.** These figures were released as an estimate by CBRE on February 22, 2017. Original research - http://bit.ly/2ktgOTw

2. **Outside the box.** Pun intended. Sometimes I can't help myself ...

3. **Dominos market share.** According to research firm NPD Crest, the brand went from a 9% share of the US market in 2009 to a 15% share just seven years later. Full story on Domino's transformation - https://bloom.bg/2yxif9S

4. **CMO spending on technology.** These figures are from Gartner research. Full research - http://gtnr.it/2xpiIWH

5. **Cova & LVMH.** This quote is from an interview with Yves Carcelle for Business Of Fashion. Full interview - http://bit.ly/2xocxXI

Chapter 19: Intersection Thinking

1. **RumChata popularity.** These claims are taken from an interview conducted on CNBC by Jim Cramer with RumChata founder Tom Maas. Full story - http://cnb.cx/2giWzU1

2. **Pluot.** While this may seem fabricated, the pluot is indeed a real fruit—and certainly not to be confused with the plumcot, which is different. If the story interests you, read more here: http://bit.ly/pluotstory

3. **Bolthouse Farms.** Bolthouse is generally credited with being the first to introduce "baby carrots" to consumers.

4. **"kind of addictive."** Full story - http://bit.ly/2wCyLR6

5. **Persuadable.** I first encountered this term when reading a book of the same title by author Ali Pittampalli.

Chapter 21: Anti-Trends

1. **Flip thinking.** This idea was first described in an Op-Ed contributed piece by Dan Pink for The Telegraph. Full story - http://bit.ly/2xoyocu

ACKNOWLEDGEMENTS

—

The concept for this book has been many years in the making – and now that it is officially an annual series, the first group of people I need to thank are the many readers of an earlier edition of this book.

As much as anyone, this book is for all of you – and if you happen to be among that group, I want to say thank you.

There are also some individuals who helped with various stages of getting this 2018 update (and previous editions) ready for publication and deserve my specific thanks:

First of all, to Paresh for jumping into the process of trend curation, working on the ideas, becoming a true partner and just being a force for good. You are the original Lifter.

To Gretchen, Matthew, Terry and Christina for offering an ongoing sounding board of editorial advice and jumping in to provide assistance when needed on updates this year and in previous years as well.

To Frank, Anton, Joss and Jessica for all your design smarts and making the visual design of the book as beautiful as it is, and to the entire design team at Faceout for the original inspiration and setting the tone for the series back in the beginning.

To Marleen, Chrys and the foreign rights team for helping to bring the ideas in Non-Obvious to so many diverse audiences around the world in their own language.

To Marnie for all your work keeping this and so many other Ideapress projects on track.

To Rich for being a great partner, always working under a crazy time-line and still getting things done like a pro.

To my wife Chhavi, who continually manages to deal with a shifting annual writing process that requires me to disappear to finish off chapters and "visualize" ideas by spreading my notes across entire rooms of the house. And then spending time reviewing and editing the whole book to make sure it is as good as it can be. You are the first person to tell me when it's working and the first to tell me when it isn't. I love that.

And finally, to my boys Rohan and Jaiden for remaining curious enough about the world to continually inspire me to observe more, judge less and always listen with both ears.

From time to time, we can all use a reminder like that.

INDEX

—

ABOUT THE AUTHOR

—

Rohit Bhargava is a trend curator, marketing expert, storyteller and the Wall Street Journal best-selling author of five books on topics as wide ranging as the future of business and why leaders never eat cauliflower. Rohit is the founder of the Non-Obvious Company, teaches marketing and pitching at Georgetown University and has been invited to speak in 32 countries around the world. Prior to becoming an entrepreneur, Rohit spent 15 years leading brand strategy at two of the largest marketing agencies in the world (Ogilvy and Leo Burnett). He lives in the Washington DC area with his wife and two boys.